D1216157

The Best Book of:
Lotus™ 1-2-3™

Related Titles

Best Book of: Framework™
Alan Simpson

Best Book of: Multiplan™
Alan Simpson

Lotus® 1-2-3® Financial Models
Elna Tymes and Tony Dowden with Charles E. Prael

Best Book of: dBASE II®/III®
Ken Knecht

Best Book of: dBASE IV
(forthcoming)
Joseph-David Carrabis

Best Book of: Microsoft® Works for the PC
Ruth Witkin

Best Book of: Quattro
Joseph-David Carrabis

Best Book of: WordPerfect®, Version 5.0
Vincent Alfieri

Best Book of: WordStar® (Features Release 4)
Vincent Alfieri

WordPerfect 5.0: Expert Techniques
Kate Barnes

Best Book of: WordStar 5.0
(forthcoming)
Vincent Alfieri

Best Book of: OS/2 Database Manager *(forthcoming)*
Howard Fosdick

Hard Disk Management Techniques for the IBM®
Joseph-David Carrabis

IBM® PS/2 Technical Guide
James A. Shields and Caroline M. Halliday

The Waite Group's Desktop Publishing Bible
James Stockford, Editor

For the retailer nearest you, or to order directly from the publisher, call 800-428-SAMS. In Indiana, Alaska, and Hawaii call 317-298-5699.

The Best Book of: Lotus™ 1-2-3™

Second Edition

Alan Simpson

HOWARD W. SAMS & COMPANY

A Division of Macmillan, Inc.
4300 West 62nd Street
Indianapolis, Indiana 46268 USA

Trademarks

Lotus 1-2-3	Lotus Development Corp.
WordStar	Micropro Inc.
SuperCalc	Sorcim Inc.
dBASE II	Ashton-Tate, Inc.
Sweet P	Enter Computer of San Diego, CA
VisiCalc	Visicorp

©1984 and 1986 by Alan Simpson

SECOND EDITION
SIXTH PRINTING — 1988

All rights reserved. No part of this book shall be reproduced, stored in a
retrieval system, or transmitted by any means, electronic, mechanical,
photocopying, recording, or otherwise, without written permission from the
publisher. No patent liability is assumed with respect to the use of the
information contained herein. While every precaution has been taken in the
preparation of this book, the publisher assumes no responsibility for errors or
omissions. Neither is any liability assumed for damages resulting from the use
of the information contained herein.

International Standard Book Number: 0-672-22563-8
Library of Congress Catalog Card Number: 86-62227

Acquired by: *James S. Hill*
Edited by: *Louis Keglovits*
Designed by: *T. R. Emrick*
Illustrated by: *Ralph E. Lund*
Cover Art by: *Celeste Design*

Printed in the United States of America

CONTENTS

Section II: 1-2-3 Graphics

Section III: Database Management

Section IV: Macros

PREFACE

Soon after its release in 1983, Lotus 1-2-3 skyrocketed to the top of the software best-seller lists—and for several good reasons. First, it was among the first of the "integrated" software packages to combine electronic spreadsheet, graphics, and information management into a single program. Second, it took advantage of the features of the modern 16-bit microcomputers (such as the IBM PC) for maximum speed and performance. Third, even with its advanced capabilities, it was (and still is) one of the easiest programs to use.

In the Fall of 1985, Lotus released Version 2.0 of 1-2-3. The new version added even more capability and flexibility, without detracting from the program's original elegance and ease of use. This second edition of the book is written for the newer 2.0 version.

If you've never used Lotus 1-2-3 or even a computer, this book will be a good starting place for you. We assume no prior experience with spreadsheets, graphics, or database management. If you already have some experience either with other spreadsheets or with earlier versions of 1-2-3, hopefully you'll find some new tips and techniques in the lessons and examples we provide.

—Alan Simpson

If you would like to use some of the sample worksheets, graphs, databases, and macros in this book, but don't want to type them all in yourself, you can purchase a copy of them on disk. The files are available in 5-1/4 inch IBM double-sided, double-density format only. To order a copy, send a check or money order for $30.00 (California residents please add appropriate sales tax) to:

SMS Software
P. O. Box 2802
La Jolla, CA 92038-2802

Make the check payable to SMS Software. Be sure to specify that you want files from Alan Simpson's The Best Book of: Lotus 1-2-3, Second Edition.

INTRODUCTION

Lotus 1-2-3 is one of the most powerful microcomputer programs available on the market today. It combines electronic spreadsheet power, graphics, information management, ease-of-use, and flexibility as no other product has before.

- As a business tool, 1-2-3 is incomparable. The powerful worksheet allows for rapid development of financial models, automated "what-if" scenarios, built-in calculations for business, statistics, trigonometry, and more.

- As a graphics package, 1-2-3 provides graphs of any data in a worksheet, supports planning graphics scenarios, and even graphic "slide shows."

- As a database management system, 1-2-3 provides sorting and searching capabilities to instantly organize and retrieve information.

- 1-2-3 includes a small programming language, so you can automate your custom worksheets.

Lotus 1-2-3 is for anyone who works with numbers, needs rapid access to information, or needs to plan. It is not just for people who are already "into" computers, but for business owners, managers, financial planners, real estate agents, insurance agents, farmers, college professors—anyone who needs information to make decisions or to make sales. The only prerequisite is a little typing skill, and even that isn't too important. 1-2-3 is as well designed for the non-typist as a software product can be.

Who should read this book? Exactly those individuals described above. Lotus 1-2-3 is easy to use, but "easy to use" is a relative term when talking about computers. You can be productive almost immediately with 1-2-3, but there are also over 300 options to choose from! To really master the worksheet, you may need to get some guidance. Although the manual is packed with useful examples, it is primarily a reference. Learning is more effective when you can develop some basic, practical skills and then build upon these to achieve mastery. Reference manuals provide necessary information; instructional texts teach. This book is for anyone who wants to learn to use 1-2-3 to its fullest potential.

If you are just thinking about buying 1-2-3 and are wondering what it can do for you, this book can help you make your decision.

GETTING READY

1. You need to *install* 1-2-3 on your computer before you can use it. (You need only perform the installation procedure once.) If you have not already done so, be sure to follow the instructions provided in the *Getting Started* manual with your copy of 1-2-3 to perform the installation. Since installation procedures vary somewhat from computer to computer, be sure to follow the appropriate instructions for your computer.

2. @1-2-3 comes with a tutorial on disk named *A View of 1-2-3*. After installing 1-2-3, you may want to try the tutorial. It is discussed in Chapter 2 of the *Getting Started* manual that came with your package.

3. On the left side of your keyboard are several keys labeled F1, F2, F3, F4, F5, etc. These are *special function* keys, and the one labeled F1 has the special function of providing help when you're working with 1-2-3. Anytime you are working with 1-2-3 and need some help, press the F1 key. The screen will provide help. When you have finished reading the Help screen, just press the Esc key. The 1-2-3 worksheet will reappear on the screen.

This book allows you to work interactively with 1-2-3 as you read. You can use the 1-2-3 Help facility in conjunction with this text whenever you feel like exploring a topic in more detail.

STRUCTURE OF THIS BOOK

This book is made up of four major sections. Section 1 contains chapters that deal specifically with the 1-2-3 worksheet. These chapters are designed to make your developing skills productive right away, then help you expand and refine those skills for faster, more fluent use of the worksheet's potential. We use fairly simple examples to explain and demonstrate new concepts and later provide more complex examples to help put your new knowledge and skills to work.

Section 2 deals with 1-2-3 graphics. It utilizes many of the skills you learned in the first section and provides an in-depth tutorial in mastering 1-2-3's graphics capabilities.

Section 3 discusses 1-2-3's database management capabilities as well as basic database management techniques and concepts. You will also find some very powerful techniques for using computerized "what if" capabilities in Section 3.

Section 4 deals with the somewhat esoteric "macro" capabilities of 1-2-3. A macro is a collection of keystrokes stored in a worksheet that can be executed by typing a single command. Macros are not essential to using 1-2-3, but they provide an added attraction that those of you interested in computer programming may want to explore.

I offer one last bit of advice before you start with Chapter 1. Learning about a new computer program is enjoyable if you allow yourself to work at a comfortable pace. One of the best techniques for learning any computer skill is to *play*. Many people are afraid to play with a computer because they fear that they will break something. If you are such a person, let me ease your mind. No matter what you type on the keyboard, even if you close your eyes and tap on random keys for half an hour, there is absolutely no possibility of your damaging the computer. There are no secret words or commands you can accidentally type to hurt the computer. So enjoy your learning. Play and experiment. The worst that can happen is that the computer will tell you that it doesn't understand what you mean. And that is only because the computer is not as smart as you are.

THE 1-2-3 WORKSHEET

Chapter 1

CREATING THE WORKSHEET

ABOUT THIS CHAPTER

This chapter discusses the basics of using 1-2-3: getting 1-2-3 up and running on your computer, positioning the *cell pointer* on the worksheet, entering some data and formulas, and saving the worksheet. By the time you finish this chapter, you will have created your first worksheet, and learned a few basic techniques along the way.

The LOTUS system includes five separate disks: System, Utility, Install, PrintGraph, and System Backup disk. 1-2-3 is stored on the one labeled System Disk. It is the main program of the system. The 1-2-3 program turns your computer into a giant worksheet which can perform calculations at amazing speeds. The worksheet has rows and columns of cells, and each row and column title provides an address for each cell. You can fill in the cells with whatever information you need: numbers, formulas for calculations, and even labels to make the display look nice.

The 1-2-3 worksheet consists of 256 columns and 8192 numbered rows. Your screen shows only a portion of the entire worksheet at any given time.

The actual worksheet is 256 columns across, and 8192 rows long. Your computer's screen can't actually display this many rows and columns, so 1-2-3 displays only a portion of the worksheet. Of course, you can move to any part of the worksheet you like by giving 1-2-3 the appropriate commands. This chapter will demonstrate some techniques which you can use to put 1-2-3 to work right away, by moving around the worksheet and filling in some cells.

GETTING STARTED

Before you try to start 1-2-3, make sure you've installed it on your computer as discussed in the Introduction to this book, and the *Getting Started* manual that came with your 1-2-3 package. Remember, you need only perform the installation once. So, if you or someone else has already installed 1-2-3 on the computer, you're ready to go.

Starting 1-2-3 on a Hard Disk

If your computer has a hard disk, follow these instructions to get 1-2-3 "up-and-running." (If your computer has two floppy disk drives, skip to the next section.)

1. Turn on the computer in the usual manner. Enter the Date and Time if the computer requests. When the DOS C> prompt appears, the computer is *booted up*.

2. Log onto the directory where 1-2-3 is stored. (For example, if 1-2-3 is stored on a directory named 123, enter the command CD\123 at the DOS C> prompt, then press RETURN.)

3. Type the command:

   LOTUS

   and press RETURN. You'll see the Access menu appear on your screen. If not, you may have spelled LOTUS incorrectly, or started from the wrong directory. Or, perhaps, you did not complete the installation instructions in the *Getting Started* manual. Refer to the *Getting Started* manual, and try again.

Starting 1-2-3 on a Floppy Disk

If your computer has two floppy disk drives, follow these steps to start 1-2-3:

To start 1-2-3, enter the command LOTUS at the DOS A> or C> prompt and press RETURN. Press RETURN once again to select 1-2-3 from the Access menu that follows.

1. Start up your computer in the usual fashion so that the DOS A> prompt appears.

2. Enter the Date and Time if necessary.

3. Remove the System Disk in drive A, and put the 1-2-3 System Disk in its place.

4. Place a formatted (preferably blank) disk in drive B.

5. Type in the command:

   LOTUS

   and press return. You should see the Access menu appear on the screen.

The Access Menu

When the Access menu appears, you'll see some instructions on the screen and a menu of options at the top of the screen, as shown below:

1-2-3 PrintGraph Translate Install View Exit

You'll have a chance to explore all the options, but for now you just want to work with 1-2-3. So, with the 1-2-3 option highlighted, just press the RETURN key to move on to the 1-2-3 worksheet.

THE SCREEN

When you first call up 1-2-3, your screen will display the upper left portion of the worksheet as shown in Fig. 1-1. All of the cells are empty, of course, because you haven't filled any of them yet. But other parts of the screen have important information in them, which will be discussed now.

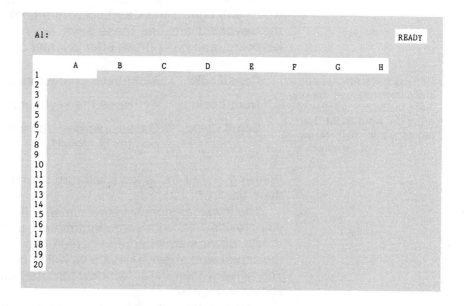

Fig.1-1. The 1-2-3 worksheet on the screen.

At the upper left corner of the screen is an area called the "control panel." The upper left corner of this area contains the symbol A1:, which indicates that the cell pointer is presently in column A, row 1. This line will also display the contents of a cell when you start filling in the worksheet. Anytime you type commands into 1-2-3, they are displayed in this section of the screen as you type. When you start working with 1-2-3 commands, menus of options and a brief explanation of each menu item will appear in the two blank lines beneath the A1: sign. In the upper right corner of the screen is a box which contains the *mode* that 1-2-3 is in at the moment. Right now, the worksheet is in the "READY" mode (Fig.1-1), indicating that it is ready to take commands from you.

Below the control panel are the worksheet *borders*. Across the top are columns A through H. Columns are labeled with letters. After column Z, columns are labeled with two letters. That is, the 27th column is AA, followed by AB, AC, etc. The columns beyond these are labeled BA through BZ, CA through CZ, etc., until the rightmost column, which is IV. There is also a border which labels the rows, numbered 1 through 20. The row numbers extend to 8192, but only 20 can fit on the screen. Just inside the border, the upper left cell is highlighted. This indicates that the *cell pointer* is in this cell. Any data that you type right now is placed in this cell. The cell is labeled A1, because it is in column A, row 1. In the upper left corner of the screen, in the control panel, the letters A1 indicate that this is indeed the position of the cell pointer.

The bottom right corner of the screen contains indicators, which will light if the Cap Lock, Num Lock or Scroll Lock keys on the keyboard are on. These keys are near the right side of the keyboard, and have these effects when on:

To use the arrow keys on the numeric keypad, make sure the Num Lock key is off. (The word NUM does not appear in right corner of the screen.)

Caps Lock: Alphabetic characters appear in uppercase.

Num Lock: Activates the keyboard's numeric keypad.

Scroll Lock: Causes screen to scroll each time the cell pointer is moved.

Pressing any of these keys will turn them on, pressing again turns them back off.

The lower left corner of the screen will display messages should you provide 1-2-3 with some information that it cannot compute.

As we've mentioned, the screen can only display a portion of the actual worksheet, as much as will fit comfortably on the screen. The screen, then, is a "window" into a section of the screen, as shown in Fig. 1-2.

You can use several keys to move around on the screen and display any portion of the worksheet you wish.

MOVING AROUND THE WORKSHEET

Use the arrow keys on the numeric keypad to move the cell pointer from one cell to another. The keypad is on the right side of

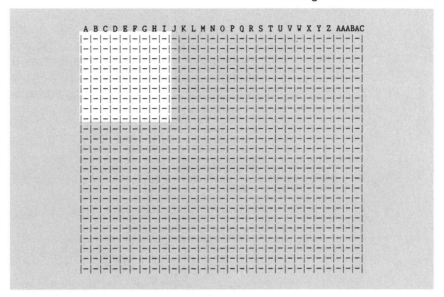

Fig.1-2. The screen shows only a portion of the worksheet.

the keyboard, as shown in Fig. 1-3. Notice that the keys labeled 8, 6, 2, and 4 also have arrows. Pressing these keys will move the cell pointer in the direction of the arrow. These *only* work if the Num Lock key is in the "off" position. If you try to move the cell pointer using these keys, and end up with numbers displayed on your screen instead, you must press the Num Lock key to activate the arrows again.

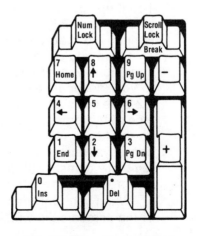

Fig. 1-3. The numeric keypad.

If you attempt to move the cell pointer beyond either the right edge or the bottom of the screen, the window simply adjusts itself accordingly. For example, if you move the cell pointer to row 20, column A (by pressing the down-arrow key 19 times), the cell pointer will be positioned as shown in Fig. 1-4.

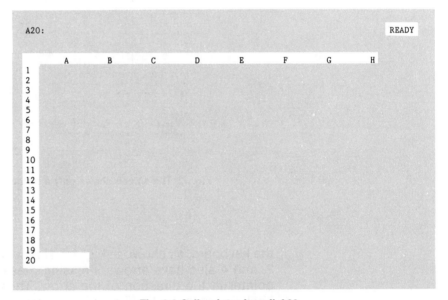

Fig. 1-4 Cell pointer in cell A20.

Now, if you again press the down-arrow key, the cell pointer will move to row 21, and the window will adjust accordingly, as in Fig. 1-5. If you attempt to move past a border, as if attempting to move to a column left of column A, the computer will beep at you to remind you that there is no cell there.

Often you need to travel much further than one cell at a time, and it isn't very efficient to continually press the arrow keys to get to your destination. Instead, you can just jump to a cell by giving 1-2-3 the cell's column and row number. Use the "GoTo" key for this type of movement. This key is special function key number five (F5) on the keyboard, as shown in Fig. 1-6. The figure shows the function keys with the 1-2-3 template installed on the keyboard. The template comes with 1-2-3 and should be used so that you don't have to memorize what all these keys do.

The GoTo key (F5) lets you quickly move the cell pointer to any cell on the worksheet.

When you first press the GoTo key, the control panel at the top of the screen asks which cell you wish to move the pointer to, like so:

Fig. 1-5. Cell pointer in cell A21.

Fig 1-6. The function keys with template.

All you need do now is type in the position of the cell you wish to jump to. For example, if you wish to position the pointer in column D, row 3, you just type in D3 and press the RETURN key. (The RETURN key is the one with the symbol ↵ on the keyboard.) The screen now looks like Fig. 1-7, with the cell pointer in column D row 3, and the control panel indicating that the pointer is in cell D3.

Fig. 1-7. Cell pointer in cell D3.

The Home key quickly returns the cell pointer to the "home" position, cell A1.

Notice that a key on the numeric keypad (shown in Fig. 1-3) is labeled "Home." Pressing this key will cause the cell pointer to return to its "home" position, cell A1. There is also a key labeled "End." That key, when pressed and followed by another press on one of the arrow keys, will move the cell pointer to the end of the worksheet. For example, typing End down-arrow will put the cell pointer to the bottom of the worksheet. Typing End → will move the pointer to the right corner of the worksheet.

Sometimes you will want to move the window to another section of the worksheet. If you consider the portion of the worksheet presently displayed on the screen as one *page* of the worksheet, you may want to move down one page or to the right one page. Several keys allow you to move the screen through the worksheet in a pagelike fashion. To move up one page, use the "PgUp" key (key number 9 on the numeric keypad). To move down one page, use the "PgDn" key (number 3 on the numeric keypad). To move the screen to the left or right, use the control key (labeled Ctrl on the keyboard) combined with an arrow key. To move the screen one page to the right, hold down the Ctrl key and press the right-arrow key. To move the screen one page to the left, hold down the Ctrl key and press the left-arrow key. Let's try an example. Right now, press the "Home" key to put the cell pointer in cell A1. If you press the PgDn key, you would see that the screen has indeed moved down a page, as shown in Fig. 1-8. Notice that the column titles are still A to H, but the row numbers are 21 to 40.

Fig. 1-8. Cell pointer in the "Home" position.

Now you can move one page to the right by holding down the Ctrl key and pressing the right-arrow key. Now the screen looks like Fig. 1-9. The row numbers are the same, but the column headings range from the letter I to P.

To move up a page, press the PgUp key, and the row numbers change back to 1 through 20, while the column headings do not change, as shown in Fig. 1-10.

Now you can move the screen to the left a page, by holding down the Ctrl key and pressing the left-arrow key, which will return you to your original page (Fig. 1-11).

You have actually completed a circle around a section of the worksheet. Fig. 1-12 shows the entire series of events that has occurred with these four page movements.

In addition, 1-2-3 also allows you to move the screen to the left

Fig. 1-9. Cell pointer in cell I21.

Fig. 1-10. Cell pointer in cell I1.

and right using other key strokes. For example, pressing the tab key (labeled with both a left and right arrow) will move the screen a page to the right (equivalent to Ctrl →). Holding down the shift key

Fig. 1-11. Cell pointer in cell A1.

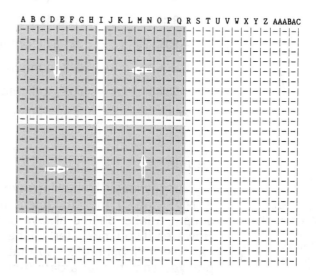

Fig. 1-12. Four "page" movements around the worksheet.

while pressing the tab key will move the screen a page to the left (identical to Ctrl ←).

Once you are familiar with moving the cell pointer and window around the worksheet, you can start filling in some cells. However, first there are a few things you need to know about how 1-2-3 views data.

TYPES OF DATA

Data on the worksheet comes in three types: "labels," "numbers," and "formulas."

Numbers

Numbers are numeric values, like quantities and dollar amounts, that begin with a number (0–9), or one of the numerical punctuations + (plus), − (minus/ hyphen), . (decimal point/period) or $ (dollar) sign.

1-2-3 considers any data entered that "looks like" a number to be a number. Therefore, the number must begin with a numeric character (0 to 9), or a plus sign, a minus sign, a decimal point, or a dollar sign. A number may contain only one decimal point and may not contain a comma or a space. Numbers cannot include alphabetic characters, except the letter E, which is used for scientific notation. Below are examples of valid and invalid numbers:

Valid Numbers	Invalid Numbers
.99	.99.1 (too many decimal points)
1234	1,234 (can't have comma)
123.45	A123.45 (has an alphabetic letter)
− 9999.99	321 34 (contains a space)
1.2E + 0	64K (contains a letter)
$123.45	(OK, indicates dollar amount)
22%	(OK, indicates percent)

Labels

Labels are nonnumeric data such as names and addresses. They should begin with a letter (A–Z), or one of the label prefixes: ' (apostrophe), " (quotation mark), ^(caret), or \ (backslash).

Specify labels by making sure that the first character in the data is NOT one of the characters used to specify a number. Quite simply, a label should always begin with an alphabetic character. However, if you must start a label with a number (i.e., 123 A St.), you can use a "label prefix" so that 1-2-3 doesn't get confused. Label prefixes specify that a data item is a label and affects the way in which the label is displayed. The label prefixes are:

'   apostrophe: left—justifies a label in a cell.

"   quotation mark: right—justifies a label in a cell.

^   caret: centers a label in a cell.

\   backslash: repeats the label within the cell.

Some valid and invalid labels are shown below:

Valid Label	Invalid Label	
January 1, 1983	**1/1/83**	(starts with a number)
'123 A St.	**123 A St.**	(starts with a number)
Interest	**– Interest**	(starts with minus sign)

Preceding a label with a backslash fills the entire cell character. For example, entering ＼ – into a cell will produce ＿＿＿＿＿＿ .

Formulas

Formulas perform calculations on other data in a worksheet, and must start with a number symbol or the @ sign.

Formulas generally contain cell reference numbers and arithmetic operators to perform math. Like numbers, formulas may not contain any spaces. The arithmetic operators that 1-2-3 uses in performing math are summarized below. These operators follow the normal order of precedence that the rules of math dictate. That is, if a formula contains both multiplication and addition, then the multiplication takes place first. Operations of equal precedence take place from left to right. The operands below are displayed in order of precedence:

( )   :parentheses used for grouping

∧   :caret used for exponentiation

–   :negative number

*   :multiplication

/   :division

+   :addition

–   :subtraction

You can see how operators are used in formulas by looking at some examples, as follows:

1 + 1	:produces 2, the sum of 1 + 1.
A1 + B1	:the sum of the contents of cell A1 plus the contents of cell B1.
A1 + A2*A3	:the contents of cell A1 added to the product of the contents of cells A2 and A3.
(A1 + A2)/A3	:the sum of the contents of cells A1 and A2 divided by the contents of cell A3.
C3∧(1/3)	:the cube root of the contents of cell C3.

Formulas follow the same rules as numbers. The examples above are "logically" correct, but some of them break the rules for defining formulas. Like a number, a formula must not begin with an alphabetic letter. A formula may begin with any of these characters:

0 1 2 3 4 5 6 7 8 9 . (@ # $ + −

Below are examples of valid and invalid formulas:

Valid Formula	Invalid Formula
+ A1 + A2	A1 + A2 (starts with a letter)
(C3 + C4)∗ @ 2	(C3 + C4)∗2 (contains a space)
10 + 10	'10 + 10 (starts with an apostrophe)

In general, if you get in the habit of beginning all formulas with a + sign or open parenthesis, you will have no trouble.

Now, before providing you with more basic information, all of this will be put together with some practical applications in mind.

ENTERING DATA INTO THE WORKSHEET

Entering data into the worksheet is a three-step process:

1. Position the cell pointer into the cell where the data will appear.

2. Type the data to be entered onto the screen.

3. Press the RETURN (↵) key, or an arrow key when finished typing the cell's contents.

You will begin with a simple example using a teacher's grade book. First, you will need a blank screen to work with, as in Fig. 1-13. Notice that the cell pointer is in cell A1.

First, type in the students' names down the left column. These will be labels, because they will not be used in any calculations, nor will they perform calculations. So here is a list of our students:

Adams
Brown
Cass
Davids
Edwards

Fig. 1-13. A blank worksheet.

First, type in Adams. As you are typing, the name appears in the control panel, as shown in Fig. 1-14.

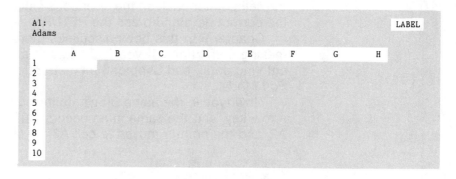

Fig. 1-14. Name typed into the control panel.

To make corrections while entering data into a cell, use the Backspace key. If 1-2-3 rejects an entry, press Escape and try again.

If you make a mistake while typing in a name (or any data into any cell, for that matter), you can use the backspace key to back up and retype your entry. The backspace key has a large, dark backward arrow ← on it.

Once Adams is typed on the screen, press the down-arrow key, which will cause his name to appear in cell A1, and the cell pointer to move down to cell A2 (Fig. 1-15).

If at any time while trying the exercises in this book you find that 1-2-3 beeps and does not accept your entry when you press the RETURN key or an arrow key, just press the Escape key (labeled Esc or Cancel on most keyboards) and try again. In fact, any time you have a problem with 1-2-3, pressing the Escape key will probably help you get out of it. (It's called the Escape key because it always lets you escape from some problem.)

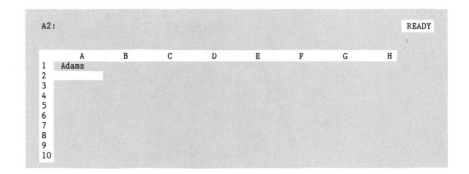

Fig. 1-15. Name entered in cell A1.

If you notice an error after you've already pressed the RETURN key or an arrow key to enter data into a cell, use the arrow keys to put the cell pointer back on the erroneous cell data. Then simply retype the correct data and press the RETURN key.

Chapter 6 in this book discusses more elegant techniques for making corrections. If you find yourself making many errors when entering data, read Chapter 6 for instructions on *editing* data in the *Edit Mode*.

Now type in the name Brown, followed by a press on the down-arrow key, and the same thing occurs, but his name goes into cell A2, and the pointer moves to cell A3, as shown in Fig. 1-16.

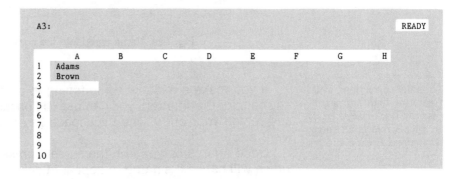

Fig. 1-16. Two names on the worksheet.

Now simply type in each name, one at a time, following each name with a press on the down-arrow key. When you're done, the screen looks like Fig. 1-17.

Now you can type in some test scores, like these:

Adams   100   90

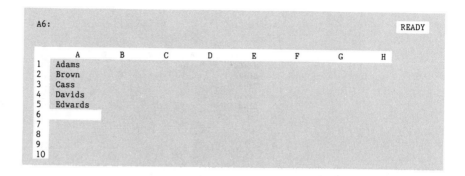

Fig. 1-17. Names in column A.

Brown	90	80
Cass	100	95
Davids	98	80
Edwards	90	75

You need to put these in the second and third columns of the worksheet. Use the arrow keys (or the GoTo key) to position the cell pointer to cell B1, as shown in Fig. 1-18.

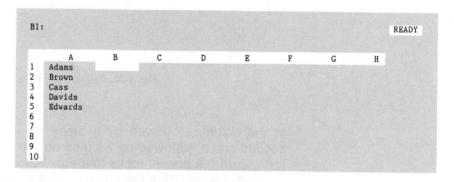

Fig. 1-18. Cell pointer in Cell B1.

Type in the numbers just as you did the labels. You can type in the first set of scores by typing in each number one at a time, following each number with a press on the down-arrow key, which will make the worksheet look like Fig. 1-19.

Notice that the cell pointer is down in row 6. To type in the next set of scores, you need to get the pointer up to cell C1, either by using some arrow keys or the GoTo key. Once that's done, the worksheet will look like Fig. 1-20.

Type in the second column of test scores using the same procedure as for the first column of scores. That is, type in the first score

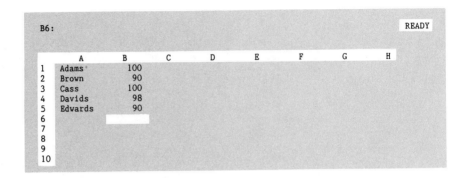

Fig. 1-19. Scores in column B.

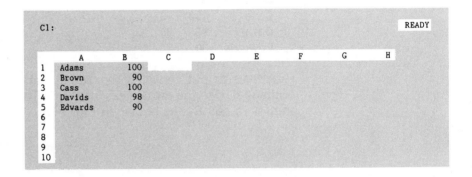

Fig. 1-20. Cell pointer in cell C1.

in the column, followed by a press on the down-arrow key; the second score, followed by a press on the down-arrow key; and so forth, until the screen looks like Fig. 1-21.

And now you have the basic data of a grade book. But you don't have the students' average test scores. You're certainly not about to figure them out by hand when you have a computer at your fingertips. We'll have to add some formulas to have 1-2-3 do this work for us.

First you need to figure out a formula. Adams' average test score is the sum of the contents of B1 and C1 divided by two. In a 1-2-3 formula, that looks like this:

(B1 + C1)/2

To type it in, position the cell pointer to column D, row 1, as in Fig. 1-22.

Next, type in the formula (B1 + C1)/2, followed by a press on the

```
C6:                                                          READY

        A        B        C        D        E        F        G        H
1   Adams      100       90
2   Brown       90       80
3   Cass       100       95
4   Davids      98       80
5   Edwards     90       75
6
7
8
9
10
```

Fig. 1-21. Scores in column C.

```
D1:                                                          READY

        A        B        C        D        E        F        G        H
1   Adams      100       90
2   Brown       90       80
3   Cass       100       95
4   Davids      98       80
5   Edwards     90       75
6
7
8
9
10
```

Fig. 1-22. Cell pointer in cell D1.

down-arrow key. This gives the result shown in Fig. 1-23. The result of the formula—not the formula itself—is displayed in that cell.

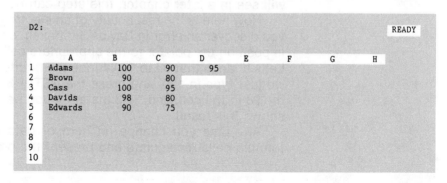

```
D2:                                                          READY

        A        B        C        D        E        F        G        H
1   Adams      100       90       95
2   Brown       90       80
3   Cass       100       95
4   Davids      98       80
5   Edwards     90       75
6
7
8
9
10
```

Fig. 1-23. Average in cell D1.

Adams' test average (95) is displayed in cell D1. The pointer is now in cell D2. The formula for Brown's average test score is:

(B2 + C2) / 2

So if you type in this formula, and press the down-arrow key, Brown's average is displayed in cell D2 (as in Fig. 1-24), and the pointer has advanced to cell D3.

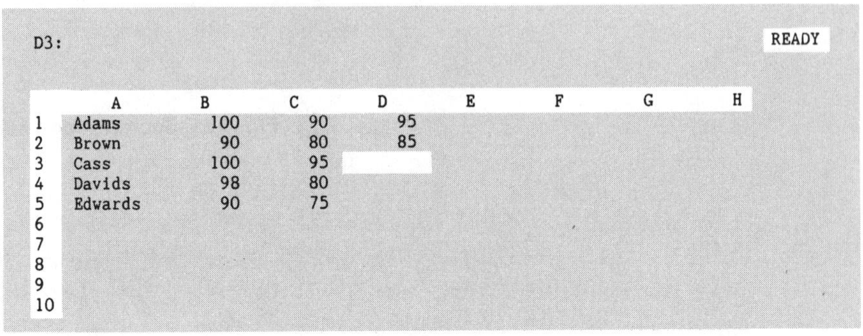

```
D3:                                                              READY

        A        B        C        D        E     F     G     H
  1  Adams     100       90       95
  2  Brown      90       80       85
  3  Cass      100       95
  4  Davids     98       80
  5  Edwards    90       75
  6
  7
  8
  9
 10
```

Fig. 1-24. The calculated averages.

Now you can type in the rest of the formulas in the usual fashion. The remaining formulas are:

(B3 + C3) / 2
(B4 + C4) / 2
(B5 + C5) / 2

As you type in each one, the result appears on the screen. (As you will see in a later chapter, this step can be simplified by copying.)

Now here is the real beauty of an electronic worksheet. Suppose you discover an error in Davids' first exam score. All you need to do is position the pointer to the appropriate cell, as shown in Fig. 1-25. Let's change that 98 to 100. Since the pointer is already in this cell, we just type in 100, and press the RETURN key. The 100 replaces the 98 in the cell, and 1-2-3 instantly updates his average! Fig. 1-26 shows this result.

Any time you change an item of data on the worksheet, all formula cells recalculate and present the proper results.

SAVING THE WORKSHEET

Whenever you enter data on a worksheet, you need to store that data on a disk file if you wish to use it again. If you turn off the

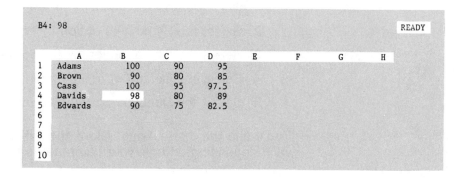

```
B4: 98                                                                    READY

         A          B         C         D        E        F        G       H
  1   Adams        100        90        95
  2   Brown         90        80        85
  3   Cass         100        95       97.5
  4   Davids        98        80        89
  5   Edwards       90        75       82.5
  6
  7
  8
  9
 10
```

Fig. 1-25. Calculated average in column D.

```
B4: 100                                                                   READY

         A          B         C         D        E        F        G       H
  1   Adams        100        90        95
  2   Brown         90        80        85
  3   Cass         100        95       97.5
  4   Davids       100        80        90
  5   Edwards       90        75       82.5
  6
  7
  8
  9
 10
```

Fig. 1-26. Instantly recalculated average.

computer, or exit 1-2-3 prior to saving your work, the data will be lost forever. Fortunately, saving a worksheet is a relatively simple task.

Before you save this particular worksheet, however, you might want to check, and perhaps change, the drive that 1-2-3 will store the file on. You need only perform this process once to set up the *default drive*. In the future, 1-2-3 will always use this drive for saving (and retrieving) worksheets.

Setting the Default Drive

Follow these steps to set up a default drive for storing worksheets:

1. Call up the 1-2-3 main menu by pressing the / key. You'll see the menu appear, which contains several options as below:

   Worksheet Range Copy Move File Print Graph Data System Quit
   Global,Insert,Delete,Column,Erase,Titles,Window,Status,Page

(we'll discuss the menus in more detail in Chapter 3).

2. Select the Worksheet option by typing the letter W.

3. Select the Global option by typing the letter G.

4. Select the Default option by typing the letter D.

5. Select the Directory option by typing the letter D.

You'll see the instructions below (though the C:\123 portion will vary, depending on how your computer is presently configured):

Directory at startup: C:\123

If you are using a hard disk, the "suggested" default drive shown (C:\123 in this example) should match the directory you start 1-2-3 from. If you are using a floppy disk system, the default drive should be B:\. If not, press the backspace key a few times to erase the suggested default drive, then type in the appropriate default drive. On a hard disk system, type C: followed by a back-slash, followed by the name of your 1-2-3 directory. On a floppy disk system, type B:\. Press RETURN after entering the new default drive. (If no changes were necessary, just press the RETURN key.)

6. Type the letter U to select the Update option from the menu to save the default directory setting.

7. Type the letter Q to select Quit and exit the menu.

As mentioned, you will not need to repeat this procedure each time you want to save a worksheet. Once the default drive is set, 1-2-3 will use that drive both to save and retrieve worksheet files. We'll discuss the menus themselves in more detail in Chapter 3.

Saving a Worksheet File

To save the gradebook worksheet you've entered in this chapter, you need to select the File Save options from the menu, and enter a file name. In more detail, here are the exact steps to follow:

1. Call up the 1-2-3 main menu by pressing the / key.

2. Select the File option, either by using the right-arrow key to highlight the File option followed by a press on the RE-TURN key, or simply by typing the letter F. This brings up a submenu, as shown below:

Retrieve Save Combine Xtract Erase List Import Directory

3. Select the Save option, either by highlighting the option

with the right-arrow key and pressing RETURN, or by typing the letter S. The control panel displays the instructions:

Enter save file name: C: \ *.wk1

Always save your work before exiting 1-2-3 or turning off the computer. To do so, select the File and Save options from the menu by typing /FS. Enter a valid file name (up to eight characters long, no spaces or punctuation).

(You might also see the names of any existing 1-2-3 worksheets previously saved on the disk.)

4. Enter a valid DOS file name. A valid DOS file name can be up to eight characters in length, and may not contain any spaces or punctuation. In this example, type in the file name GRADES and press the RETURN key. A copy of the worksheet will be stored on disk, and will also remain on the screen.

Safety Warning

If you (or anybody else) has previously saved a worksheet with the file name GRADES, you'll see the safety warning:

Cancel Replace
Cancel command—Leave existing file intact

If you attempt to save two worksheets with the same file name, the worksheet currently displayed on the screen will replace the worksheet already stored with that file name. Before replacing an existing worksheet with the one on your screen, 1-2-3 warns you that you are about to replace another worksheet. If you decide to use a different file name for the new worksheet, select the Cancel option, then type /FS once again and enter a new file name. If it's OK to overwrite the existing file, just select the Replace option by typing R.

Once you've saved a worksheet, anytime that you save the worksheet again in the future, 1-2-3 will "suggest" the same file name, as below:

Enter save file name: C: \ GRADES

You can just press RETURN to use the suggested file name over again. Of course, 1-2-3 will present the Cancel and Replace options before overwriting the previously saved copy of the worksheet. If you've simply made changes or improvements on the worksheet, select the Replace option. If you wish to save the original worksheet, and the new one separately, you'll need to select Cancel, then type /FS again and assign a new name for the new copy (such as GRADES2).

EXITING 1-2-3

Before turning off computer, save your worksheet with /FS, then type /Q to Quit 1-2-3. Select Exit from the Access menu to return to the DOS prompt.

Once you've saved your worksheet, you should still exit 1-2-3 before turning off the computer. Here are the simple steps required to do so:

1. Call up the menu by typing /.

2. Select the Quit option by typing Q.

3. Answer yes, by typing the letter Y, when 1-2-3 double-checks your request.

4. When the ACCESS menu appears, type E to select the Exit option.

When you've successfully exited 1-2-3, you'll see the DOS A> or C> prompt appear on the screen. This is the safe time to remove any floppy disks from their drives and turn off the computer.

RETRIEVING A WORKSHEET

To retrieve a previously saved worksheet, select the File and Retrieve options from the 1-2-3 main menu by typing /FR. Highlight the name of the worksheet to retrieve, and press RETURN.

In the future, you can access any worksheet that you've saved by first getting 1-2-3 up-and-running. Use the techniques we discussed at the beginning of this chapter to do so. On a floppy disk system, be sure to put your data disk in drive B.

When you see a blank 1-2-3 worksheet on the screen, follow these steps to retrieve your worksheet:

1. Type / to call up the main menu.

2. Type F to select the File option.

3. Type R to select the Retrieve option.

1-2-3 will display a list of 1-2-3 worksheets that have previously been saved. Each file name has the *extension* .WK1 after it, which 1-2-3 adds to any worksheet file name that you assign. To retrieve one, use the left- and right-arrow keys to highlight the worksheet name (GRADES.WK1 in this example), then press RETURN. (Optionally, you can just type in the file name, GRADES, then press RETURN.) Your worksheet will appear on the screen, looking exactly as it did when you saved it.

WHAT HAVE YOU LEARNED?

1. To get 1-2-3 up-and-running on a hard disk system, log onto the appropriate directory on your hard disk, if necessary, and enter the command LOTUS at the C: prompt. Select 1-2-3 from the ACCESS menu.

2. To get 1-2-3 up-and-running on a floppy disk system, put your 1-2-3 system disk in drive A, and a data disk in drive B. Enter the command LOTUS at the A> prompt. Select 1-2-3 from the ACCESS menu.

3. The screen displays only a portion of the entire worksheet, which is 256 columns wide, and 8192 rows long. The keys on the numeric keypad, the Tab key, and the GoTo (F5) key allow you to move the cell pointer about the entire worksheet.

4. There are three main types of data that you enter on worksheets, nonnumeric data called *labels*, numeric data, such as quantities and dollar amounts, and formulas, which perform calculations.

5. To enter data on a worksheet, position the cell pointer to where you want the data to be stored, type in the data, then press the RETURN key or one of the arrow keys.

6. To make corrections while entering data, use the backspace key. If 1-2-3 refuses to accept an entry, press Escape and try again.

7. To save a worksheet, call up the menu and select the File and Save options (by typing /FS). Enter a file name of up to eight characters long, and press RETURN.

8. To retrieve a worksheet, call up the menu and select the File and Retrieve options (by typing /FR). Highlight the name of the worksheet to retrieve, and press RETURN. (Optionally, type in the name of the worksheet to retrieve, then press RETURN.)

QUIZ

1. The command that you enter at the DOS A> or C> prompt to get 1-2-3 "up-and-running" on your computer is:
   a. 1-2-3
   b. LOTUS

    c. ACCESS

    d. RUN

2. The actual size of the 1-2-3 worksheet is:
   a. 8 columns by 20 rows
   b. 8 rows by 20 columns
   c. 256 columns by 8192 rows
   d. 8192 columns by 256 rows

3. The arrow keys on the numeric keypad work only if:
   a. The Scroll Lock key is on
   b. The Scroll Lock key is off
   c. The Num Lock key is on
   d. The Num Lock key is off

4. To quickly move the cell pointer to a specific cell, press the
   a. GoTo key (F5)
   b. End key
   c. PgUp key
   d. Calc (F9) key

5. Which of the following is a valid label entry?
   a. 123 Apple St.
   b. 1/12/86
   c. — Quarter 1 —
   d. Smith

6. How would the label ^Qtr 1 be displayed in a cell?
   a. Qtr 1, left justified
   b. Qtr 1, right justified
   c. Qtr 1, centered
   d. ^Qtr 1, left justified

7. Which of the following is a valid number entry?
   a. 123 Apple St.
   b. – 355.67
   c. 12,876
   d. .991.32

8. A formula may NOT begin with which of the following characters?
   a. A plus (+) sign
   b. An open parenthesis (()
   c. A number (0–9)
   d. A letter (A–Z)

9. To save a worksheet, select the File and Save options from the menu by typing which keystrokes?
   a. F5FS
   b. \FS
   c. /FS
   d. MFR

10. To retrieve a worksheet, select the File Retrieve options by typing which keystrokes?
    a. F5FR
    b. \ FR
    c. /FR
    d. F2

Chapter 2

FUNCTIONS AND FORMULAS

ABOUT THIS CHAPTER

This chapter summarizes all of the *functions* that you can use in your 1-2-3 worksheets. These functions perform calculations beyond simple addition (+), subtraction (−), multiplication (*), division (/) and exponentiation (^) that the formula operators provide. Though you will probably never use all of the functions that 1-2-3 has to offer, it's a good idea to get acquainted with their availability. If you would like to try some of the examples in this chapter, clear the worksheet by pressing the / key and selecting Worksheet Erase Yes. (Just type /WEY to do so.)

USING FUNCTIONS

If your pocket calculator cost more than $1.98, or came as a prize in a breakfast cereal box from a reputable company, chances are it has some built-in function keys on it, such as a square-root key, or perhaps even some trigonometric functions. These are provided because it is pretty difficult to do these calculations using add, subtract, multiply, and divide. The 1-2-3 worksheet has many built-in functions too. However, you don't press a key to use a 1-2-3 function. You type the name of the function (preceded by the @ symbol) into a cell, and 1-2-3 handles it from there.

Most functions require an *argument*. An argument in computer jargon is simply some value for the function to work upon. (Personally, I have had other types of arguments with my computer—none of which I've ever won.) The argument to a function is always placed in parentheses after the function. For example, the function to determine the square root of a number in 1-2-3 is @SQRT. The function can't do much by itself, it needs to know what to find the square root of. That is, it needs an argument. To ask 1-2-3 for the square root of nine, simply put this formula (the function with its argument) into any cell of the worksheet:

@**SQRT(9)**

Whichever cell you place this formula into will display the number 3, the square root of nine. The (9) is the argument. The argument need not be a specific number. It can be another cell's value. For example, if cell A1 contained the number 64, then the formula:

@**SQRT(A1)**

would display 8, the square root of 64.

The argument need not be a single cell either. For example, if cell A1 contained the number 90, and cell A2 contained the number 10, then the formula:

@**SQRT(A1 + A2)**

The argument to a function can be real data, a reference to a cell, a reference to a group of cells, a formula, or another function.

would display 10, the square root of cell A1 (90) plus A2 (10).

In some cases, the argument may actually be a whole row or column of numbers. For example, the SUM and AVG (average) functions are usually used with numerous arguments. Fig. 2-1 shows a worksheet with a column of numbers typed in.

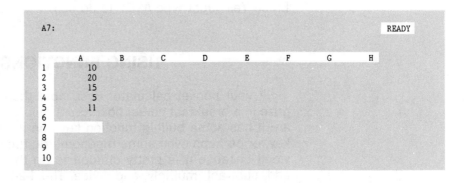

Fig. 2-1. Numbers on a worksheet.

A group (or range) of cells is specified with two periods, such as A1..Z28.

You can use the symbol .. to stand for "all the values between one cell and another." Therefore, to sum all of the values between A1 and A5 (inclusive), type in the formula:

@**SUM(A1..A5)**

More specifically, position the cell pointer A7 (as shown in Fig. 2-1), type in the formula @SUM(A1..A5), press RETURN, and get the result displayed in Fig. 2-2. The sum is displayed in cell A7.

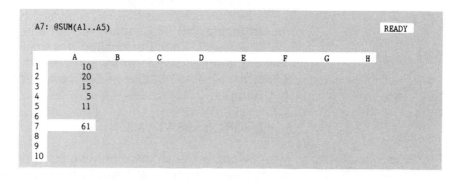

Fig. 2-2. Sum calculated with @SUM (A1..A5).

Similarly, to place the cell pointer to cell A8, type in the formula:

@AVG(A1..A5)

press RETURN, and the average of the column of numbers would appear in cell A8, as shown in Fig. 2-3.

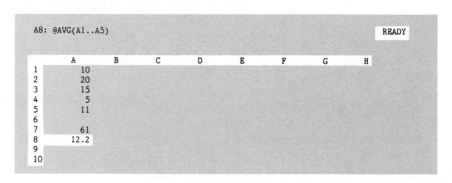

Fig. 2-3. Average calculated with @AVG (A1..A5).

You selected cells A7 and A8 at random. No rule states that these formulas must appear at the bottom of the column or even in the same column. You could have placed these formulas in any cell on the entire worksheet and still come up with the same answer.

Functions can also use other functions as their argument. For example, the @ ABS function converts a number to its absolute value (i.e., if it is a negative number, ABS will change it to a positive number). So, if cell A1 contained the number -90, and cell A2 contained the number -10, then the function:

@SQRT(@ABS(A1 + A2))

would display 10, the square root of the absolute value of -100 ($-90 + -10$). These are called *nested* functions because one is inside the other. Any formula that contains parentheses must have exactly the same number of open and closed parentheses. Hence the formula:

@SQRT(@ABS(A1 + A2)

A formula must have the same number of open and closed parentheses.

won't work, because there are two open parentheses, and only one closed parenthesis. 1-2-3 would beep at you if you typed in this formula, and wouldn't accept it until it was fixed.

When 1-2-3 rejects formula, it will beep and you'll be in Edit mode (as indicated by the word EDIT in the upper right corner of the screen). You can use the left- and right-arrow keys to move the cursor and make corrections. The Del key will delete the character above the cursor. After correcting the formula, press RETURN to enter it into the cell. Optionally, pressing Escape will erase the formula from the control panel so you can start over from scratch. (Editing is discussed in detail in Chapter 6.)

A quick easy way to make sure you have equal parentheses in a formula is to start counting from zero at the left, add one for each open parenthesis, and subtract one for each closed parentheses. If you end up with zero at the end, you have entered the formula correctly. For example, when you try it with the formula below, the end result is zero:

@SQRT(@ABS(A1 + A2))
   ↑   ↑   ↑   ↑ ↑
   0   1   2   1 0

However, with this formula, the end result is one because a closed parenthesis is missing:

@SQRT(@ABS(A1 + A2)
   ↑   ↑   ↑   ↑
   0   1   2   1

This concentration on precision may seem trivial now, but when you nest functions five or six deep, parentheses can become a real chore. Programmers use this technique all the time when writing software because it is easy, and it works.

Arguments may also be quite complex. For example, the following formula:

@ABS(@SUM(A1..A5 + G7/4)

states that the absolute value of the sum of columns A1 through A5, plus the quotient of cell G7 divided by four, is to be displayed. Again, notice that an equal number of open and closed parentheses occur within the argument list.

Functions do not always display results in a cell immediately. For example, the function:

@SQRT(@ABS(A1))

only displays the square root of the absolute value of the contents of cell A1. The absolute value, per se, is never displayed. It is used only to calculate the absolute value before the square root calculation takes place. Therefore, the term *returns* is often used when discussing the effect of a function on a value. That is, you "send" the function some numeric value, and it "returns" another value. In the expression below:

@SQRT(81)

You send the value (81) to the SQRT function, and it returns the value, 9 (the square root of 81). We'll use the term "returns" often throughout this chapter.

Functions are a tool you can use with your worksheet. Before you start to build a worksheet, it's good to know what tools you have available to work with. In this chapter, we'll summarize the 1-2-3 functions. Don't worry about memorizing them. Just scan through and make a mental note of those which you may want to use in your profession.

As in the foregoing examples, some functions require only a single argument. Others require a range of values (e.g., A1..A5), while others require combinations of single arguments and ranges.

The various functions will be separated into types to help you more easily spot functions relevant to your particular needs. The 1-2-3 manual discusses all the functions in more technical detail. For on-screen help with functions while using 1-2-3, press the Help key (F1) and use the down-arrow key to highlight Help Index. Press RETURN, highlight the @ Functions option, and press RETURN again. Press Escape to return to the worksheet.

SUMMARY OF FUNCTIONS

This summary shows the name and proper argument for many of the 1-2-3's more commonly used functions. Some functions operate on entire ranges of numbers (either a row, column, or even a block). When this is the case, we use the word "range" in the argument list [e.g., @SUM(range)]. Otherwise, we use a single variable name [e.g., @SQRT(x)]. Some functions require two or three arguments in which case we separate the arguments with commas [e.g., @IRR(guess, range)]. Some functions require no arguments, and appear without an argument list (e.g., @RAND).

Wherever a single argument is required, the argument can be either an actual number or a reference to a cell. Whenever a range is required, you should use the beginning and end points in the range (e.g., A1..A10).

The remainder of this chapter provides a brief description of each function along with examples of proper *syntax* (grammatical rules). The words "calculates," "displays," and "returns" are used interchangeably.

GENERAL MATHEMATICAL FUNCTIONS

1-2-3 provides these general mathematical functions:

@SUM(range)

Sum of a Group of Numbers
Returns the sum of a group of numbers specified in the range. Example: @SUM(A1..A25) gives the sum of all numbers in the column A1 to A25.

@AVG(range)

The Mathematical functions perform basic arithmetic on numbers.

Average of a Group of Numbers
Returns the average of a group of numbers (including zeros, but not blanks). Example: @AVG(A1..Z1) returns the average of all numbers in row A1 to Z1.

ABS(x)

The Absolute Value of a Number
Returns the absolute value of a number or a single cell. Example:@ABS(B2) returns the absolute value of the contents of cell B2.

@ROUND(x,places)

Round a Number
Rounds the value to the number of places specified. Example: @ROUND(9.129,2) returns the value, 9.13. Either *x* or *places* may be cell locations. [@ROUND(A1,A2)].

@INT(x)

Integer Portion of a Number
Removes the decimal portion of a number. Example: If cell B1 contains 1.23456, @INT(B1) returns 1.

@RAND

Random Numbers
Returns a random number between 0 and 1. Does not use an argument. Example: @RAND returns the value 0.147506 or any other number between 0 and 1.

@SQRT(x)

Square Root
Displays the square root of a number. Example: @SQRT(J11) returns the square root of the number stored in cell J11.

FINANCIAL FUNCTIONS

The financial functions perform calculations that are useful in any business setting.

The financial functions, as the name implies, perform calculations commonly used in financial applications. The main trick to using the financial functions is getting interest rates and periods to match. For example, if you use an *annual* percentage rate to calculate a *monthly* payment on a loan, the results will be incorrect. The examples shown in this section will demonstrate correct manipulations of interest rates and periods.

Some examples will show the results of calculations rounded to two decimal places. If you try out the examples, your screen may show more decimal places. Chapter 3 in this book shows techniques for controlling the display, including decimal places, of numbers.

@CTERM(interest,fv,pv)

Compounding Periods
Calculates the number of compounding periods required for an investment at a present value (pv) to reach a future value (fv) earning a fixed interest rate (interest) per compounding period. Example: How long does it take to turn $10,000 into $20,000 at a fixed rate of 10% per year, compounded monthly. (Since the interest is compounded monthly, the rate needs to be divided by 12.) The answer is calculated with the formula @CTERM (10%/12,20000,10000). The answer is 83.52 months (or about 7 years).

@DDB(cost,salvage,life,period)

Double-Declining Depreciation
Calculates the depreciation

allowance on an asset at a specific period of time using the double-declining balance method. Example: Your office pays $5,000 for a machine that will have a salvage value of $1,000 at the end of 5 years. What is the depreciation in the first year? The formula to find out is @DDB(5000,1000,5,1), which returns $2,000, the depreciation allowance for the first year. The formula, @DDB(5000,1000,5,3), returns $720.00, the depreciation allowance for the third year.

@FV(payment,interest,term)

Future Value

Computes the future value of an investment based on a number of equal payments, each earning interest at a periodic rate, over a specified term. Example: You deposit $4,000 annually into an account which earns 10% annually. What is the value of the account after 25 years? The formula @FV(4000,0.1,25) calculates the result, $393,388.24.

@IRR(guess,range)

Internal Rate of Return

Calculates the internal rate of return of an investment, and series of calculations, based on an initial guess. Example: Cell A1 contains the initial investment —50000 (entered as a negative number because it is outflow). Cells A2..A14 each contain the number 500, representing payments returned on the investment. Cell A16 contains the number .01, a first guess for the internal rate of return. The formula @IRR(A16,A1..A14) displays the result .039, the internal rate of return for the cash flows in column A.

@NPV(interest,range)

Net Present Value
Calculates the net present value of a series of future cash flows discounted at a fixed period interest rate. Example: Cells A10..A14 each contain the number 1200, each representing a cash flow. What is the net present value of the cash flows given a discount rate of 15%? The formula   @NPV(0.15,A10..A14) displays the result $4,022.59— the present value of the future cash flows.

When calculating monthly financial results from yearly financial data, remember to divide the annual interest by 12, and to multiply the years by 12.

@PMT(principal,interest,term)

Payment on a Loan
Calculates the payment on a loan, given the principal, periodic interest rate, and number of terms. To calculate *monthly* payments given an *annual* percentage rate, and a term in years, divide the interest rate by 12, and multiply the term by 12. For example, what is the monthly payment on a loan of $147,000.00, given a 9.375% annual interest rate, and a term of 20 years? The   formula   @PMT (147000,9.375%/12,20 * 12)   returns the correct monthly payment, $1358.26.

@PV(payment,interest,term)

Present Value
Computes the present value of a series of equal payments discounted at a periodic interest rate for a term. Example: You are considering buying a second trust deed, wherein the lender pays $2000 a year for 25 years. Given that you could earn 12% by investing your money elsewhere, what is the present value of the loan, including the 12% interest that you won't earn if you buy the loan. The formula @PV(2000,12%,25)   returns

$15,686.28, the cash value of the loan in today's dollars.

@RATE(fv,pv,term)

Periodic Interest Required
Calculates the periodic interest required for an investment at a present value (pv) to reach a future value (fv) within a certain period of time (term). Twenty five years from now, you want to retire with $1,000,000.00 in the bank. You have $50,000 to put away in a retirement account. How much interest (compounded monthly) will you need to earn to accumulate a million dollars? The answer is given by the formula @RATE(1000000, 50000,25*12). The answer is .010035 per month. (Multiply that by 12 to get the annual interest rate 12.04%).

@SLN(cost,salvage,life)

Straight-Line Depreciation
Computes the straight-line depreciation allowance of an asset for any given period. Example: You buy a computer for $5,000 that has a salvage value of $1,000 in five years. In any given year, the depreciation allowance is given by the formula @SLN(5000,1000,5), which returns $800.00.

@SYD(cost,salvage,life,period)

Sum-of-Years Depreciation
Determines the depreciation allowance for a given year using the sum-of-years-digits method. Example: You purchase a $5,000 computer that has a salvage value of $1,000 after five years. The depreciation allowance for the first year is given by the formula @SYD(5000,1000,5,1), which return $1333.33. The depreciation allowance for the third year is given by the formula

@SYD(5000,1000,5,3), which returns $800.00.

@TERM(payment,interest,fv)

Required Term
Computes the number of periods required for regular payments, at a fixed periodic interest rate, to reach a future value (fv). Example: Given that you can invest $4,000 a year into a retirement account, at 10% annual interest, how long will it take to accumulate $500,000.00? The formula @TERM(4000,10%,500000) returns the answer, 27.3 years.

STATISTICAL FUNCTIONS

1-2-3 includes a number of functions for performing basic statistical analyses of data. Section III of this book discusses additional statistical functions that are used with 1-2-3's database management capability.

@COUNT(range)

Count the Items in a List
Counts how many nonblank cells there are in a range of cells, and returns that number. Example: @COUNT(A1..A10) would return 10 if all cells were filled. It would return 6 if four cells were blank.

@STD(range)

Standard Deviation
Returns the standard deviation of a range of numbers (it ignores blank cells in the list). Example: @STD(Z1..Z28) provides the standard deviation of all values between cells Z1 and Z28 (inclusive).

@VAR(range)

Variance
Calculates the variance in a series of numbers. Example: @VAR(A1..A5) determines the variance of the numbers in cells A1 to A5. Ignores blank cells.

@MIN(range)

Smallest in a Range
Displays the smallest number in a series of numbers. Example: @MIN(A1..A20) displays the smallest value in the series from cell A1 to cell A20.

@MAX(range)   **Largest in a Range**
Displays the largest number in a series of numbers. Example: @MAX(A1..A20) displays the largest value in the series from cell A1 to cell A20.

TRIGONOMETRIC FUNCTIONS

The trigonometric functions perform calculations that are useful in electronics and engineering.

In the trigonometric functions such as sine, cosine, and tangent, angles are always expressed as radians both in the argument function, and in the results. (You can convert degrees to radians by multiplying the degrees by @PI/180. To convert radians to degrees, multiply the number of radians by 180/@PI.

@ACOS(x)   **Arc Cosine**
Calculates the arc cosine of an angle expressed in radians. Example: @ACOS(0.123) returns 1.447484 (the angle, in radians, whose cosine is 0.123).

@ASIN(x)   **Arc Sine**
Computes the arc sine of an angle expressed in radians. Example: @ASIN(0.987) returns 1.409375, the angle whose sine is 0.987 in radians.

@ATAN(x)   **Arc Tangent**
Calculates the 2-quadrant arc tangent of an angle. Example: @ATAN(123) returns 1.562666; the angle whose tangent is 123.

@ATAN2(x,y)   **4-quadrant Arc Tangent**
Returns the 4-quadrant arc tangent of an angle whose tangent is y/x. Example: @ATAN2(-3,2) returns 2.553590.

@COS(x)   **Cosine**
Returns the cosine of the angle in radians. Example: to calculate the cosine of a 45-degree angle, convert degrees to radians as in the formula @COS(45*@PI/180). The result is 0.707106781 radians. The formula @COS(0.7853981) returns 0.707106896 radians.

@EXP(x)   **Number *e***
Returns the number *e* raised to the power expressed in *x*. Example: @EXP(1) returns 2.718281; @EXP(10) returns 22046.6.

@**LN(x)**   **Natural Logarithm**
                    Computes the natural logarithm (base *e*) of the
                    number *x*. Example: @LN(2.7182818285) returns
                    1.

@**LOG(x)**   **Logarithm**
                    Computes the logarithm (base 10). Example:
                    @LOG(10) returns 1.

@**MOD(x,y)**   **Modulo**
                    Returns the remainder (modulo) of x after divi-
                    sion by y. Example: @MOD(9,2) returns 1 (nine
                    divided by 2 is 4, remainder 1). Often used to
                    determine if a number is evenly divisible by some
                    other number. For example, @MOD(A1,2) will re-
                    turn 0 if an even number is stored in cell A1.

@**PI**   **Pi**
                    Returns the number pi (approximately
                    3.141592653). This function takes no argument.
                    Example: @PI returns 3.141592. The formula
                    @ASIN(0.987)*(180/@PI) returns 80.75129, the
                    arc sine of an angle of 0.987 radians expressed
                    in degrees. The formula @PI*16^2 returns
                    804.247, the area of a circle whose radius is 16.
                    The formula (@ASIN(45*(@PI/180)))*(180/@PI)
                    returns the value 51.757518516, the arc sine, in
                    degrees, of an angle of 45 degrees.

@**SIN(x)**   **Sine**
                    Returns the sine of an angle expressed in radi-
                    ans. Example: @SIN(1.6) returns 0.999573603.
                    The formula @SIN(90*@PI/180) returns 1.

@**TAN(x)**   **Tangent**
                    Returns the tangent of an angle expressed in
                    radians. Example: @TAN(0.785398) returns
                    0.999999673. The formula @TAN(45*@PI/180) re-
                    turns the tangent of a 45 degree angle, 1.

LOGICAL FUNCTIONS

The logical functions allow a worksheet to make decisions based upon types of data, and relationships between data items.

The logical functions are used to make decisions within the worksheet. The IF function allows you to use a number of *logical operators* for making decisions. These are:

=   Equal

<   Less than

≤	Less than or equal to
>	Greater than
≥	Greater than or equal to
< >	Not equal to
#NOT#	Not
#AND#	And
#OR#	Or

We'll see some examples of their use after the summaries below.

@IF(condition,true,false)

Make a Decision
The @IF function first determines whether or not the *condition* portion is true or false. If the condition is true, then the @IF function performs the *"true"* argument. If the condition is false, the @IF function performs the *"false"* argument. Example: @IF(A1> = 10,"Bigger", "Smaller") will display the word "Bigger" if cell A1 contains a number greater than or equal to 10. If cell A1 contains a number smaller than 10, then the formula displays the word "Smaller."

@CHOOSE(x,options...)

Choose from many options
@CHOOSE selects an item from a list, based upon a single criterion. If the *x* argument is zero, @CHOOSE selects the first item, if the *x* argument is 1, @CHOOSE selects the second argument. Example: @CHOOSE(@MOD(@NOW,7),'Saturday", "Sunday", "Monday", "Tuesday", "Wednesday", "Thursday", "Friday") displays the day of the week in English. The 1-2-3 @NOW function calculates a *serial date*. The remainder (modulus) of this number when divided by seven yields a value between zero and six. This number indicates the day of the week, where zero is Saturday, 1 is Sunday, and so forth.

@ISNUMBER(x)

Test for a Number
Returns 1 (True) if the referenced cell contains a number or is blank. Otherwise, it returns 0 (False). Example: @IF(@ISNUMBER(A1), "Yes","No") will display Yes if cell A1 contains a number. Otherwise, it displays No.

@ISSTRING(x)

Test for a Label
Returns 1 (True) if the referenced cell contains a label otherwise returns 0 (False). Example: @IF (@ISSTRING(A1),A1," ") displays the contents of cell A1 if cell A1 contains a label. Otherwise, it displays nothing (a blank space).

@TRUE

True
Makes a cell "true" in the logical sense, but displays the number 1. Example: @IF(A3 = "Yes",@TRUE, @FALSE) calculates to 1 (True) if cell A3 contains the word Yes. Otherwise, it returns 0 (False).

@FALSE

False
Makes a cell "false" in the logical sense, but displays the number 0. Example: @IF(A3 = "Yes",@TRUE, @FALSE) calculates to 0 (False) if cell A3 does not contain the word Yes. Otherwise, it returns a 1 (True).

@ISERR

Is an Error
Returns a True value (1) if the referenced cell contains an error (ERR). Otherwise it returns a False (0). Example: The formula @IF(@ISERR (J22),"Error!",X1/J22) displays the word "Error!" if cell J22 contains an error. Otherwise, the formula displays the quotient of cell X1 divided by cell J22.

@ISNA

Is Not Available
Returns a True value (1) if the referenced cell contains NA (not available). Otherwise, returns False (0). Example: The formula @IF(@ISNA

(J22),"No Data!",X1/J22) displays the message "No Data!" if cell J22 contains NA. Otherwise, the formula displays the quotient of cell X1 divided by cell J22.

With the addition of logical operators in the logical functions, you can be very specific about making decisions in the spreadsheet. Some examples of decision-making formulas and their English equivalents are listed below:

Formula	English Equivalent
@IF(B4<>C4,A1,A2)	If cell B4's contents do not equal cell C4's contents, display the contents of cell A1. Otherwise, display the contents of cell A2.
@IF(B4>1#AND#C4>1,A1,A2)	If both cell B4 and C4's contents are greater than 1, display cell A1. Otherwise, display cell A2.
@IF(B4>1#OR#C4>1,A1,A2)	If either cell B4 or C4's contents are greater than 1, display cell A1. Otherwise, display cell A2.

You'll see some practical applications for these functions in Chapter 9.

TABLE FUNCTIONS

The table functions can find answers by looking up information in a table.

Sometimes an exact mathematical relationship does not exist between two related sets of numbers. For example, the tax tables have an income range and a base tax fee and percentage rate for each income. To determine your taxes, we need to look them up in the table; there is no direct mathematical correlation. 1-2-3 can also look up information in tables, using the table functions.

@VLOOKUP(x,range,column)   **Vertical Table Lookup**
This function looks up data in one column of data, and returns a value from another column. For example, take a look at the small worksheet below:

	A	B	C	D
1	Part No.	Part Name	Qty.	Unit Price
2	--------	--------	--------	--------
3	A-100	Spark Plug	40	1.56
4	A-101	Radiator Cap	22	5.88
5	A-102	Condenser	37	4.33
6	A-103	Points	121	5.44
7	B-111	Tire	88	72.11
8	B-112	Battery	42	65.44
9	Z-999	Jack	65	55.66

The entire range of data in the table is in the range of cells A3..D9. (The column headings and underlines are not actually data.) If one were to ask you the part name for part number A-103 you could easily find this from the table. 1-2-3 could perform this same task given the formula @VLOOKUP("A-103",A3..D9,1), which returns "Points". The formula tells 1-2-3 to "look up the part number "A-103" in the leftmost column of the data in the cells A1..D9, and return whatever is stored exactly one column to the right."

The formula @VLOOKUP("A-103",A3..D9,3) returns 5.44, which is the unit price for part number A-103. The last argument, 3, tells 1-2-3 to return data from 3 columns to the right.

The formula @VLOOKUP("Tire",B3..D9,2) returns 72.11, the unit price of a tire. In this example, the formula needs to look up the part name, rather than the part number, so the defined range is B3..D9 rather than A3..D9.

Note that if you are looking up a number and 1-2-3 cannot find an exact match for the number, it selects the number that is closest to, but less than, the number being sought. For example, look at the small sample worksheet below:

	A	B	C	D
1	Income	Tax		
2	==============			
3	10000	123		
4	20000	234		
5	30000	345		
6	40000	456		
7	50000	567		
8	60000	678		
9				

The formula @VLOOKUP(35000,A3..B8,1) returns 345 because there is no value exactly matching 35,000. Therefore, 1-2-3 displays 345, the number one column to the right of 30,000.

@HLOOKUP(x,range,row)   **Horizontal Table Lookup**
This function is similar to the @VLOOKUP function, except that it seeks a value across a row, and the corresponding value in another row below. For example, look at the worksheet below:

	A	B	C	D	E
1					
2		1984	1985	1986	1987
3	Apples	3454.76	8735.54	3435.54	3254.34
4	Bananas	4975.49	1936.87	4862.45	4582.12
5	Cherries	5465.23	4522.23	8245.32	5842.25
6					

The formula @HLOOKUP(1986,B2..E5,2) returns 4862.45, the value two rows beneath 1986.

@INDEX(range,column,row)   **Display a Value from a Table**
This function displays data from a table based upon the intersection of a row and column number. For example, the formula @INDEX (A3..E5,3,1) returns 4862.45 which is in the third column, first row of the range of cells extending from A3 to E5. (The top row is row 0, and the leftmost column is column zero.) The formula @INDEX(A3..E5,0,0) returns Apples, the contents of the cell in the upper left corner of the range A3..E5.

DATE FUNCTIONS

The Date functions let you manage dates and times in a worksheet.

Computers usually have some difficulty dealing with calendar dates. The unusual rules of dates, such as "Thirty days hath September, April June and November...) don't fit neatly into a simple numbering system. However, Lotus 1-2-3 offers *serial dates* to help with this problem. Serial dates begin with 1 at January 1, 1900. Each day thereafter is assigned a number, larger by one, up to December 31, 2099 which has a serial date of 73050.

Within any given day, the time is assigned a fractional number. Midnight is 0, noon is .5, and 11:59:59 PM (just before midnight) is .999999.

The date functions discussed in this section will display dates in serial format (such as 32355) when entered. As we'll see in the next chapter, however, you can use the Range Format commands to display dates and times in the more familiar 12/31/86, and 12:00:00 PM formats.

@DATE(year,month,day)
Calculate a Serial Date
Converts three arguments—the Year, Month, and Day—to a serial date. Example: @DATE(86,3,31) returns 31502, the serial number date for March 31, 1986.

@DATEVALUE(date)
Calculate a Serial Date
Converts a single argument into a serial date. Example: @DATEVALUE("03/31/86") returns 31502, the serial date for March 31, 1986. If cell A1 contains the label '03/31/86, then the formula @DATEVALUE(A1) also returns the serial date 31502.

@DAY(serial date)
Day of the Month
Isolates the day of the month from a serial date. Example: If cell A1 contains the formula @DATE(86,3,31), then the formula @DAY(A1) returns 31.

@NOW
System Date and Time
Returns the system date and time from the computer, usually entered when first starting up the computer, or maintained automatically in other computers. Example: @NOW returns 31523.31 if the current date is April 21, 1986. The decimal portion (.31) is the fractional time.

@TIME(hour,minute,second)
Fractional Time
Returns the fractional time from three arguments representing the hour, minute, and second. Example: @TIME(15,30,45) returns 0.646354, the fractional time for 3:30:45 PM. (Uses military 24-hour clock.)

@TIMEVALUE(time)
Fractional Time
Returns the fractional time from a

single argument. Example: if cell A1 contains the label '15:30:45, then the formula @TIME-VALUE(A1) returns 0.646354, the fractional time for 3:30:45.

@HOUR(serial date)

Hour of Day
Returns the hour from a serial date or fractional time. Example: @HOUR(@NOW) displays the current hour.

@MINUTE(serial date)

Minute
Returns the hour from a serial date or fractional time. Example: @MIN-UTE(@NOW) displays the current minute.

@SECOND(serial date)

Second
Returns the second from a serial date or fractional time. Example: @SECOND(@NOW) displays the current second. Pressing the CALC key (F9) once each second demonstrates this functions time-keeping ability.

The String functions let you manipulate label data.

STRING FUNCTIONS

The string functions perform calculations on labels in much the same way that the other functions perform calculations on numbers. The word "string" comes from a computer term meaning a "string of characters with no numeric value." The word "label" means the same thing, so these could just as easily have been called the label functions.

These functions allow you to combine labels, separate labels, change uppercase and lowercase, convert numbers to labels, and so on. At first glance, these functions might seem quite impractical. However, the string functions come in handy in many applications, particularly in database management applications that print mailing labels and form letters.

@CHAR(x)

ASCII/LICS Characters
Returns the ASCII/LICS character associated with a number (1-255). The characters include the usual numeric and alphabetic characters, as well as the special set of foreign letters, currency signs, and graphic symbols. Ex-

amples: @CHAR(162) returns a cent sign. @CHAR(163) shows the British Pound sign. @CHAR(165) shows the Yen currency sign. @CHAR(173) displays pi. @CHAR(176) shows the degrees symbol. @CHAR(189) displays 1/2. Appendix A of the Lotus 1-2-3 manual shows all the ASCII/LICS codes.

@CODE(x)

ASCII/LICS Code
Opposite of @CHAR, this function shows the numeric ASCII/LICS number associated with a character. Example: @CHAR("*") displays 42, because the ASCII code for an asterisk is 42.

@EXACT

Exact Label Match
Returns 1 (True) if two labels match exactly. Otherwise, it returns 0 (False). Example, if cell D3 contains 'Smith, and cell E3 contains 'SMITH, then the formula @IF(@EXACT(D3,E3), "Yes", "No") displays "No" because the cases are different. Without using @EXACT, as in the formula @IF(D3 = E3, "Yes", "No"), returns Yes because the = sign is not sensitive to uppercase and lowercase.

@FIND(x,y,start)

Find a Character
Searches a label for a character, or group of characters. If a match occurs, it returns the number where the match starts. Otherwise, it returns a 0. Example: If cell D6 contains "John Smith" then the formula @FIND(" ",D6,0) returns 4 because the space is the fourth character from the left. (The first character is always 0). The *start* argument tells where the search for the matching pattern begins. For example, the formula @FIND(" ",D6,5) returns 0, because there is no blank space to the right of the fifth character in "John Smith".

@LEFT(string,n)

Leftmost Characters
Returns the leftmost characters of a string, *n* spaces wide. Example: If cell D6 contains "John Smith", @LEFT(D6,4) returns "John". The formula @LEFT(D6,@FIND(" ",D6,0)) also returns "John", but does so by calculating the length using the @FIND function.

@LENGTH(string)

Length of a Label
Returns the length of a label. Example, if cell D6 contains "John Smith" then the formula @LENGTH(D6) returns 10.

@LOWER(string)

Lowercase Equivalent
Converts all uppercase letters in a label to lowercase. Example: If cell D6 contains "John Smith," then the formula @LOWER(D6) returns "john smith".

@MID(string, start, stop)

Portion of a Label
Returns a portion of a *string* starting at a *start* position, extending to a *stop* position. Example: The formula @MID("hahaheheho",2,4) returns "hahe". (@MID considers the first character to be zero.)

@N(range)

Corner of a Range
Determines if the upper left corner of a group of cells (range) is a number, and returns that number. Example, if cells D11..F14 contain the numbers 1 through 8, with 1 in cell D11, then the formula @N(D11..F14) returns a 1.

@PROPER(string)

Proper Case
Converts the first letter of a word to uppercase, and all other letters to lowercase. Example: If cell A9 contains "john smith", then the formula @PROPER(A9) returns "John Smith".

@REPEAT(string,n)

Repeat a Character
Repeats the character(s) in *string n* number of times. Example: @RE-

PEAT("-",70) creates a line of hyphens across the entire screen.

@REPLACE
(string,start,n,new string)

Replace Characters
Puts *new string* into *string* starting at *start*, replacing *n* characters. Examples: If cell D14 contains "JanFebApr" and cell E14 contains "Mar", the formula @REPLACE(D14,6,3,E14) returns JanFebMar (three characters were replaced). The formula @RE-PLACE(D14,6,0,E14) returns JanFeb MarApr, placing the new Mar string into the original string without replacing any of the original characters.

@RIGHT(string,n)

Rightmost Characters
Displays the right "*n*" characters from *string*. Example: @RIGHT ("ABCDEFG",3) displays EFG. If cell D6 contains the label "John Smith" then the formula @RIGHT(D6, @LENGTH(D6) − @FIND("   ",D6,0)) displays "Smith."

@S(range)

Corner of a Range
Determines if the upper left corner of a group of cells (range) is a label, and returns that label. Example, if cells D11..F14 contain the letters A through H, with "A" in cell D11, then the formula @N(D11..F14) returns A.

@STRING(x,dec)

Converts a Label to a Number
Converts a number, *n*, to a label with *dec* number of decimal places. Example: @STRING(12.95555,2) returns '12.96. If cell Z28 contains 123.45, then the formula + @CHAR(165)& @STRING(Z28,2) displays 123.45 with a Yen currency sign in front.

@TRIM(string)

Remove Blank Spaces
Removes extraneous blank spaces from a label. Example: The formula @TRIM("Before   and   after Spaces") returns "Before and after spaces."

@UPPER(string)   **Convert to Uppercase**
                        Converts all lowercase letters in a la-
                        bel to uppercase. Example: If cell D6
                        contains "John Smith" the formula
                        @UPPER(D6) returns JOHN SMITH.

@VALUE(string)   **Convert Label to Number**
                        Converts a label, containing numeric
                        characters, to a numeric value. Also
                        converts any fractions to decimals.
                        Example: @VALUE("5 2/3") returns
                        5.6666666667.

SPECIAL FUNCTIONS

The Special functions are used in advanced worksheets and macros.

The special functions are used primarily in advanced worksheets, and *macros* in particular (discussed in Section 4 of this
book). We'll cover these lightly here, and demonstrate them in more
detail in the later chapters of the book.

@@(cell-address)   **Pointer to a Cell**
                        Returns the contents of a cell whose
                        address is the argument. For exam-
                        ple, cell E1 contains the label 'H1,
                        and cell H1 contains the word "Hel-
                        lo" then the formula @@(E1) dis-
                        plays "Hello" (the contents of cell
                        H1).

@CELL(attribute,range) **Attribute of a Cell**
                        Returns information about a particu-
                        lar cell. Example: If cell E1 contains
                        the label 'Hello, then the formula
                        @CELL("prefix",E1..E1) displays an
                        apostrophe, the label prefix in cell
                        E1.

@CELLPOINTER(attribute) **Attribute of the Highlighted Cell**
                        Returns attribute information for the
                        currently highlighted cell. Example:
                        @CELLPOINTER("contents") dis-
                        plays Hello when the cell pointer is
                        resting on a cell that contains the
                        label 'Hello.

@COLS(range)   **Number of Columns in a Range**
                        Returns the number of columns in a
                        group (range) of cells. Example:

@COLS(B1..E20) returns 4, because there are four columns between B and E (inclusive).

@ROWS(range)

Number of Rows in a Range
Returns the number of rows in a group (range) of cells. Example: @ROWS(B1..E20) returns 20 because there are twenty rows between 1 and 20 (inclusive).

@ERR

Error
Makes the value of a cell ERR. Example: @IF(J22>0,X1/J22,@ERR) will display the quotient of cell X1 divided by cell J22 if cell J22 is greater than zero. Otherwise, the cell displays ERR.

@NA

Not Available
Makes the value of a cell NA. Example: @IF(J22>0,X1/J22,@NA) will display the quotient of cell X1 divided by cell J22 if cell J22 is not blank. Otherwise, the cell displays NA.

SAMPLE WORKSHEETS USING FUNCTIONS

Take some time now to look at some useful worksheets that combine numbers, labels, formulas, and functions. For purposes of illustration, we'll display the actual formulas on the screen in some cases rather than their output, so you can analyze the worksheet's actual contents. 1-2-3, of course, will just display the calculated value.

The first is a simple loan-analysis worksheet that calculates the payment on a loan for various terms, 1 to 5 years. This worksheet appears in Fig. 2-4.

Notice that there is a separate formula for each term:

@PMT(B1,B2/12,A?*12)

This formula calculates the payment for the principal, stored in cell B1; interest rate divided by 12 (months), which is stored to cell B2; and the term (times 12 months); which is stored in column A for this particular row.

Of course, what you type in will not appear as you typed it, because 1-2-3 always shows the results of a formula rather than the formula itself. If you position to cell pointer to each location where

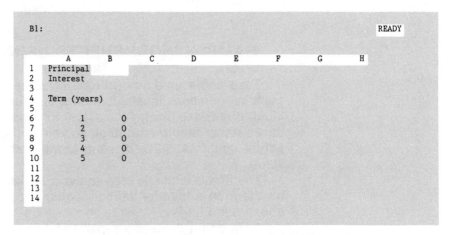

```
B1:                                                        READY


           A        B        C        D        E        F        G        H
1   Principal
2   Interest
3
4   Term (years)
5
6          1   @PMT(B1,B2/12,A6*12)
7          2   @PMT(B1,B2/12,A7*12)
8          3   @PMT(B1,B2/12,A8*12)
9          4   @PMT(B1,B2/12,A9*12)
10         5   @PMT(B1,B2/12,A10*12)
11
12
13
```

Fig. 2-4. Payment formulas in the worksheet.

something appears in Fig. 2-4, and type in the displayed labels and formulas, you will end up with a worksheet that looks like the one in Fig. 2-5. Notice that all values are presently 0, because we've only typed in the labels and formulas.

```
B1:                                                        READY


           A        B        C        D        E        F        G        H
1   Principal
2   Interest
3
4   Term (years)
5
6          1        0
7          2        0
8          3        0
9          4        0
10         5        0
11
12
13
14
```

Fig. 2-5. Loan worksheet with no data.

To use the worksheet position the cell pointer to cell B1 and type in a principal amount, say 5000 and press RETURN. Then move the cell pointer to cell B2 and type in an interest rate, say 16.5% (don't forget the percent sign, since this is a percentage figure). The result, shown in Fig. 2-6, is the monthly payment for the loan for each of the five possible terms.

Of course, if you were to change any of the assumptions (princi-

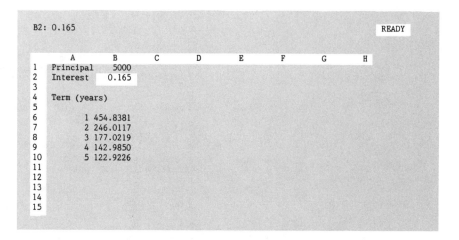

```
B2: 0.165                                                        READY

         A          B        C        D        E        F        G        H
 1  Principal     5000
 2  Interest      0.165
 3
 4  Term (years)
 5
 6            1  454.8381
 7            2  246.0117
 8            3  177.0219
 9            4  142.9850
10            5  122.9226
11
12
13
14
15
```

Fig. 2-6. Payments on a loan with varying terms.

pal, interest, or term), the calculated cells would recalculate immediately, and display the new results.

To save this small worksheet, call up the menu and select File
Save (type /FS). Enter a name, such as SLOAN (for Small Loan) and
press RETURN.

To start with a clean slate for the next worksheet, call up the
menu and select Worksheet Erase Yes (type /WEY). The worksheet
currently on the screen will disappear. (Since you just saved it on
the disk, however, you can always get it back later using the File
Retrieve commands.)

Statistical Worksheet

Let's look at another worksheet that uses some of the statistical functions, and deals with rows and columns of data. Fig. 2-7
displays another grade book example, but with many calculations.

Notice that the cells in column E1 to E6 calculate the averages
for each student. The cells in row B8 to D8 calculate the average
score on each exam. The cells in row B10 to D10 and C10 to D10
calculate the highest (MAX) and lowest (MIN) scores on each exam.
Row B13 to D13 calculates the standard deviation for each exam.
This worksheet would actually look like the one in Fig. 2-8 with just
the labels and formulas typed in. Note that the results of all formulas are ERR because there is no data in the grade book.

When you fill in some test scores, the proper results of the
formulas will appear as shown in Fig. 2-9. And of course, if you
make any changes to existing scores, 1-2-3 will update all calculations immediately.

There are quite a few more decimal places than you need on

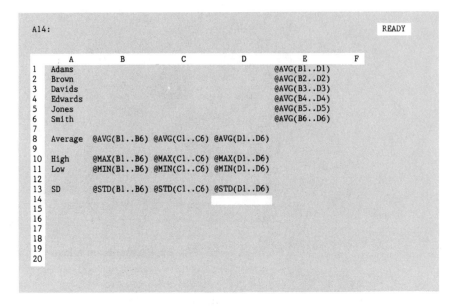

```
A14:                                                                    READY

          A            B              C              D              E           F
 1   Adams                                                      @AVG(B1..D1)
 2   Brown                                                      @AVG(B2..D2)
 3   Davids                                                     @AVG(B3..D3)
 4   Edwards                                                    @AVG(B4..D4)
 5   Jones                                                      @AVG(B5..D5)
 6   Smith                                                      @AVG(B6..D6)
 7
 8   Average   @AVG(B1..B6)  @AVG(C1..C6)  @AVG(D1..D6)
 9
10   High      @MAX(B1..B6)  @MAX(C1..C6)  @MAX(D1..D6)
11   Low       @MIN(B1..B6)  @MIN(C1..C6)  @MIN(D1..D6)
12
13   SD        @STD(B1..B6)  @STD(C1..C6)  @STD(D1..D6)
14
15
16
17
18
19
20
```

Fig. 2-7. Formulas for the statistical worksheet.

```
A1: 'Adams                                                              READY

          A            B              C              D              E           F
 1   Adams                                                      ERR
 2   Brown                                                      ERR
 3   Davids                                                     ERR
 4   Edwards                                                    ERR
 5   Jones                                                      ERR
 6   Smith                                                      ERR
 7
 8   Average   ERR           ERR            ERR
 9
10   High      ERR           ERR            ERR
11   Low       ERR           ERR            ERR
12
13   SD        ERR           ERR            ERR
14
15
16
17
18
19
20
```

Fig. 2-8. Statistical worksheet with no data.

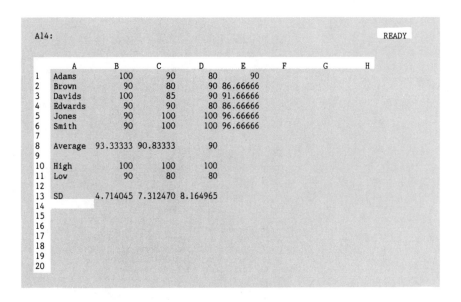

Fig. 2-9. Completed statistical worksheet.

most calculations. Perhaps two would be sufficient, and would certainly clean up the display. Formatting displays is the topic of the next chapter.

To save the statistical worksheet, select File and Save from the menu (type /FS), and enter a name file name such as STATS. Then press RETURN.

To start with a clean slate for the next worksheet, select Worksheet Erase Yes from the Menu (type /WEY). The next worksheet will be a bit trickier than the previous two.

Tax Table Lookup

Let's look at an example of 1-2-3's ability to look up data in a table now. We'll use the classic example of a tax table. In this case, you need to put in the tax table at the outset, so the worksheet looks like the one in Fig. 2-10. Notice that most formulas refer to cell B16 as a piece of data. This is the cell into which you type an individual's income to figure his taxes. Let's study this worksheet in more detail before trying it out.

Notice that cells in the table from A4 to C14 contain the actual tax table. Column A of the table holds a range of incomes, column B holds the base tax rate, and column C holds the percentage figure for calculating taxes on the amount of income over the base rate. Cells B17 to B20 do all the calculating.

Cell B16 will contain an income. Cell B17 contains this formula:

```
B1:  'Tax                                                              READY

           A          B        C        D        E        F        G
 1    Taxable     Tax       Plus %
 2    Income      Owed      Over
 3    ...............................
 4             0        0     0.01
 5          3120     31.2     0.02
 6          5450     77.8     0.03
 7          7790      124     0.04
 8         10160    242.8     0.05
 9         12500    359.8     0.06
10         14850    500.8     0.07
11         17170    663.2     0.08
12         19520    851.2     0.09
13         21860   1061.8      0.1
14         24200   1295.9     0.11
15
16    Income:                   <-- Enter income here.
17    Base Owed:  @VLOOKUP(B16,A4..C14,1)
18    Plus:       +B16-@VLOOKUP(B16,A4..C14,0)
19    Percent:    @VLOOKUP(B16,A4..C14,2)
20    Total Tax:  +B17+(B18*B19)
```

Fig. 2-10. Tax table worksheet with visible formulas.

@VLOOKUP(B16,A4..C14,1)

The formula looks up the income stored in B16 in the tax table. It returns the base tax rate, because the third argument (1) instructs the formula to return the value in column B (1 column to the right of column A). If the formula can't find the exact income in the tax table, it picks the next-lowest income in the range of incomes (e.g., if income is 15000, the table lookup will select 14850). The formula will then return the base tax rate for 14850, (which is 500.8), and place that amount into cell B17.

In cell B18, the formula determines how much over the income cutoff the individual made. It looks like this:

+B16 − @VLOOKUP(B16,A4..C14,0)

This formula subtracts the cutoff value in the table from the actual income. For example, if actual income were 15000, then this formula would become 15000 − 14850, because the @VLOOKUP value of 15000 with a zero offset is 14850 (closest to, and below 15000).

Cell B19 looks up the appropriate percentage rate for the actual income. The formula looks like this:

@VLOOKUP(B16,A4..C14,2)

This is basically the same as looking up the base tax rate, however the offset argument is two, so the value returned is the percentage figure from column C. Therefore, if the actual income were 15000, then the percentage rate returned by this formula will be 0.07.

Finally, cell B20 determines the total tax owed. Its formula looks like this:

+ B17 + (B18*B19)

which simply adds the base tax owed to the percentage figure times the amount over.

The worksheet, without an income figure in it, will look like Fig. 2-11. The Income cell is empty, and calculations are zero (except for the percentage figure, which is 0.01, and correctly so).

```
B16:                                                        READY

         A          B          C       D      E      F      G
1    Taxable     Tax        Plus %
2    Income      Owed       Over
3    -------------------------------
4            0          0      0.01
5         3120       31.2      0.02
6         5450       77.8      0.03
7         7790        124      0.04
8        10160      242.8      0.05
9        12500      359.8      0.06
10       14850      500.8      0.07
11       17170      663.2      0.08
12       19520      851.2      0.09
13       21860     1061.8       0.1
14       24200     1295.9      0.11
15
16   Income:                <-- Enter income here.
17   Base Owed:        0
18   Plus:             0
19   Percent:       0.01
20   Total Tax:        0
```

Fig. 2-11. Tax table with no data.

If you position the cell pointer to cell B16, and type in a hypothetical income, such as 15000, 1-2-3 will immediately calculate the entire tax due, as shown in Fig. 2-12.

To save the tax table worksheet, select File Save from the menus (type /FS), and enter a file name such as TAXES. Press RETURN. To clear the workspace, select Worksheet Erase Yes (type /WEY).

The worksheets displayed here are relatively small and simple, 1-2-3 allows us to create worksheets of enormous size and complexity. With the knowledge gained so far, you can probably create

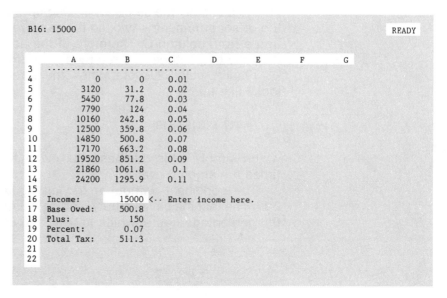

Fig. 2-12. Calculated taxes.

just about any worksheet your heart desires. It is simply a matter of positioning the cell pointer to where you want to add data, and typing in whatever label, number, or formula you wish. It helps to know what functions you have available to you to make the work easier.

In the next chapter, we'll discuss techniques for formatting the worksheet.

WHAT HAVE YOU LEARNED?

In this chapter you have seen that Lotus 1-2-3 offers many *functions* for performing calculations. The functions can be categorized by the type of service they perform. Some categories perform somewhat familiar tasks, such as general math, date and time calculations, statistics, financial calculations, trigonometry, and table lookups. Others perform tasks that are more unique to the computer's view of data, like the string, special, and logical functions.

1. The Mathematical functions perform general arithmetic.

2. The Statistical functions calculate averages, highest and lowest values, and other statistics.

3. The Financial functions provide a variety of calculations for business applications.

4. The Trigonometric functions calculate data useful in engineering and electronics.

5. The Logical functions make decisions about the relationships among data.

6. The Table functions look up data in tables.

7. The Special functions are used to perform fancy tricks in more advanced worksheets.

QUIZ

1. In the formula @SQRT(9), the 9 is called the:
   a. Function
   b. Argument
   c. Separator
   d. Cell reference

2. In the formula @SUM(A1..A25), the A1..A25 refers to:
   a. The two cells A1 and A25 separately
   b. The contents of cell A1 times cell A25
   c. All the cells between A1 and A25 (inclusive)
   d. The contents of cell A1 divided by cell A25

3. If cell A6 contains -64, then the formula @SQRT(@ABS (A6)) returns:
   a. ERR
   b. 64
   c. -64
   d. 8

4. For assistance with functions while using 1-2-3, you can press the Help key (F1), and select the options:
   a. Help Index and @Functions
   b. @Functions and Arguments
   c. Return and Continued
   d. Formula or Number

5. Which formula accurately calculates the *monthly* payment on a 20-year loan at 10% annual interest rate with a principal of $5,000.00?
   a. @PMT(5000,10%,20)
   b. @PMT(5000,10%*12,20/12)
   c. @PMT(5000,10%/12,20*12)
   d. @PMT(5000,10%/12,20)

6. Which of the following functions does *not* calculate a depreciation allowance?
   a. @DDB
   b. @SLN
   c. @STD
   d. @SYD

7. If cell A1 contains the number 10, then the formula @IF(A1<10,"Bobbi","Billie") will display:
   a. Bobbi
   b. Billie
   c. ERR
   d. Nothing

8. If cell A1 contains the number 100, and cell B1 contains the number 200, then formula @IF(A1>10#AND#B1>1000, "Yes","No") will display:
   a. Yes
   b. No
   c. ERR
   d. Nothing

9. A date entered with an @NOW or @DATE function is likely to be displayed in numeric format such as 31523. This numeric format is called a(n)
   a. Serial date
   b. Fractional date
   c. Format date
   d. Error

10. When a worksheet needs to look up information in a table (as in the case of tax tables), you can use the:
    a. @INDEX and @CHOOSE functions
    b. @CELL and @CELLPOINTER functions
    c. @MAX and @MIN functions
    d. @HLOOKUP and @VLOOKUP functions

Chapter **3**

```
┌─────────────────────────────────────────────────────┐
│                                                       │
│          FORMATTING THE                               │
│          WORKSHEET                                    │
│                                                       │
└─────────────────────────────────────────────────────┘
```

ABOUT THIS CHAPTER

In this chapter we'll discuss techniques for formatting the worksheet so that it looks exactly as you want it to. You'll also have the opportunity to work with the 1-2-3 menus and commands in more detail. The menus will open doors to many more powerful techniques, as we'll see in the coming chapters.

THE MAIN MENU

To call up the menu at any time, just press the slash (/) key.

You've used the menu briefly in earlier chapters to save worksheets and perform a few other tasks. As you may recall, you press the slash (/) key to bring the menu onto the screen. The menu appears above the worksheet as in Fig. 3.1.

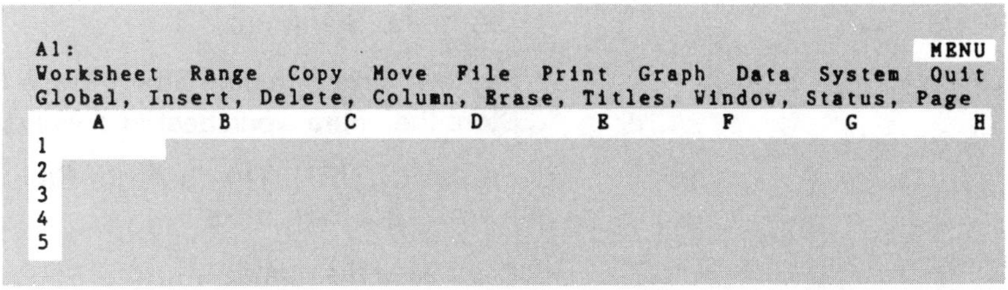

Fig. 3-1. The main menu on the worksheet.

Notice that the prompt in the upper right corner of the screen now reads "Menu," indicating that you are in the menu mode. There is a cell pointer in the menu itself, and right now it is highlighting the menu option Worksheet. Worksheet is a command that has a whole series of subcommands associated with it. These are displayed just below the main menu. You can use the left- and right-arrow keys to move the menu pointer to other options. If you move the menu pointer to Range, a submenu of commands that go along with the Range command appears in the control panel. To select a command, position the pointer to the appropriate option and press the RETURN key.

For example, in the first chapter we used the /FS (File Save) command to save a worksheet. We could have optionally done the following:

1. Type in a slash (/), which would make the Main Menu appear as such:

   Worksheet Range Copy Move File Print Graph Data System Quit
   Global, Insert, Delete, Column, Erase, Titles, Window, Status,
   Page

2. Press the right arrow key four times until the menu pointer is highlighting the File command, as below:

   Worksheet Range Copy Move File Print Graph Data System Quit
   Retrieve, Save, Combine, Xtract, Erase, List, Import, Directory

3. Press RETURN, which makes the File subcommand menu replace the main menu, like so:

   Retrieve Save Combine Xtract Erase List Import Directory
   Erase the current worksheet and display the selected worksheet

   Now the Retrieve subcommand is highlighted, and a brief description of its purpose is displayed beneath the menu.

4. Press the right arrow key once, so the pointer moves to the Save option. Now its purpose is briefly described beneath the menu, as such:

   Retrieve Save Combine Xtract Erase List Import Directory
   Store the entire worksheet in a worksheet file

5. Press RETURN. This selects Save as the command to perform. 1-2-3 then asks:

   Enter save file name:

   Also, any existing file names are displayed below this prompt. At any point, you can type in a file name, press RETURN. 1-2-3 saves the file and returns to the Ready mode.

To select an item from a menu, highlight the item and press RETURN, or simply type the first letter of the option.

So you actually have two methods of giving commands to 1-2-3. One is by typing in a slash and the first letter of each command. For example, to save a file, you could quickly type in /FS, and the control panel would ask for the name of the file to save. The second method, as described above, is to type in commands by pointing to menu options. That is, type in a slash to display the Main Menu, then move the menu pointer to appropriate command and press RETURN. You may prefer the latter until you have memorized the commands, or if you are not a good typist.

For the sake of simplicity, we'll use the following method of expressing commands in this book: Whenever a new command is introduced, we'll display both its abbreviated form and longer pointing form in parentheses. For example, when you see a command like this:

/FS (File Save)

you can use either method. You can either type in the /FS, or you can type in the slash, move the menu pointer to the File command in the main menu, and press RETURN. Then move the menu pointer to the Save command in the next menu, and press return again. Whichever method you prefer is up to you.

Remember, we'll always present commands in this format:

/WGF (Worksheet Global Format)

abbreviated commands └── Menu words for pointing

In this second example, you can either type in /WGF, or type in a slash, press RETURN when the menu pointer is highlighting the word Worksheet; move the menu pointer to the word Global in the next menu that appears, then press RETURN; then move the pointer to the word "Format" in the next menu to appear on the screen, and press RETURN again.

To work backwards through a series of incorrect menu selections, press the Escape key repeatedly.

If you ever get a bit lost using the pointing method of selecting menu options, press the Escape (Esc) key. The Escape key unselects commands. So now, just remember this saying:

If in doubt, ESCape key out.

If you're ever lost, just keep pressing the Escape key until you are back in familiar territory.

OK, now let's get on with the business of custom formatting the worksheet to our liking.

When you first call up 1-2-3, it displays a blank worksheet with an initial format: each column is nine spaces wide. Labels are automatically left-justified in a cell, and numbers appear with as many decimal places as will fit in the cell. Formulas display results rather than themselves. You can change one or all of these format settings for a single cell, a column, or *globally* (on the entire worksheet).

FORMATTING COLUMNS

Setting Column Widths

There are several ways to format a column in the worksheet. The simplest is to define a new width for the entire column. 1-2-3 usually assigns a standard width for the entire column. 1-2-3 usually assigns a standard width of nine characters to each column on the worksheet, but you can change that. For example, in the grade book worksheet, nine characters is a little slim for displaying the students' names. A column width of 20 would be better for the names. The /WCS (Worksheet Columns Width) commands allow you to assign a column a width of one (minimum) to 240 (maximum) characters.

Fig. 3-2 shows part of a blank worksheet that has not been formatted in any fashion.

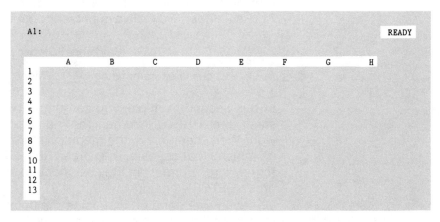

Fig. 3-2. A blank unformatted worksheet.

To change the width of a column, move the cell pointer to the column and type /WCS (Worksheet Column Set-Width).

To widen column 1 to 20 characters, perform the following steps:

1. Position the cell pointer to the column you wish to format. (The cell pointer is already in cell A1, so you need not do anything in this case.)

2. Type in the command /WCS. The screen will display four options: Set-Width, Reset-Width, Hide, and Display. Select Set-Width. 1-2-3 asks you to:

Enter column width (1..240): 9

and displays the current column width.

3. Type in the new column width, 20 and press RETURN.

The column width adjusts accordingly, as in Fig. 3-3.

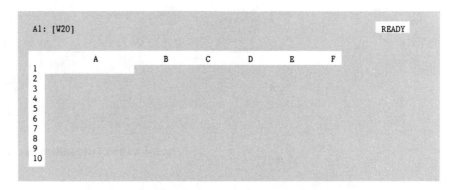

Fig. 3-3. Column A widened to 20 spaces.

Note that columns G and H have been bumped off the screen, because the additional width in column A takes up more room in the window.

Another way to set the column width is to position the pointer to the column and type in the /WCS commands. When 1-2-3 asks for a new column width you can use the right-arrow key to widen the column, and the left-arrow key to slim it. Each time you press an arrow key, the column will widen or shrink by one space. Press RETURN when the column is at the desired width.

Another option on the /WCS menu is Reset. If you select this option, the column will be reset to the initial width of nine.

Label Justification

You can also format the way in which numbers and labels are displayed in columns. For example, you can specify that all labels in a given cell be either left-justified, centered in the column, or right-justified. You can specify that labels be right-justified, like so:

Adams
Brubaker
Carlson
Decker
Smithsonian

For this type of formatting use the /RL (Range Label) command.

This command only works with labels that are already in the column as shown in Fig. 3-4.

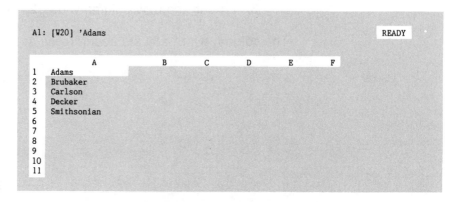

Fig. 3-4. Labels left-justified in column A.

Here are the steps for realigning the labels:

1. Type in the command /RL.
2. Select Right.
3. Type in the Range (in this case, A1..A5) and press RETURN.

All labels shift to right-justification as shown in Fig. 3-5.

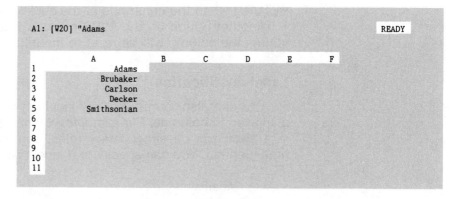

Fig. 3-5. Labels right-justified in column A.

The Center option from the /RL menu of choices centers all the labels in the column, as shown in Fig. 3-6.

Table 3-1. Numbers Formats

Format	Description	Examples
General	Zeros after the decimal point are not displayed. Very large and small numbers are displayed in scientific (exponent) format.	123.456 123.45 1.2E + 12 9999.99
Fixed	Numbers are displayed with a fixed number of decimal places (between 0 and 5, inclusive). Zeros behind the decimal point are displayed.	123456 1234.5 123.45 12.345
Scientific	Numbers are expressed in scientific notation. You can specify the number of decimals in the multiplier (from 0 to 15). Exponent of 10 from −99 to +99.	1.23E + 04 −1.2E−00 1.234E + 15 −3.45E−24
Currency	Numbers are displayed in "dollars and cents" formats, with a dollar sign in front and commas between units of 1000. Negative numbers are displayed inside parentheses. Fixed number of decimal places (0-5) with zeros after the decimal point are displayed.	$123.45 $1,234.00 ($123.45) $1,234.10 $99.01 ($1.00)
,(comma)	Numbers are displayed in the same fashion as in the currency format, except the dollar sign is not displayed.	123.45 1,234.00 (123.45) 99,999,999.99
Percent	Displays the value of the cell, multiplied by 100, followed by a percent sign. Decimal places displayed can range from 0 to 15.	12.00% 10% 123.45% .00001%
Text	Formulas are shown as entered (as in the worksheet examples in the previous chapter). Numbers are displayed in the General format.	@AVG(A1..A5) 95 @SQRT(A1) 123.456
+/−	Each digit in the integer portion of the number is displayed as a + (if positive), −(if negative), or decimal point (if zero). Creates a small horizontal bar graph.	+ + + + + + ++ − − − − − − . . .
Hidden	Hides data so that nothing is displayed.	
Reset	Resets numbers to General format.	

To realign a label (or group of labels) use the Range Label (/RL) commands.

Keep in mind that only the existing labels will be right-justified or centered. Any new labels added to the column will be left-justified, because 1-2-3 "naturally" aligns labels this way.

Formatting Numbers

You can format columns of numbers in a similar fashion. While labels may be centered or left- or right-justified, numbers can be formatted in 9 different ways. 1-2-3 naturally displays numbers in the General format, given in Table 3-1, but you can change that to

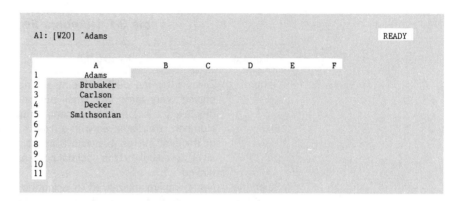

Fig. 3-6. Labels centered in column A.

any of the other eight options. Table 3-1 shows the options for formatting numbers.

Fig. 3-7 displays a worksheet with individuals' names and some sales figures.

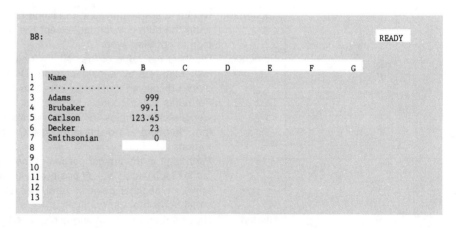

Fig. 3-7. Worksheet with names and numbers.

To format a number (or range of numbers), use the Range Format (/RF) commands. You can choose from 9 different numeric formats.

The numbers in this example would look better if displayed in the Currency format. The command for format an existing column of numbers is /RF (Range Format). Here are the steps involved:

1. Select the /RF command.

2. From the menu of choices, move the pointer to the Currency option. Press RETURN. 1-2-3 will ask:

   Enter number of decimal places (0..15):2

3. The number of decimals for the numbers is displayed as 2.

You could change this by typing in another number, but since 2 is adequate just press RETURN. 1-2-3 asks:

Enter range to format: XX..XX

4. Specify the range of numbers to be formatted, in this case B1..B7 and press RETURN.

The numbers in column B are redisplayed in currency format, as in Fig. 3-8.

```
B8:                                                              READY

          A              B        C        D        E        F        G
 1   Name
 2   ................
 3   Adams            $999.00
 4   Brubaker          $99.10
 5   Carlson          $123.45
 6   Decker            $23.00
 7   Smithsonian        $0.00
 8
 9
10
```

Fig. 3-8. Numbers in currency format.

*If a cell displays *******, you need to use /WCS (Worksheet Column Set-Width) to widen the column.*

If you end up with a symbol like ********* in a cell instead of the number, that means that the column is not wide enough to display the number. Use the /WCS (Worksheet Column Set-Width) command described before to widen the column.

These commands only affect the format in which the numbers appear. 1-2-3 still performs calculations in full precision, about 15 decimal places of accuracy.

Date Formats

To format serial dates, use the /RFD (Range Format Date) commands.

You can select from a variety of formats for dates and times. As mentioned earlier, a serial date displayed with an @DATE or @NOW function will appear as number (such as 31253) until formatted. The table on the next page shows the same serial date in nine other formats.

To format a date use the /RFD (Range Format Date) commands. For example, if cell A1 contains the function @NOW, and you format cell A1 using /RFD1, then the date appears in 21-Apr-86 format. If cell D7 contains the @NOW function, and you format cell D7 using /RFDT1 (Range Format Date Time 1), the date appears as a time in 09:23:40 AM format.

To try an exercise, follow these steps:

Format	Commands Used
21-Apr-86	/RFD1 (Range Format Date 1)
21-Apr	/RFD2 (Range Format Date 2)
Apr-86	/RFD3 (Range Format Date 3)
04/21/86	/RFD4 (Range Format Date 4) (Long Intn'l)
04/21	/RFD5 (Range Format Date 5) (Short Intn'l)
09:23:40 AM	/RFDT1 (Range Format Date Time 1)
09:23 AM	/RFDT2 (Range Format Date Time 2)
09:23:40	/RFDT3 (Range Format Date Time 3) (Long Intn'l)
09:23	/RFDT4 (Range Format Date Time 4) (Short Intn'l)

1. Move the cell pointer to cell E1.

2. Enter the formula @DATE(86,12,31) and press RETURN.

3. Move the cell pointer to cell E2.

4. Enter the function @NOW and press RETURN.

5. To reformat the serial dates, type /RFD1 (Range Format Date 1).

6. Press up arrow to highlight both cells E2 and E1.

7. Press RETURN.

8. To widen the column, use the /WCS (Worksheet Column Set-Width) command.

9. Press right arrow, then press RETURN.

You'll see both dates in 31-Dec-86 format.

The Long International and Short International (Intn'l) settings can be modified for various foreign formats, as discussed in Appendix A.

FORMATTING THE ENTIRE WORKSHEET

In this section, we'll discuss commands for formatting the entire worksheet. As with single columns, you can format column widths, label justification, and number displays. We'll begin by formatting all the columns on the worksheet.

Global Column-Width

1-2-3 always presents a new worksheet with 9 characters per column, and a worksheet typically displays columns A through H on the screen. We can change this to any column width between one and 240 characters. The command we use to do so is /WGC (Worksheet Global Column-Width). Here are the steps:

To *globally* set all column widths, use /WGC (Worksheet Global Column-Width).

1. Type in the command /WEY to start with a new worksheet.

2. Type in the command /WGC. 1-2-3 will display the current width setting and ask for the new column width.

3. Type 20 and press RETURN. The worksheet is redisplayed with the appropriate column widths, as in Fig. 3-9.

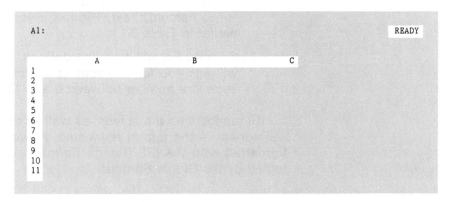

Fig. 3-9. All columns widened to 20 spaces.

Global Column-Width

As you can see, only columns A to C are now displayed on the screen, because these are all that will fit in the 1-2-3 window.

If you prefer, you can use the left- and right-arrow keys to draw the column width on the screen, rather than typing in the number for column width. To do so, select the /WGC command, then press the arrow keys to either expand or shrink the column. 1-2-3 will display the effect of the arrow keys on the screen. When the columns appear to be the width you desire, press the RETURN key.

The /WGC command will format all the column widths on the screen, except those which have already been set by a /WCS (Worksheet Column Set-Width) command.

Global Formats

To globally align all labels to be entered into a worksheet, use the /WGL (Worksheet Global Label-Prefix) commands.

You can format all labels in the worksheet also, using the command /WGL (Worksheet Global Label-Prefix). Here is how to do that:

1. Type in the command /WGL. This will display three options: Left, Right, Center.

2. Choose the format you desire by moving the pointer or typing in the first letter of the desired format.

Any labels that are presently on the worksheet will not be affected. However, any new labels that you type in will be displayed in the format requested in step 2 above.

You can also specify a format for displaying numbers on the entire worksheet. To do so, use the /WGF (Worksheet Global Format) command. Here are the steps involved:

1. Type in /WGF. This will display your options for displaying numbers: Fixed, Scientific, Currency, ,(comma), General, +/−, Percent, Text, Hidden, Reset. (We described these earlier in Table 3-1.)

2. Select a Format from the options. For some formats, 1-2-3 will ask you for the number of decimal places to display. Type in a number between 0 and 15.

All numbers on the screen, as well as any new numbers added, will appear in the format requested. However, any cells you have formatted with the /RF (Range Format) command will not be affected by the Global Format.

ZERO DISPLAY

To suppress the display of zeros in a worksheet, use the /WGZY (Worksheet Global Zero Yes) commands.

Usually, any formula that results in a zero value will display the number 0. For example, the formula @SUM(A1..A3) will display the number 0 if cells in A1..A3 are all blank.

You can suppress the display of the number 0 using the /WGZ (Worksheet Global Zero) commands. When you use /WGZ, the screen displays the options Yes and No. Select Yes to suppress displays of the number 0. Select No to display the number 0 as usual.

CLOCK DISPLAY

You can alter the display of the clock that appears in the lower left corner of the screen. The /WGDOC (Worksheet Global Default Other Clock) commands present the options:

Standard International None

The Standard option displays the date and time in the standard format that you usually see on the 1-2-3 screen. The International setting displays the date in the Long International Format (Date 4), and the time in the Short International Format (Time 5). You can gain control over these formats using other commands, as discussed in the next section and Appendix A.

If you select the None option, the date and time are not displayed at the bottom of the screen.

Select Quit from the submenu to return to the READY mode.

INTERNATIONAL FORMATS

If your work extends beyond the borders of the United States, you may need to use numeric and date formats other than those provided on the general menus. You can use the /WGDOI (Worksheet Global Default Other International) options to modify the formats presented by the /RF (Range Format) and /WGF (Worksheet Global Format) commands. For more information, see the Appendix in this book.

WHAT HAVE YOU LEARNED?

1. To call up the main menu, type a slash (/).

2. You can select menu items either by highlighting and pressing RETURN, or by typing the first letter of the menu option.

3. To back-out of a menu selection, press the Escape key.

4. To change the width of a column, use the /WCS (Worksheet Column Set-Width) commands.

5. To format a cell, or group of cells, use the /RF (Range Format) commands.

6. Use /RL (Range Label) to realign labels.

7. Use /RF (Range Format) to choose from many options for formatting numbers.

8. Use /RFD (Range Format Date) to format dates and times.

9. To globally format the worksheet, use the /WG (Worksheet Global) commands.

QUIZ

1. Pressing which key calls up the menu?
   a. Backslash (\)

  b. Slash (/)
  c. F10
  d. Equal (=)

2. To "unselect" a series of menu selections, you would press which key repeatedly?
    a. Break
    b. Ctrl
    c. Escape
    d. Num Lock

3. To change the width of a single column, you would move the cell pointer to that column and enter the commands:
    a. /RFC (Range Format Column)
    b. /RFGC (Range Format Global Column-Width)
    c. /WGCS (Worksheet Global Column Set-Width)
    d. /WCS (Worksheet Column Set-Width)

4. To display the number 1234.56 as $1,234.56, you would need to use which menu commands?
    a. /RFC2 (Range Format Currency 2)
    b. /RF,2 (Range Format Comma 2)
    c. /RFP2 (Range Format Percent 2)
    d. /RFF4 (Range Format Fixed 4)

5. To display the number 1234.56 as 1234.5600, you would need to use which menu commands?
    a. /RFC4 (Range Format Currency 4)
    b. /RF,4 (Range Format Comma 4)
    c. /RFP4 (Range Format Percent 4)
    d. /RFF4 (Range Format Fixed 4)

6. To globally display all numbers on the worksheet in scientific notation with two fixed decimal places, you would use which commands?
    a. /RFS2 (Range Format Scientific 2)
    b. /WGFS2 (Worksheet Global Format Scientific 2)
    c. /WSNE (Worksheet Scientific Notation Everywhere)
    d. /RGF2 (Range Global Format 2)

7. To display the formula @DATE(86,06,15) as a date in 15-Jun-86 format, you would use the commands:
    a. /RFD1 (Range Format Date 1)
    b. /RFD2 (Range Format Date 2)
    c. /RFD3 (Range Format Date 3)
    d. /RFD4 (Range Format Date 4)

8. To display the function @NOW as a time in HH:MM AM/PM format, you would use the commands:
    a. /RFDT1 (Range Format Date Time 1)
    b. /RFDT2 (Range Format Date Time 2)

    c. /RFDT3 (Range Format Date Time 3) (Long Intn'l)

    d. /RFDT4 (Range Format Date Time 4) (Short Intn'l)

9. If a date or number appear as asterisks (********) in a cell you must:

    a. Use /RF (Range Format) to select a different format

    b. Erase the cell and start over

    c. Move the contents to a new cell

    d. Use /WCS (Worksheet Column Set-Width) to widen the column

10. The commands /WGZY (Worksheet Global Zero Yes) will

    a. Display all numbers with leading zeros

    b. Display all numbers with trailing zeros

    c. Display all cells that contain zero as the number 0

    d. Display all cells that contain zero as blanks

Chapter 4

RANGES

ABOUT THIS CHAPTER

So far we've been working with either individual cells, or the worksheet as a whole. You can also work with groups, or *ranges* of cells on the worksheet. In this chapter we're going to learn many techniques for working with ranges. You'll find that these techniques really boost your productivity when developing your own custom worksheets.

A range is any group of adjacent cells on the worksheet.

A range is simply a rectangular collection of cells on the worksheet. The smallest possible range is a single cell, the largest possible range is the entire worksheet. Fig. 4-1 shows several possible ranges on a worksheet. Note that each has an even, rectangular shape.

We've used ranges in several formulas already, such as @SUM(A1..A10). This formula displays the sum of all numbers in the range of cells from A1 to A10. Let's look at some other interesting ways to put ranges into formulas.

RANGES IN FORMULAS

In this exercise, we'll discuss techniques for "drawing" the contents of a range into a formula. For example, Fig. 4-1 has a column of 10 numbers, A1 to A10. If you want to put the formula @SUM(A1..A10) into cell A12, you could just type it in as you have in the past. But let's explore a new technique.

With the cell pointer in cell A12, type the first portion of the formula into the control panel as such:

VALUE
@SUM(

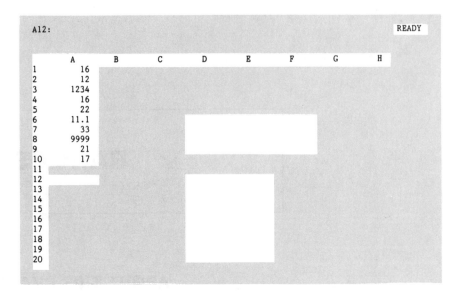

Fig. 4-1. Examples of ranges.

Notice that the upper righthand corner of the control panel informs you that you are entering a value, and that the cursor is precisely in the position into which you are about to enter the range to sum. Now we can draw the range into the formula following these steps:

1. Press the up-arrow key 11 times. The mode indicator changes to POINT, and as the cell pointer moves up the column, it places each column's value into the formula on the control panel. After 11 key presses, the cursor is in cell A1, and the formula in the control panel reads @SUM(A1, as Fig. 4-2 shows.

2. Now press the period key to begin typing in the rest of the range in the sum. Now the formula in the control panel looks like this:

                                                          POINT
@**SUM(A1..A1**

3. Now, press the down-arrow key 9 times. With each press of the down-arrow key, the cell pointer expands downward, and the second value in the control panel changes accordingly. When you reach cell A10, the control panel formula reads @SUM(A1..A10, and the worksheet looks like Fig. 4-3.

4. Now, to finish the formula, type in a closing parenthesis [ )].

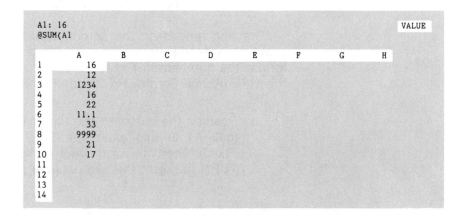

Fig. 4-2. Portion of formula entered on worksheet.

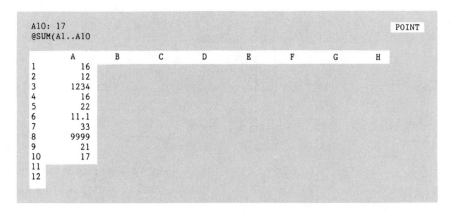

Fig. 4-3. Range highlighted on the worksheet.

The completed formula, @SUM(A1..A10), appears in the control panel and the cell pointer returns to its normal size.

5. Pressing the RETURN key enters the formula into the cell, and the sum of the values in the drawn range appears in the cell A12.

When specifying ranges in formulas (like A1..Z3), you can *point* with the arrow keys rather than type in the cell references.

This way of entering formulas into the worksheet has the advantage of allowing you to see the contents of the formula. It is also a great way to enter information if you are not a good typist.

RANGES IN COMMANDS

Drawing ranges on the screen works just as well with menu commands as with formulas. Let's try out another example. Let's format the numbers in Fig. 4-3 to two fixed decimal places using the /RFF (Range Format Fixed) command.

1. Position the cursor to the top of the range to be formatted (cell A1 in this example). Type in /RFF (Range Format Fixed). Then the worksheet looks like Fig. 4-4. Press RETURN to select the two decimal places option.

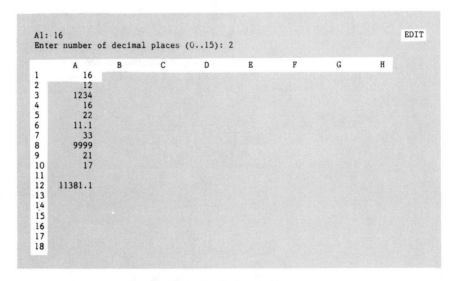

Fig. 4-4. First step in formatting a range.

2. 1-2-3 asks you to:

   Enter range to format: A1..A1

   Press the End key then the down-arrow key three times so that the pointer extends to cell A12. The control panel range becomes A1..A12, and 1-2-3 draws this same range on the worksheet as shown in Fig. 4-5.

3. Press RETURN. The cell pointer shrinks back to its original size, and the numbers in the drawn range are formatted with two fixed decimal places (Fig. 4-6).

When drawing ranges, one cell is always the *anchor* cell, simply because it does not move. The cell diagonally across from the

```
A12: @SUM(A1..A10)                                                POINT
Enter range to format: A1..A12

          A         B       C       D       E       F       G       H
 1       16.0
 2       12.0
 3     1234.0
 4       16.0
 5       22.0
 6       11.1
 7       33.0
 8     9999.0
 9       21.0
10       17.0
11
12    11381.1
13
14
15
16
```

Fig. 4-5. Range to format is highlighted.

```
A12: (F2) @SUM(A1..A10)                                           READY

          A         B       C       D       E       F       G       H
 1       16.00
 2       12.00
 3     1234.00
 4       16.00
 5       22.00
 6       11.10
 7       33.00
 8     9999.00
 9       21.00
10       17.00
11
12    11381.10
13
14
15
16
17
18
19
20
```

Fig. 4-6. Numbers formatted with fixed decimal places.

anchor cell is the *free cell*, because you can move it anywhere on the screen. In the control panel, the anchor cell is the first cell displayed in the range, the free cell is the second cell in the range, like this:

Enter range to format: A1..A12

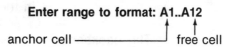

anchor cell ─────────────────┘ free cell

When highlighting a range, the *anchor cell* stays in one place, while the arrow keys move the *free cell*.

The arrow keys move the free cell to draw the range. You can use other keys with ranges too, mostly for anchoring and unanchoring cells. The way in which these keys behave depends upon whether or not a cell is already anchored.

If a cell is not already anchored, 1-2-3 displays only one cell address in the control panel, like this:

Enter (start of range): A1

The following keys have these effects on the unanchored cell:

When the control panel refers to a single cell (e.g. Z5), pressing the period key changes that to a range (e.g. Z5..Z5).

(Period)	Anchors the cell named in the control panel (A1 in this example), and allows you to draw the range with arrow keys. Also, changes the single cell address to a range (A1..A1 in this example).
(Any Arrow Key)	Moves the cell pointer, and changes the cell address in the control panel, but does not draw a range. Useful for moving to the beginning cell in a range you wish to create.
Esc (Escape)	Eliminates the entire prompt from the control panel, and moves to the previous prompt. That is, cancels the entire command.

If a cell is already anchored, these keys have a much different effect. You can tell that a cell is already anchored if it is displayed in the control panel with two coordinates, like this:

Enter (start of range): A1..A1

Now these keys will have these effects:

When highlighting a range, pressing the period key changes the location of the free cell.

(Period)	Moves the anchor to the nearest corner in a clockwise direction.
(Any Arrow Key)	Expands the cell pointer in the direction of the arrow, thereby drawing the range on the screen. The second address in the control panel changes as the pointer expands, to match the lower right corner of the range.
Esc (Escape)	Unanchors the cell, and returns to a single cell address in the control panel. This is handy for moving the beginning cell address in the range to a new location.

The backspace key also affects ranges you may be drawing.

Whether or not a cell is already anchored, the backspace key will cancel the range you are currently drawing on the screen and will return the cell pointer to its original position before you began drawing the range.

You can also use the End key on the numeric keypad to draw a range. For example, when the control panel asks:

Enter range to copy TO: A1..A1

pressing the End key, followed by pressing the down-arrow key, will extend the cell pointer to the last nonblank cell in the range. Any time you press the End key, followed by a press on an arrow key, the cell pointer will move to the last nonblank cell in the direction of the arrow key. If the cell pointer is already anchored, it will expand accordingly. If the cell pointer is not already within an active range when you press an End-key, arrow-key combination, the cell pointer will travel to the far corner of the worksheet in the direction specified.

An Exercise in Ranging

Let's try a little exercise in controlling the range highlighter. Follow the steps below, and experiment on your own a little after you get going.

1. Type /WEY (Worksheet Erase Yes) to start with a blank worksheet.

2. Press GoTo (F5), type in C4, and press RETURN. This will move the cell pointer to cell C4.

3. Enter the commands /RFC2 (Range Format Currency 2) and press RETURN. Notice that the control panel is ready to highlight a range starting at C4..C4.

4. Press right-arrow key 4 times. Notice that the highlight extends to the right, and the control panel changes to C4..G4.

5. Press down-arrow key 13 times. The highlighter extends into a large box covering the range C4..G17.

6. Now press each of the arrow keys a few times, and notice how the box grows and shrinks from the lower right corner (where the blinking cursor is).

7. Press the period key once. Notice that the blinking cursor moves to the lower left corner. Press the arrow keys a few times each and notice how the highlighter expands and shrinks from the lower left corner.

8. Press the period key again. The blinking cursor moves to

the upper left corner, and the arrow keys cause the high-lighter to expand and shrink from that corner.

9. Now experiment with the period and arrow keys on your own until you get the feel for how to control the expanded highlighter. Notice also that the PgUp, PgDn, Home, and End keys also work in sizing the highlighter.

Just press RETURN when done experimenting. Of course, any numbers that you now enter into the area that was highlighted on the screen will appear in currency format. (The purpose of this exercise was to experiment with the range highlighter, so don't bother with the number formats right now.)

Once you have practiced a bit, drawing (and undrawing) ranges is as simple as 1-2-3! If you should get lost while drawing a range on the screen, you can use the usual escape procedure to get back to more familiar territory. Just keep in mind our now familiar plati-tude:

As with everything else in 1-2-3, pressing Escape will get you out of a mess while highlighting a range.

If in doubt, Escape key out!

NAMING RANGES

You can assign names to individual cells, and ranges of cells, to make working with your worksheet a little easier. Range names let you use more English-like variable names in formulas, as below:

@PMT(Principal,Interest/12,Term∗12)

rather than plain cell references as in the formula below:

@PMT(A2,B2/12,C2∗12)

Creating Range Names

Use /RNC (Range Name Create) to assign a name to a range of cells.

Fig. 4-7 shows a sample worksheet with numbers and labels only (no formulas yet), which we'll use to demonstrate range names. If you want to try this example, use /WEY (Worksheet Erase Yes) to start with a blank worksheet. Then move the cell pointer to column B and use /WCS (Worksheet Column Set-Width) to make the column five spaces wide. Note that in this worksheet column B is empty, and only serves as space between column A and the other columns.

Type in the numbers and labels as they appear on the work-sheet. (Hint: use \ - and \ = to create the underlines in the work-sheet).

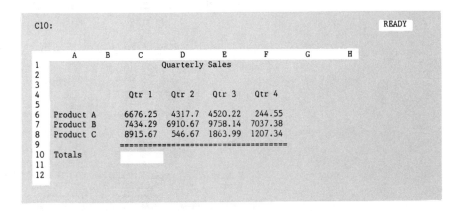

Fig. 4-7. Sample worksheet with labels and numbers.

Here are the steps to assign the range name "Qtr1" to the first quarter data, and use that range name in a formula:

1. Move the cell pointer to cell C6.

2. Type /RNC (Range Name Create).

3. Type in the range name Qtr1 and press RETURN.

4. Press the down-arrow key twice to highlight C6..C8, as in Fig. 4-8, then press RETURN.

```
           A        B        C          D          E          F          G
1                             Quarterly Sales
2
3
4                           Qtr 1      Qtr 2      Qtr 3      Qtr 4
5                        ............................................
6   Product A            6676.25     4317.70     4520.22      244.55
7   Product B            7434.29     6910.67     9758.14     7037.38
8   Product C            8915.67      546.67     1863.99     1207.34
9                        ====================================
10  Totals
11
12
```

Fig. 4-8. The range C6..C8 highlighted on the worksheet.

At this point cells in the range C6..C8 now have the name Qtr1. You can use this in a formula, as in the steps below:

5. Move the cell pointer to cell C10.

6. Type in the formula @SUM(Qtr1) and press RETURN.

The total for the column appears in cell C10, as shown in Fig. 4-9.

```
C10: @SUM(QTR1)                                                    READY

          A       B       C       D       E       F       G       H
 1                             Quarterly Sales
 2
 3
 4                          Qtr 1   Qtr 2   Qtr 3   Qtr 4
 5
 6    Product A           6676.25   4317.7  4520.22  244.55
 7    Product B           7434.29  6910.67  9758.14  7037.38
 8    Product C           8915.67   546.67  1863.99  1207.34
 9                        =====================================
10    Totals             23026.21
11
12
```

Fig. 4-9. Total in cell C10.

Try repeating the same process for columns D, E, and F, naming the ranges Qtr2, Qtr3, and Qtr4 respectively. Use the Qtr2, Qtr3, and Qtr4 range names in @SUM formulas in cells D10, E10, and F10. Fig. 4-10 shows the completed worksheet with totals in row 10.

```
F10: @SUM(QTR4)                                                    READY

          A       B       C       D       E       F       G       H
 1                             Quarterly Sales
 2
 3
 4                          Qtr 1   Qtr 2   Qtr 3   Qtr 4
 5
 6    Product A           6676.25   4317.7  4520.22  244.55
 7    Product B           7434.29  6910.67  9758.14  7037.38
 8    Product C           8915.67   546.67  1863.99  1207.34
 9                        =====================================
10    Totals             23026.21 11775.04 16142.35  8489.27
11
12
```

Fig. 4-10. Totals calculated in the worksheet.

Range Labels

You can assign names to individual cells using labels in adjacent cells. For example, look at the simple worksheet in Fig. 4-11. At the moment, it consists only of the simple labels Principal,

Interest, Term, and Payment. We'll put data into the adjacent cells to the right of these labels.

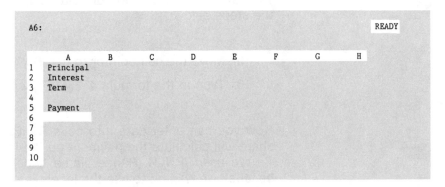

Fig. 4-11. Worksheet with labels in column A.

Use /RNL (Range Name Labels) to use labels on the worksheet as range names for adjacent cells.

First, however, we can use the labels in column A as range names for adjacent cells in column B. To assign labels as range names, you use the /RNL (Range Name Labels) commands, as in the steps below:

1. Press Home to put the cell pointer in cell A1.

2. Type /RNL (Range Name Labels).

3. Select Right, because you want to assign range names to cells on the right (in column B).

4. Press down-arrow key twice to highlight A1..A3, as in Fig. 4-12, then press RETURN.

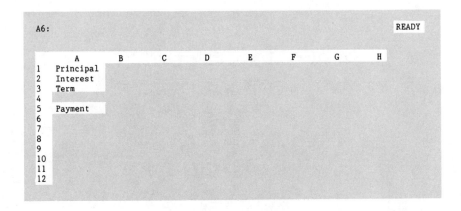

Fig. 4-12. Range labels highlighted on the screen.

Now cell B1 has the range name Principal. Cell B2 has the range name Interest, and cell B3 has the range name Term. Now you can enter the @PMT formula using these range names, as in the steps below:

5. Move the cell pointer to cell B5.

6. Type in the formula @PMT(Principal,Interest/12,Term*12).

Now you can enter data into cells B1, B2, and B3, and the worksheet will calculate the payment on the loan.

We used /RNLR (Range Name Labels Right) in this example because we wanted to use the labels in column B as range names for cells to the right. The /RNLL (Range Name Labels Left) will assign labels as range names to cells on the left. /RNLD (Range Name Labels Down) will assign names to cells beneath the range labels, and /RNLU (Range Name Labels Up) will assign names to cells above the labels.

Viewing Range Names

Use /RNT (Range Name Table) to view the names and locations of named cells and ranges.

If your worksheet grows large, and you start to forget the names of all your ranges, the Range Table commands can help. Just move the cell pointer to some out-of-the-way cell that has many blank rows beneath it, and a blank column to the right. Then enter the command /RNT (Range Name Table), and press RETURN. The names, and locations, of all named ranges will appear on the screen, as in Fig. 4-13.

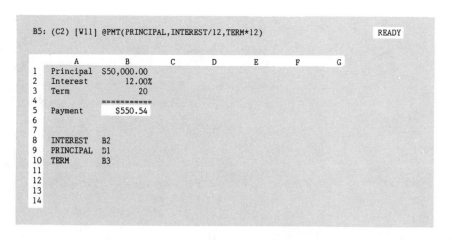

Fig. 4-13. Range names in rows 8-10.

Deleting Range Names

Whenever you select the /RN (Range Name) options from the menu, you are given the options:

Create Delete Labels Reset Table

Use /RND (Range Name Delete) to delete a single range name. Use /RNR (Range Name Reset) to delete all the range names.

The Delete option displays all existing range names in a menu, and lets you delete one by highlighting and pressing RETURN. If you delete a range name that is used in a formula, 1-2-3 will "fix" the formula so that it still works. For example, if you were to delete the range name "Principal" in the small loan payment worksheet, 1-2-3 would automatically change the payment formula to:

@PMT(B1,Interest/12,Term∗12)

The Reset option under the Range Name menu deletes *all* the range names in the current worksheet, and adjusts all the formulas accordingly.

Finding Named Cells and Ranges

Named ranges can help you find your way around large worksheets. For example, suppose you wanted to move the cell pointer to the "cost of sales" figure for 1986 in a large worksheet. Unfortunately, you couldn't remember where the number is. If the cell (or range) has no name, you'd have to hunt around using the arrow and GoTo keys.

Had you named the cell (or range) previously using /RNC (Range Name Create) or /RNL (Range Name Labels), you could just press the GoTo (F5) key. When 1-2-3 asks that you:

Enter address to go to:

you could then press the Name key (F3). 1-2-3 will show the names of all named ranges on a menu. Then you just highlight the name of the range to move the cell pointer to and press RETURN. The cell pointer will jump directly to your destination.

To jump to a named cell or range, press GoTo (F5), then Name (F3). Highlight a name and press RETURN.

Unfortunately, many 1-2-3 users do not appreciate the value and convenience of named ranges until they've developed very large worksheets of their own. One might waste many hours looking around for a cell that could just as easily have been assigned a name and jumped to immediately. Many hours might be spent trying to fix errors in worksheets that have formulas like @PMT(X2, J33/12,Z1∗12) rather than simpler formulas like @PMT(Principal, Interest/12, Term∗12). Keep these range naming capabilities in mind. Someday, you'll wonder how anybody could ever get along without them.

WHAT HAVE YOU LEARNED?

In this chapter, we've discussed techniques for working with groups of adjacent cells on the worksheet, called *ranges*. The main purpose of the various range capabilities is to simplify the use of the worksheet. 1-2-3 let's you visually work with a group of cells by highlighting, and also to work with groups of cells (or single cells) through names rather than cell coordinates.

1. A range is any group of adjacent cells on the worksheet, forming a rectangular or square pattern.

2. When using ranges as arguments in functions (or formulas), you can *draw* the range on the worksheet by highlighting, rather than typing in coordinates like A1..C3.

3. When drawing ranges, the *anchor cell* stays put. The *free cell* moves in the direction of the arrow key pressed.

4. To change a cell reference in the control panel, (such as A1) to a range, (such as A1..A1), press the period key.

5. To "unanchor" a range and reposition the anchor cell (changing a range reference like A1..A1 to a cell reference like A1), press the Escape or Backspace key. Reposition the anchor cell and press period to start drawing the range again.

6. When drawing a range, you can press the period key to change the free cell.

7. The /RNC (Range Name Create) commands let you assign a name to any range of cells on the worksheet.

8. The /RNL (Range Name Labels) commands let you use existing labels as range names for adjacent cells above, below, to the right, or left of the labels.

9. /RND (Range Name Delete) and /RNR (Range Name Reset) delete existing range names.

10. You can use the GoTo (F5) and Name (F3) keys to move the cell pointer immediately to any named cell or range.

QUIZ

1. When drawing ranges on the worksheet, which cell contains the blinking cursor?
   a. The anchor cell
   b. The free cell

   c. The named cell

   d. The label cell

2. To change the free cell when highlighting a range, you press which key?
   a. Escape
   b. Tab
   c. Any arrow key
   d. Period

3. To convert a single cell reference in the control panel (such as Z1) to a range (such as Z1..Z1), you press which key?
   a. Escape
   b. Tab
   c. Any arrow key
   d. Period

4. To assign a name to a range of cells on the worksheet, you would use:
   a. /RNLR (Range Name Labels Right)
   b. /RNC (Range Name Create)
   c. /RNT (Range Name Table)
   d. /RNR (Range Name Reset)

5. To use the label in cell J4 as the name for cell J5 (the cell immediately below), you would use the commands:
   a. /RNLR (Range Name Labels Right)
   b. /RNLL (Range Name Labels Left)
   c. /RNLD (Range Name Labels Down)
   d. /RNLU (Range Name Labels Up)

6. To display the names and locations of all named ranges on the worksheet, use the commands:
   a. /RNLR (Range Name Labels Right)
   b. /RNC (Range Name Create)
   c. /RNL (Range Name List)
   d. /RNT (Range Name Table)

7. To delete a single range name, use the commands:
   a. /RNR (Range Name Reset)
   b. /RND (Range Name Delete)
   c. /RNL (Range Name Lose-It)
   d. /WEY (Worksheet Erase Yes)

8. To move the cell pointer quickly to a named range or cell, press the F5 key, then press which key?
   a. F1
   b. F2
   c. F3
   d. F4

Chapter **5**

COPYING RANGES

ABOUT THIS CHAPTER

As you begin to develop more complex worksheets of your own, you'll soon find that entering a similar formula into many different cells is both tedious and time consuming. In this chapter, you'll see how to end the tedium and save lots of time using the /C (Copy) commands.

One of the greatest advantages to using ranges is that you can copy parts of the worksheet to other locations, which saves a great deal of typing effort. To demonstrate, you'll fill in a large number of cells by copying the contents of a single cell.

COPYING DATA

To copy any data on the worksheet, use the /C (Copy) command.

Fig. 5-1 shows a worksheet with only one cell filled. To place this same value in some more cells, use the /C (Copy) option. First, select the /C option. The control panel requests that you:

Enter range to copy FROM: A1..A1

Since the cell pointer is already in cell A1, the A1 also appears in the control panel. That is, 1-2-3 "assumes" that the cell to copy from is the range A1..A1 (a single cell). Press RETURN to indicate that this is indeed the cell to copy from. The control panel then requests that you:

Enter range to copy TO: A1

Fig. 5-1. One number on the worksheet.

Now you can determine as large an area as you wish. First, press the period key, which changes the control panel to this:

Enter range to copy TO: A1..A1

Now, press the right-arrow key six times, expanding the cell pointer to cell G1, as shown in Fig. 5-2. Now expand the cell pointer downward by pressing the down-arrow key. The cell pointer will expand to include the rows, and the range specified in the control panel will extend to the lower-right corner of the highlighted range (G11), as shown in Fig. 5-3 (assuming you've pressed the down-arrow key 10 times).

The range you are copying to is the size of the entire highlighted area. So if you now press RETURN, you will see a copy of cell A1's contents in each cell in the drawn range, as shown in Fig. 5-4. This is a quick and easy method for filling a lot of cells (as long as all the cells need the same contents).

When specifying ranges to copy FROM and TO, you can point using the arrow keys, or type in the cell references (e.g. A1..Z5).

Using the pointing method is not necessary, however. You could just as easily type in the /C command, press the RETURN key when the control panel asks for the range to copy FROM. Then, rather than pointing, just type in A1..G11 to indicate the lower right corner of the copy-to-range, then press the RETURN key.

Copying ranges of labels is exactly the same as copying numbers. Simply position the cell pointer to the cell you want to copy, select the /C (Copy) command, and define the FROM and TO copy ranges. Copying formulas, however, is a bit different, and we will discuss that now.

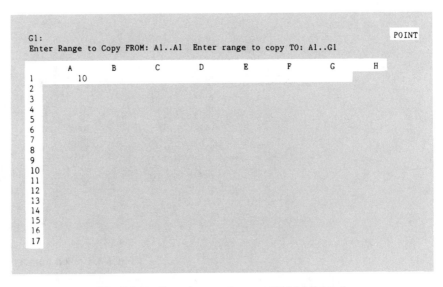

Fig. 5-2. Portion of range to copy TO highlighted.

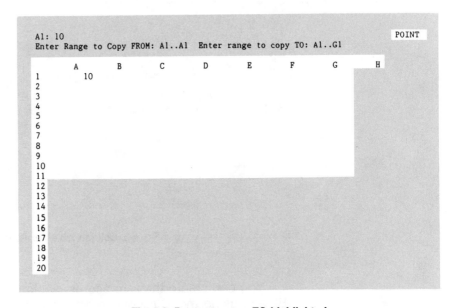

Fig. 5-3. Range to copy TO highlighted.

COPYING FORMULAS

For our example of copying formulas, we'll use the familiar grade book example. Type in /WEY. Starting with a blank worksheet, leave the left-most column available for filling in the student's names. Then, create a range of zeros for test scores. The beginnings of our grade book worksheet will look like Fig. 5-5.

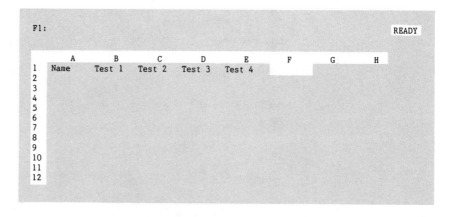

```
A1: 10                                                          READY

        A        B        C        D        E        F        G        H
 1     10       10       10       10       10       10       10
 2     10       10       10       10       10       10       10
 3     10       10       10       10       10       10       10
 4     10       10       10       10       10       10       10
 5     10       10       10       10       10       10       10
 6     10       10       10       10       10       10       10
 7     10       10       10       10       10       10       10
 8     10       10       10       10       10       10       10
 9     10       10       10       10       10       10       10
10     10       10       10       10       10       10       10
11     10       10       10       10       10       10       10
12
13
14
```

Fig. 5-4. Copied numbers.

```
F1:                                                             READY

        A        B        C        D        E        F        G        H
 1   Name     Test 1   Test 2   Test 3   Test 4
 2
 3
 4
 5
 6
 7
 8
 9
10
11
12
```

Fig. 5-5. Column labels in Row 1.

You can create the zero scores by simply placing a zero in cell B2 and using the /C (Copy) command to fill in the range, as in the example above where we did the same with tens. Copy from cell B2..B2 to cells B2..E12.

Unless you specify otherwise, copied formulas will attempt to retain their original "meaning."

Assume you want averages across each student, and down each test. You could fill in the necessary formulas one at a time, but there is a better method. First, put the formula @AVG(B2..E2) in cell F2 as shown in Fig. 5-6.

You can use the /WGFT (Worksheet Global Format Text) command to have the worksheet display the actual formula, rather than its calculated results. Move the cell pointer to column F, and use /WCS to widen the column to 15 spaces. Next, rather than typing

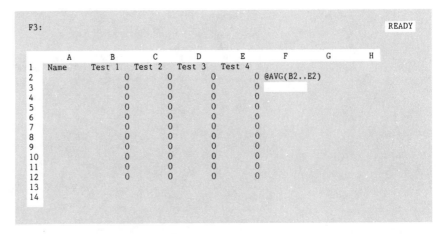

Fig. 5-6. Formula in cell F2.

the appropriate formula into each cell, just copy this one into the appropriate range. Here's how to do so:

1. With the cell pointer still in cell F2, select the /C (Copy) command. The control panel asks:

   Enter range to copy FROM: F2..F2

   The cell pointer is already in cell F2, so just press RETURN, since this is the formula we wish to replicate. The control panel then requests you to:

   Enter range to copy TO: F2

2. Press the down-arrow key to move the cell pointer down to cell F3. The control panel reads:

   Enter range to copy TO: F3

3. Press the period (.) key, so that the control panel reads:

   Enter range to copy TO: F3..F3

4. Now stretch out the cell pointer to cell F12 by pressing the down-arrow key nine times, until the expanded cell pointer looks like Fig. 5-7.

5. Now just press the RETURN key, and magically the appropriate formulas are displayed in this column, as shown in Fig. 5-8.

Notice that the formula in each row has been properly corrected to perform an average for its particular row. That is, the original formula is still @AVG(B2..E2), while the formula in row 3 has auto-

```
F2: '@AVG(B2..E2)                                              READY
```

	A	B	C	D	E	F	G	H
1	Name	Test 1	Test 2	Test 3	Test 4			
2		0	0	0	0	@AVG(B2..E2)		
3		0	0	0	0			
4		0	0	0	0			
5		0	0	0	0			
6		0	0	0	0			
7		0	0	0	0			
8		0	0	0	0			
9		0	0	0	0			
10		0	0	0	0			
11		0	0	0	0			
12		0	0	0	0			
13								
14								
15								

Fig. 5-7. Range to copy TO is highlighted.

```
F2: (T) [W15] @AVG(B2..E2)                                    READY
```

	A	B	C	D	E	F	G
1	Name	Test 1	Test 2	Test 3	Test 4		
2		0	0	0	0	@AVG(B2..E2)	
3		0	0	0	0	@AVG(B3..E3)	
4		0	0	0	0	@AVG(B4..E4)	
5		0	0	0	0	@AVG(B5..E5)	
6		0	0	0	0	@AVG(B6..E6)	
7		0	0	0	0	@AVG(B7..E7)	
8		0	0	0	0	@AVG(B8..E8)	
9		0	0	0	0	@AVG(B9..E9)	
10		0	0	0	0	@AVG(B10..E10)	
11		0	0	0	0	@AVG(B11..E11)	
12		0	0	0	0	@AVG(B12..E12)	
13							
14							

Fig. 5-8. Copied formulas in column F.

matically been corrected to @AVG(B3..E3). Also, the formula in row four has been corrected to @AVG(B4..E4), and so forth.

Try it again with the columns for average scores on each exam. Position the cell pointer to B14 and type in the formula @AVG (B2..B12), so the worksheet looks like Fig. 5-9 (only a portion of the formulas may appear).

Now spread the formula across all columns using the /C command. Specify cell B14 as the cell to copy FROM when prompted. Then specify the range C14..E14 as the range to copy TO, as shown in Fig. 5-10.

You may want to use the /WGC (Worksheet Global Column-

```
B15:                                                              READY

          A        B        C        D        E        F          G
   1  Name      Test 1   Test 2   Test 3   Test 4
   2              0        0        0        0  @AVG(B2..E2)
   3              0        0        0        0  @AVG(B3..E3)
   4              0        0        0        0  @AVG(B4..E4)
   5              0        0        0        0  @AVG(B5..E5)
   6              0        0        0        0  @AVG(B6..E6)
   7              0        0        0        0  @AVG(B7..E7)
   8              0        0        0        0  @AVG(B8..E8)
   9              0        0        0        0  @AVG(B9..E9)
  10              0        0        0        0  @AVG(B10..E10)
  11              0        0        0        0  @AVG(B11..E11)
  12              0        0        0        0  @AVG(B12..E12)
  13
  14      @AVG(B2..B12)
  15
  16
  17
```

Fig. 5-9. Formula in cell B14.

```
B14: '@AVG(B2..B12)                                               READY

          A        B        C        D        E        F          G
   1  Name      Test 1   Test 2   Test 3   Test 4
   2              0        0        0        0  @AVG(B2..E2)
   3              0        0        0        0  @AVG(B3..E3)
   4              0        0        0        0  @AVG(B4..E4)
   5              0        0        0        0  @AVG(B5..E5)
   6              0        0        0        0  @AVG(B6..E6)
   7              0        0        0        0  @AVG(B7..E7)
   8              0        0        0        0  @AVG(B8..E8)
   9              0        0        0        0  @AVG(B9..E9)
  10              0        0        0        0  @AVG(B10..E10)
  11              0        0        0        0  @AVG(B11..E11)
  12              0        0        0        0  @AVG(B12..E12)
  13
  14      @AVG(B2..B12)
  15
  16
  17
  18
  19
  20
```

Fig. 5-10. Range of cells to copy TO.

Width) command to widen the columns so that the entire formula can be seen in its cell.

So now you have a general *template* for a grade book. The word "template" in electronic spreadsheet jargon means a worksheet preformatted for a specific purpose. That is, the grade book template is much the same as a blank page in a typical grade book. The advantage of the worksheet's template, of course, is that it does the calculations automatically. Mere paper cannot compete with this.

Absolute vs. Relative Cell References

Only relative cell references adjust when a formula is copied.

What is particularly important to learn from this exercise is the concept of *relative cell reference*. When you originally typed in the formula @AVG(B2..E2) into cell F2, you told 1-2-3 to display the average of all cells from four positions to the left of this point to one position to the left. So when you copied the formula, each new copy assumed you meant the average of the appropriate number of cells to the left. That is, 1-2-3 wisely decided that you did not want it to show the average score for the first student in each row. Rather, you wanted to show each student's average in the appropriate place. Therefore, 1-2-3 adjusted accordingly.

Absolute cell references (marked by the $ symbol) do not change when the formula is copied.

However, you may not always want 1-2-3 to make this kind of assumption. You can easily tell 1-2-3 when it should not make such an assumption, by referencing *absolute* cells. For this example, we'll set up a worksheet that calculates the monthly payment on a loan with a fixed principal and interest rate and varying terms as shown in Fig. 5-11. In the upper lefthand portion of the screen, you can type in the principal and interest. Then the spreadsheet calculates the monthly payments for various terms, and displays them in the table near the middle of the screen.

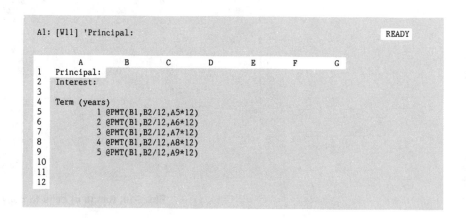

Fig. 5-11. Sample worksheet with formulas exposed.

You'll be interested to see how quickly you can build such a spreadsheet using ranges and copying. In cells A1 and A2, simply type in the labels Principal: and Interest:. In cell A4, type in the label Term (years). In cells A5 through A9 type in the numbers 1 through 5.

Now to calculate the payment for a 12-month loan you need to type into cell B5 the formula:

@PMT(B1,B2/12,A5∗12)

because cell B1 will contain the principal, cell B2 will hold the interest, and cell A5 holds the term. Fig. 5-12 displays the worksheet with the labels and a formula typed in.

```
B6:                                                      READY

        A         B      C      D      E      F      G
1  Principal:
2  Interest:
3
4  Term (years)
5          1 @PMT(B1,B2/12,A5*12)
6          2
7          3
8          4
9          5
10
11
12
```

Fig. 5-12. Payment formula in cell B5.

The appropriate formulas for all cells are displayed below.

@PMT(B1,B2/12,A5∗12)
@PMT(B1,B2/12,A6∗12)
@PMT(B1,B2/12,A7∗12)
@PMT(B1,B2/12,A8∗12)
@PMT(B1,B2/12,A9∗12)

However, if you use the /C (Copy) command to copy the formulas into their cells, we end up with this set of formulas:

@PMT(B1,B2/12,A5∗12)
@PMT(B2,B3/12,A6∗12)
@PMT(B3,B4/12,A7∗12)
@PMT(B4,B5/12,A8∗12)
@PMT(B5,B6/12,A9∗12)

1-2-3 automatically corrects the formulas for *all* cells, yet only the last argument in the formulas actually needed to vary. The principal and interest need to remain constant, since they are stored in cells B1 and B2 only. You need to make these cell addresses *absolute*, so that when you copy the formula, only the term varies in each formula. Use the $ symbol to make a cell "absolute" (constant) rather than "relative" (variable) when you copy cells in this fashion. Let's work through the problem step by step.

1. First, position the cell pointer to cell B5 and type in this formula:

   @PMT($B$1,$B$2/12,A5*12)

   This assures that when you make copies of the formula, references to cells B1 and B2 remain constant, and only the reference to cell A5 varies in each row. Leave the cell pointer in cell B5.

2. Type in the /C (Copy) command. The control panel asks:

   Enter range to copy FROM: B5..B5

   Since this is the cell we want to copy, just press RETURN.

3. The control panel asks:

   Enter range to copy TO: B5

   Press the down arrow, so that the cell pointer moves to cell B6, and the control panel reads:

   Enter range to copy TO: B6

4. Press the period (.) key to anchor the cell. The control panel reads:

   Enter range to copy TO: B6..B6

5. Press the down-arrow key three times, so that the cell pointer extends to cell B9 and the control panel reads:

   Enter range to copy TO: B6..B9

6. Now press RETURN, and 1-2-3 properly fills all the cells, as Fig. 5-13 shows. (You can use \WGFT and \WCS to see the actual formulas on your own screen.)

Notice that the $B$1 and $B$2 cell addresses are unchanged, yet the cell A5 address is properly adjusted for each row. That is, cells B1 and B2 are absolute (they don't change), and the A5 cell is relative (it varies properly with each row).

The ABS Key

You can use the ABS key (F4) to enter the $ in a cell reference without actually typing the $. A simple example will best demonstrate. Put the cell pointer on any cell, and type in the partial formula:

```
B10: [W25]                                                          READY

            A                B              C        D        E        F
 1   Principal:
 2   Interest:
 3
 4   Term (years)
 5             1 @PMT($B$1,$B$2/12,A5*12)
 6             2 @PMT($B$1,$B$2/12,A6*12)
 7             3 @PMT($B$1,$B$2/12,A7*12)
 8             4 @PMT($B$1,$B$2/12,A8*12)
 9             5 @PMT($B$1,$B$2/12,A9*12)
10
11
12
```

Fig. 5-13. Copied formulas with absolute references.

@PMT(B2

Before moving the cursor, press the ABS key (F4). The B2 will turn to an absolute reference, as below:

@PMT($B2

Press the ABS key again to mix the reference, as below:

@PMT($B$2

Press the ABS key once again to remix the reference, as below:

@PMT(B$2

You can press the ABS key as many times as you wish.

You don't actually need this partial formula, so you can just press the Escape key to erase the formula from the control panel.

You can even change a cell reference after the formula has already been entered into a cell. To try this, move the cell pointer to cell B5, and press the EDIT (F2) key. Use the left-arrow key to move the cursor to beneath any cell reference, as below:

@PMT($B$1,$B$2/12,A5*12)

Each time you press the ABS key, the dollar sign symbols will change. Press RETURN when done to enter the modified formula back into the cell. (We'll discuss the EDIT key in more detail in the next chapter.)

To change the cell
references in a formula
from relative to absolute
to mixed, use the ABS
(F4) key.

To recap: There are two ways to copy formulas. In one method cell addresses are relative. When you copy the formulas, the cell addresses are automatically updated in the cells you copy to. This method preserves the "meaning" of the formula (e.g., sum across a row). In the second method, cell references are absolute. That is, when you copy the formulas, the cell references do not adjust to their new cell locations. You create absolute references placing a $ in front of cell addresses that must remain constant. You can mix these relative and absolute cell addresses in a formula, as we have just shown. You can even make a cell address half relative, half absolute (e.g., B$1) in which case the column address (B) will vary, but the row (1) will remain constant. Similarly, the cell address $B1 will remain constant in terms of column (B), but the row (1) will vary in the copied cells. This last type of address is referred to as a *mixed* address, because it contains one relative and one absolute coordinate.

CELL LABELS

You can use relative and absolute references with range and cell names as well. A simple exercise with the current worksheet will demonstrate. Follow these steps to assign the name "Principal" to cell B1, and the name "Interest" to cell B2:

1. Move the cell pointer to cell A1.

2. Type /RNLR (Range Name Labels Right).

3. Press down-arrow key to highlight the range A1..A2, then press RETURN.

When you highlight the formulas in the range B5..B9, you'll see in the control panel that the cell names are now used in the formulas, along with the absolute reference signs, as below:

@PMT($PRINCIPAL:,$INTEREST:/12,A5/12)

Fig. 5-14 shows how the formula would appear before copying. Fig. 5-15 shows the formula after copying. Like the absolute cell references, the range-name references with $ symbols remain constant even after copying.

WHAT HAVE YOU LEARNED

Absolute and Relative
Range Names and Cell
Labels can be used in
formulas in place of cell
references.

In summary, you can use the Copy commands to make copies of individual cell contents. When formulas are involved, they will be properly adjusted to their new locations. In some cases, however, you will not want the cells to adjust. In those cases, make the references absolute by including dollar signs in the cell addresses.

```
B5: (T) [W38] @PMT($PRINCIPAL:,$INTEREST:/12,A5*12)                    READY

             A                        B                      C        D
     1   Principal:
     2   Interest:
     3
     4   Term (years)
     5             1  @PMT($PRINCIPAL:,$INTEREST:/12,A5*12)
     6             2
     7             3
     8             4
     9             5
    10
    11
    12
```

Fig. 5-14. Payment formula with range names.

```
B10: [W38]                                                             READY

             A                        B                      C        D
     1   Principal:
     2   Interest:
     3
     4   Term (years)
     5             1  @PMT($PRINCIPAL:,$INTEREST:/12,A5*12)
     6             2  @PMT($PRINCIPAL:,$INTEREST:/12,A6*12)
     7             3  @PMT($PRINCIPAL:,$INTEREST:/12,A7*12)
     8             4  @PMT($PRINCIPAL:,$INTEREST:/12,A8*12)
     9             5  @PMT($PRINCIPAL:,$INTEREST:/12,A9*12)
    10
    11
    12
    13
    14
    15
```

Fig. 5-15. Copied formula with absolute references.

1. The /C (Copy) command copies any data in the worksheet.

2. When copying, you can draw ranges to copy FROM and TO using the usual arrow keys.

3. When copying formulas, cell references within the formulas will retain their "meaning" by adjusting to to new columns and rows.

4. To keep formulas from adjusting, you can make the cell references in the formula *absolute* by typing in dollar ($) signs.

5. As an alternative to typing dollar signs into formulas, you can use the ABS (F4) key.

6. You can also make named cells and ranges absolute using the ABS (F4) key.

QUIZ

1. To copy any item of data on the worksheet, use which command?
   a. /RC (Range Copy)
   b. /WC (Worksheet Copy)
   c. /C (Copy)
   d. /D (Duplicate)

2. Which of the formulas below contains *only* relative cell references?
   a. @PMT(A1,B1/12,C1*12)
   b. @PMT($A$1,$B$1/12,$C$1*12)
   c. @PMT($A$1,$B1/12,$C1*12)
   d. @PMT(A$1,B$1/12,C$1*12)

3. Which of the formulas below contains *only* absolute cell references (without any mixed references)?
   a. @PMT(A1,B1/12,C1*12)
   b. @PMT($A$1,$B$1/12,$C$1*12)
   c. @PMT($A$1,$B1/12,$C1*12)
   d. @PMT(A$1,B$1/12,C$1*12)

4. If you copy the formula @SUM(A$5..C$5), what will happen to the cell references:
   a. Both row and column references will change
   b. Neither the row or column references will change
   c. Only the row references will change
   d. Only the column references will change

5. When specifying relative and absolute references in a formula, you can use which key to insert/delete dollar signs?
   a. CALC (F9)
   b. WINDOW (F6)
   c. ABS (F4)
   d. NAME (F3)

6. In the formula @SUM($Qtr1), the argument to the @SUM function is most likely:
   a. The range name Qtr1 as an absolute reference
   b. The range name Qtr1 as a relative reference
   c. The single cell name $Qtr1
   d. An error

Chapter 6

EDITING THE
WORKSHEET

ABOUT THIS CHAPTER

When developing a worksheet, there is often the need to change, or *edit*, its contents. There may be several reasons for doing so. We all make typographical errors from time to time that need to be corrected. Sometimes we put the right data in the wrong place, or the wrong formula in the right place, and so forth. And sometimes, we just change our minds about how we want the worksheet to look on the screen, so we move things around or add and delete rows and columns. In this chapter, we'll discuss 1-2-3's many editing capabilities.

THE EDIT MODE

To modify the contents of a cell, move the cell pointer to the cell and press the EDIT (F2) key.

Whenever you type something into a cell that 1-2-3 can't digest, 1-2-3 automatically beeps and goes into its *edit mode*. You can also enter the edit mode yourself by positioning the cell pointer to the cell whose content you wish to edit, and pressing Edit (F2) key. When you're in the Edit mode, the upper-right corner of the screen displays the word EDIT. You can use many keys in this mode to change a cell's contents. These keys and their effects are:

← **(backspace)**	Moves the cursor back one space, and erases a character in the entry as it moves.
Del	Erases the character above the cursor.
Esc	Cancels any changes and returns the unedited data to the cell.

Home	Moves the cursor to the first character in the entry.
End	Moves the cursor to the last character in the entry.
Ins	Toggles between Insert and Overwrite modes.
← (left-arrow)	Moves the cursor to the left one character without erasing anything.
→ (right-arrow)	Moves the cursor to the right one character without erasing.
⊢←	Moves the cursor 5 characters to the left.
→⊣	Moves the cursor 5 characters to the right.
↵ (return)	Completes the editing of the entry and goes back to previous mode.

To practice with this, position the cell pointer to any cell, and type in the formula:

@SUM(A1..A51)

Now suppose you realize that there is an error in this formula. It was supposed to be @SUM(A1..A15). Here is a quick way to fix it.

1. Move the cell pointer to the cell with the erroneous contents. Press the F2 (Edit) key. The cell's contents appear in the control panel, along with the cursor, like this:

   @SUM(A1..A51)_

2. Use the left-arrow key to back up to the 5 in A51, like this:

   @SUM(A1..A51)

3. Press the 1 key. This inserts the one in front of the present 5, as below:

   @SUM(A1..A151)

4. Move the cursor to the right one place so that it is under the second one in the formula, like this:

   @SUM(A1..A151)

5. Now press the Del at the bottom of the numeric keypad. This deletes the character over the cursor, like this:

   @SUM(A1..A15)

6. Press the RETURN key, and the corrected formula goes back to its original cell.

Insert vs. Overwrite

The Ins key switches between Insert and Overwrite mode when editing with the F2 key. To see how this works, press the EDIT (F2) key once again so that the formula:

@SUM(A1..A15)

appears on the screen. Press the left-arrow key so that the cursor is beneath the 1 in 15, as below:

@SUM(A1..A15)

Next, press the Ins key (next to the Del key) to switch to Overwrite mode. You'll see the overwrite symbol (OVR) appear at the bottom of the screen. Next type the numbers 51. You'll notice that rather than inserting the new characters into the formula, 123 overwrote the existing characters, as below:

@SUM(A1..A51)

The Ins key acts as a toggle. Each time you press it 1-2-3 switches between the Insert and Overwrite modes.

You can use the F2 Edit key to change numbers, labels, or formulas.

MOVING BACKWARD THROUGH COMMANDS

To "unselect" a menu option, press the Escape key.

Whenever you type in a series of commands, 1-2-3 always re-members each command. Once in a while, you may find that you've typed in the wrong commands and gotten yourself lost. For example, suppose you mean to type in the command /WGFT (Worksheet Global Format Text). By accident, you type in /GFT. This places you in the graph menu, and the mysterious prompt:

Enter sixth data range: t

appears on the control panel. What to do? Escape key out! Just keep pressing the escape key until you get back to familiar territory, such as the Ready mode, and try again. That's all there is to it.

You can undo an entire series of commands with the Break key. When you discover you've taken a wrong path in a series of com-mands, simply hold down the Ctrl key and press the Scroll Lock key. This will send you back to the Ready mode immediately. 1-2-3 will forget the whole series of commands that led you down the wrong path.

EDITING ROWS AND COLUMNS

Sometimes you need to edit the actual worksheet, not just a single entry or a series of commands. There are several options from the Range and Worksheet modes that allow you to do so. Fig. 6-1 shows a simple worksheet with some names in alphabetical order and some sales figures.

```
A1: [W11] 'Name                                                    READY

           A        B         C        D        E        F        G
    1   Name     Sales
    2   ...........................
    3
    4   Bliss      $9,932.91
    5   Blomgren   $8,983.04
    6   Kenney    $11,983.32
    7   Mohr       $8,932.00
    8   Newell     $8,888.08
    9   Rosiello   $6,232.11
   10
   11
   12
   13
   14
   15
   16
```

Fig. 6-1. Sample worksheet with labels and numbers.

Suppose you wish to add the name Clement to the list, and keep it in alphabetical order. The /WI (Worksheet Insert) command allows you to do so. Here are the steps:

1. Position the cell pointer to the row position (cell A6 in this example).

2. Select the /WI (Worksheet Insert) command. It asks if you wish to insert a column or a row. Select Row.

3. 1-2-3 then asks:

   Enter row insert range: A6..A6

The /WIR (Worksheet Insert Row) and /WIC (Worksheet Insert Column) commands let you insert rows and columns into the worksheet.

This is precisely where you wish to insert a row, so just press RETURN. All rows below A6 move down one to make room for the new row, as shown in Fig. 6-2.

Now you can just type Clement, and his sales amount, into the new row.

The Column option works in the same way. Simply position the cell pointer to where you want the new column to appear. Then

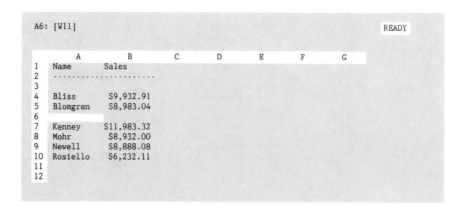

```
A6: [W11]                                                         READY

                A          B         C         D         E         F         G
     1  Name          Sales
     2  ......................
     3
     4  Bliss         $9,932.91
     5  Blomgren      $8,983.04
     6
     7  Kenney        $11,983.32
     8  Mohr          $8,932.00
     9  Newell        $8,888.08
    10  Rosiello      $6,232.11
    11
    12
```

Fig. 6-2. New row inserted on the worksheet.

select the /WIC (Worksheet Insert Column) option, and press RE-TURN. All columns to the right of the new one move to the right.

When you insert a new row or column, all existing formulas are adjusted accordingly. However, the formulas are not automatically placed in the new rows or columns. Use the /C copy command to fill in formulas when appropriate.

The /WDR (Worksheet Delete Row) and /WDC (Worksheet Delete Column) commands let you delete rows and columns from the worksheet.

The /WD (Worksheet Delete) option eliminates rows or columns from the worksheet. Suppose you decide to eliminate Blomgren from the list of names. To do so, simply position the pointer to her name in cell A5. Select the /WD (Worksheet Delete) command. It again asks if you wish to delete a column or a row. Select Row. When it asks for the range to delete, you can simply press the RETURN key, since the cell pointer is already positioned in the appropriate row. All rows below Blomgren's name will move up a row to fill in the blank space.

CLEANING UP

To erase a cell, or group of cells, use the /RE (Range Erase) commands.

Sometimes a worksheet just needs some cleaning up. Use the /RE (Range Erase) command for this. For example, suppose you wanted to erase all sales figures but wanted to keep the column there for future use. Select /RE (Range Erase), and specify the range, either by typing or drawing. In this example, the range will be B4 to B9. Press RETURN, and the cell entries are replaced with blanks (Fig. 6-3). You may want to use the highlighting method of drawing ranges when erasing, so you can see exactly what is to be erased.

If any of the cells in the specified range is protected, and the protection is on, then 1-2-3 will beep at you and ignore your request.

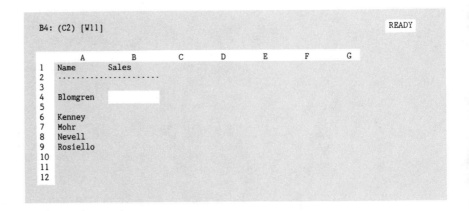

Fig. 6-3. Sales figures in B4..B9 erased.

To override, we need to type in the /WGP (Worksheet Global Protection) option, and select Disable. Then again type in the Range Erase command and specify the range. (Worksheet protection is discussed later in this chapter.)

You can erase the entire worksheet's contents, changing all cells to blanks. The /WE (Worksheet Erase) command provides this capability. However. It also sets all column widths back to their original 9 spaces. Column formats and protection fences are also set back to their original widths. The /WE command is usually used when you've created and saved one worksheet, and want to start building another one from scratch. Be careful. Once the worksheet is erased from the screen, it is erased permanently. If you have a copy of the worksheet on disk, however, the /WE will not affect the disk file.

MOVING SECTIONS OF THE WORKSHEET

To move the contents of cells, use the /M (Move) command.

Another method for redesigning a worksheet is to move a range of cells from one location on the spreadsheet to another. For example, suppose you had a long list of names and numbers as shown in Fig. 6-4.

Notice that only rows 12 through 31 are on the screen, since we must scroll down this far to see the total in row 31. There are additional names above in rows one through 11.

This worksheet would be better displayed in four columns rather than two. You can easily move this half of the list so that it appears next to top half of the list. Use the /M (Move) command to do so. Here are the steps:

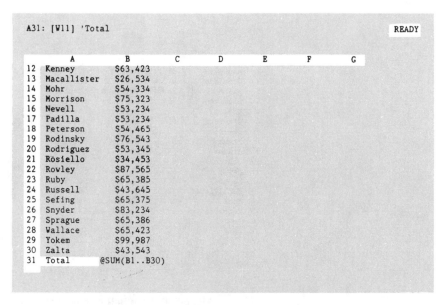

Fig. 6-4. Bottom half of a worksheet.

1. Position the cell pointer to the top left corner of the range to be moved. Since there are thirty rows in this example, we'll split them into two columns of 15 rows each, so move the cell pointer to cell A16.

2. Select the /M (Move option). The control panel asks:

   Enter range to move FROM: A16..A16

   Press the right arrow key once to expand the cell pointer to cell B16, then press the End key followed by the down-arrow key to quickly expand the cell pointer to the entire range to be moved. The control panel now specifies the entire range of cells to move, A16..B31. Press RETURN.

3. The control panel then requests:

   Enter range to move TO: A16

   Move the cell pointer up to cell C1, which causes the prompt to read:

   Enter range to move TO:C1

4. Press the period key and the right arrow key to expand the cell pointer and prompt to C1..D1.

5. Press RETURN. The named range is moved over to columns C1 and D1, as shown in Fig. 6-5.

```
C16: [W10] 'Total                                                    READY

            A           B          C            D          E      F      G
 1    Andrews       $23,412 Newell       $53,234
 2    Berriuno      $23,423 Padilla      $53,234
 3    Bliss         $65,434 Peterson     $54,465
 4    Blomgren      $54,354 Rodinsky     $76,543
 5    Clement       $53,243 Rodriguez    $53,345
 6    Crawford      $56,434 Rosiello     $34,453
 7    Davis         $53,234 Rowley       $87,565
 8    Frank         $32,434 Ruby         $65,385
 9    Gilmore       $43,342 Russell      $43,645
10    Johnson       $87,433 Sefing       $65,375
11    Jolly         $53,254 Snyder       $83,234
12    Kenney        $63,423 Sprague      $65,386
13    Macallister   $26,534 Wallace      $65,423
14    Mohr          $54,334 Yokem        $99,987
15    Morrison      $75,323 Zalta        $43,543
16                          Total        @SUM(B1..D15)
17
18
19
```

Fig. 6-5. Bottom half of a worksheet moved up and over.

Notice that the second argument in the @SUM formula has adjusted itself accordingly. The /M (Move) command usually makes the correct adjustment for a formula, however what 1-2-3 views as the correct adjustment and what you feel is the correct adjustment might not always match. After moving a range, check your formulas to make sure they still contain the appropriate references.

CHANGING CALCULATION PROCEDURES

The /WGR (Worksheet Global Recalculation) commands let you change the worksheet's recalculation procedures.

1-2-3 automatically recalculates all formulas on the worksheet any time you change or add data to a single cell on the worksheet. This is great for immediate feedback, and is especially wonderful for projections and playing with "What-if" questions. However, if there are many calculations to be performed in the worksheet, and it takes a long time to perform them all, then it is suddenly not so pleasant. It means that each time you add or change data in a cell, you have to wait for all the recalculations to take place. You can change 1-2-3 so that recalculations only take place when you want them to.

Fig. 6-6 shows a worksheet which calculates some basic statistics on a range of numbers (A1 to A20). The numbers do not exist yet. As you type each number in, the cells with formulas in them will recalculate and display the results each time you add another number to the list. This can be somewhat bothersome, and also meaningless if you are only concerned with the statistics on the entire set of numbers. You can change the recalculation procedure from automatic to manual using the /WGR (Worksheet Global Recalculation) command.

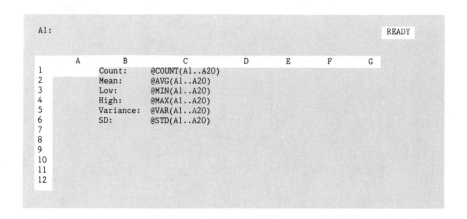

Fig. 6-6. Sample worksheet with formulas exposed.

The formulas are displayed in the worksheet because the /WGFT (Worksheet Global Format Text) command is in effect. Use the /WGFG (Worksheet Global Format General) command to make the formulas display their results, which is all zeros and ERRs until there are some data in the A1..A20 range.

Now, select /WGR (Worksheet Global Recalculation). This presents a menu of subcommands:

Natural Columnwise Rowwise Automatic Manual Iteration

Select Manual.

Now when you add numbers to the range (as in Fig. 6-7), the calculations remain zeros and ERRs even through the numbers are typed in. The CALC symbol is displayed in the lower right portion of the screen. This is to remind you that these data have not been calculated yet.

Once you have typed some numbers into Column A, you can have 1-2-3 do the calculations by pressing the Calc key (Function key F9). 1-2-3 then does all the calculations, and displays the results as shown in Fig. 6-8. Furthermore, the CALC reminder is no longer displayed in the lower righthand portion of the screen because there is no need to recalculate.

If you were to change any of the values in column A, there would not be an automatic recalculation. However, the CALC reminder would immediately reappear on the screen, reminding you once again that a change has occurred in the data, and to see that change you must press the Calc key.

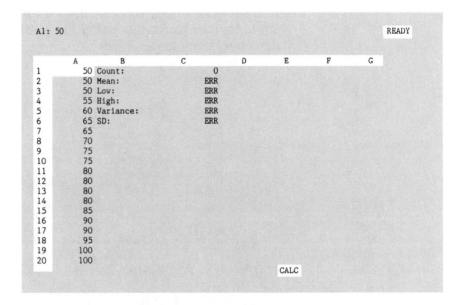

Fig. 6-7. Sample data in the range A1..A20.

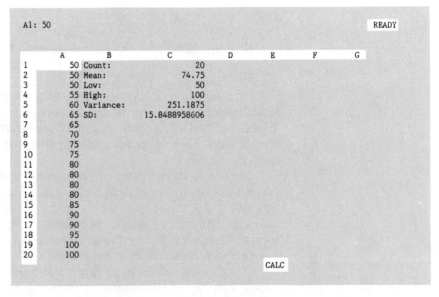

Fig. 6-8. Calculated results after pressing Calc key (F9).

To return to Automatic recalculation mode, simply select the /WGR command again, and choose Automatic from the options.

The /WGR command also allows you to change the order in which calculations take place. In its "natural" state, 1-2-3 calculates all formulas exactly as they should be calculated. For example, if calculation "A" requires information from calculation "B," 1-2-3 will naturally perform calculation "B" first. You can change the natural setting to either Columnwise or Rowwise by selecting these options from the /WGR menu. However, there is very rarely a need to do so, and unless a peculiar application absolutely demands it, it's best not to stray from the Natural calculation procedure.

PROTECTING CELLS FROM ACCIDENTAL CHANGE

You can format cells in the worksheet so that they are protected from accidental change. You will find this feature especially useful for cells with formulas in them, where you don't want to accidentally erase the formula by mistakenly typing a number directly into the cell. If you're going to let other people use your worksheets, then you'll probably end up liking this feature (and the people who use your worksheet) even more.

It helps to think of cells as being for either *input* or *output*. Cells with labels and numbers in them are usually input cells. That is, you enter data into them, such as entering names and test scores into our electronic grade book. Cells with formulas are typically output cells. That is, they display the results of calculations based upon numbers in the cells, such as our average scores in the grade book example. Generally, you should protect output cells, and leave the input cells unprotected for easy data entry and modification.

The analogy to electric fences used in the 1-2-3 manual is good for envisioning what happens when you protect cells. Initially, all cells have the equivalent of an electronic fence around them, but the electricity is off (Fig. 6-9). Since the power is off in the electric fence, it is easy to "jump in" and change the cell's contents.

You can "turn on the juice" in any cell, range of cells, or even all the cells on the screen, which makes it difficult to "jump in" and modify the contents of the cell. In Fig. 6-10, Cell B1 has the power in the fence turned on, and therefore is protected from accidental modification or deletion.

In its normal state each cell in the worksheet has an electronic fence built around it, but the electricity is turned off. 1-2-3 has four commands for protecting cells. Some turn the electricity on and off in the fences, others tear down and rebuild fences around cells. A summary of the commands follows:

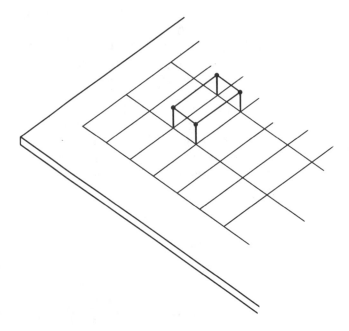

Fig. 6-9. Power is off in the electronic fence.

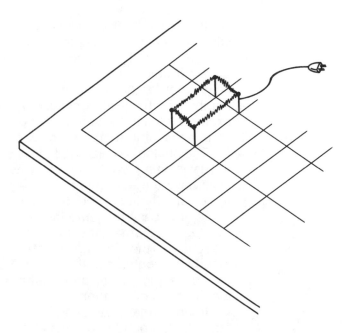

Fig. 6-10. Cell is protected because power is on.

/RP   Range Protect: Builds electronic fences around a range of cells, but does not "turn on the juice."

/RU   Range Unprotect: Tears down the electronic fences around a range of cells.

/RI   Range Input: Makes it impossible to move the cell pointer into protected cells.

/WGP   Worksheet Global Protection: Turns the electricity on and off in all cells in the worksheet that have electronic fences around them.

Fig. 6-11 shows the loan payment worksheet with the formulas displayed in their cells. (You created this worksheet at the end of Chapter 2, and saved it with the file name SLOAN.) Since you have not tampered with the protection facilities at all yet, all cells are in their natural state. That is, each has an invisible electronic fence around it, but the power is off. You only need fences around the Output fields (the cells with formulas in them), so let's begin by first tearing down all the electronic fences, and then building fences around only the output cells.

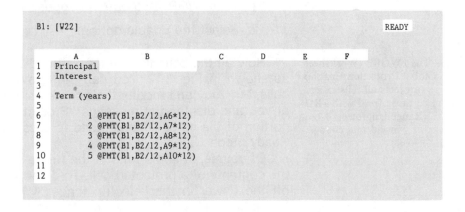

Fig. 6-11. Sample worksheet with formula exposed.

The /RU (Range Unprotect) commands remove protection from cells in a specified range.

The /RU (Range Unprotect) command will tear down the electronic fences. Here is the procedure:

1. Type in the Command /RU. 1-2-3 asks that you:

   Enter range to unprotect: XX..XX

2. Enter the Range to tear down the fences on. (For the sake of example, tear down all the fences.) The range, in this case, is A1..B10. Press RETURN.

At this point, none of the cells have electronic fences around them. You may notice that the display got a little brighter, or perhaps changed color. Unprotected cells are always displayed at a brighter intensity or in a contrasting color.

To put some fences around the formula cells, use the /RP (Range Protect) command. Here are the steps:

1. Type /RP (Range Protect). 1-2-3 asks that you:

   Enter range to protect: XX..XX

2. Specify the Range to protect. In this example, we'll want to protect the formulas in cells (B6..B10). Type in B6..B10 and press RETURN.

The cells in the protected range will return to their normal intensity or color. At this point, the formula cells all have electronic fences around them, but the power is off so you can still jump in.

You can turn on the juice in the electric fences with the /WGP (Worksheet Global Protection) command, following these steps:

1. Type /WGP. Two options appear, Enable and Disable.

2. Select the Enable option.

The /WGPE (Worksheet Global Protection Enable) protects all cells except those freed with /RU (Range Unprotect) from accidental change.

Now all the cells with fences around them have the power on, as shown in Fig. 6-12. You can still move the pointer into those cells, but you can't modify their contents. If you try, 1-2-3 will beep at you and display the message "Protected cell" in the lower left portion of the screen. You'll need to press Esc to get back to the Ready mode.

Of course, at some time in the future you may need to change the contents of a protected cell. To do so, you merely have to turn off the power in the "electric fences." This is accomplished by typing in the /WGP command, and selecting the Disable option from the menu choices. When done changing the formula in the protected cell, type in the /WGP command again, select Enable, and once again all output cells are protected.

You can carry it a step farther and make it impossible to even put the cell pointer in the protected cells. Use the /RI (Range Input) command for this. Here are the steps:

1. Type in the /RI command. 1-2-3 asks that you:

   Enter data input range: XX..XX

2. Type in the range of the entire worksheet (A1..B10) and press RETURN.

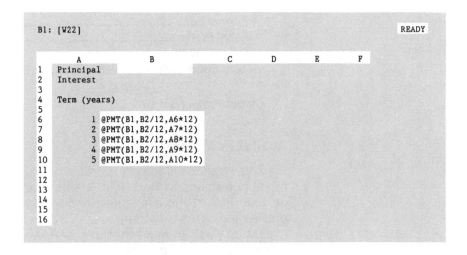

Fig. 6-12. Range of cells to protect is highlighted.

When you move the cell pointer around the worksheet, it will skip over cells in the range not specified in the /RI command.

To terminate the Range Input command, press the Esc key prior to filling data into a cell.

STATUS OF THE WORKSHEET

The /WS (Worksheet Status) command shows the status of various worksheet settings.

You can quickly check the status of the worksheet at any time using the /WS (Worksheet Status) commands. When you type /WS, you'll see a display as below:

Available Memory:
Conventional .... 247312 of 250080 Bytes (98%)
Expanded .... (None)

Math Co-processor: (None)

Recalculation:
Method .... **Automatic**
Order .... **Natural**
Iterations 1

Circular Reference: (None)

Cell Display:
Format .... (G)
Label-Prefix .... '
Column-Width 9
Zero Suppression .... Off

Global Protection: Off

Available Memory

The Available Memory portion of the display tells how much memory remains to work with. In this example, the worksheet takes up only 2% of the available Random Access Memory (RAM). The display indicates that there are 247312 bytes of 250080 (or 98%) still available. Keep in mind that this is RAM memory, (not disk space) where the active worksheet is stored and all the work takes place. Disks are only used for storing worksheets that are not in use at the moment.

The Conventional memory portion of the display refers to the RAM memory that came with your computer. The Expanded memory portion of the display refers to any additional memory boards you may have added to gain more RAM memory. The Math Co-processor portion of the display refers to any boards you might have added to speed processing, such as the 8087 processor.

Recalculation

The recalculation portion of the display shows the status of the recalculation method in use. In this example, the worksheet uses the usual Automatic, Natural recalculation with a single iteration. The /WGR (Worksheet Global Recalculation) options from the menu allow you to change this.

Circular Reference

The Circular Reference portion of the display shows the address of any formulas that refer to themselves. For example, if cell A1 contained the formula, +A1+B1, this would be a circular reference because the formula refers to its own location on the worksheet (cell A1). Circular references generally cause problems because they grow each time the worksheet recalculates. (When a formula contains a circular reference, the word CIRC appears at the bottom of the screen.)

The Circular Reference portion of the Worksheet Status display only shows the address of a single cell containing a circular reference. If you change the formula and the CIRC indicator still appears at the bottom of the screen, check the Worksheet Status display again. It will show the location of the next circular reference that needs to be fixed.

Cell Display

The Cell Display portion of the Worksheet Status screen shows the default format for displaying numbers. In the sample screen shown, the default display is the General (G) format. You can change this to Fixed, Currency, Scientific, or any of the other available number formats using the /WGF (Worksheet Global Format) commands.

The Label-Prefix option shows the default label prefix, and apostrophe (left-justified) in this example. This can be altered with the /WGL (Worksheet Global Label-Prefix) commands.

The Column-Width portion shows the default column width, nine in this example. The /WGC (Worksheet Global Column-Width) commands will change this setting.

The Zero Suppression portion tells whether zeros are displayed on the worksheet (Off), or if the zeros are invisible, showing only a blank cell rather than the 0 (On). Use the /WGZ (Worksheet Global Zero) options to turn the zero suppression on and off.

Global Protection

The Global Protection portion tells the status of the worksheet's protection capabilities, which are controlled by the /WGP (Worksheet Global Protection) commands.

WHAT HAVE YOU LEARNED?

1. To edit the contents of a cell, move the cell pointer to the cell and press F2. Use the editing keys to make changes, and press RETURN when done editing.

2. Use /WIC (Worksheet Insert Column) to insert new columns into the worksheet. Use /WIR (Worksheet Insert Row) to insert new rows.

3. To erase a cell, or range of cells, use the /RE (Range Erase) commands.

4. To move a section of the worksheet, use /M (Move).

5. To change the calculation procedures on the worksheet, use /WGR (Worksheet Global Recalculation).

6. To protect cells from accidental change or deletion, use the /WGPE (Worksheet Global Protection Enable) commands.

7. To leave some cells unprotected in a worksheet, use /RU (Range Unprotect) before using /WGPE (Worksheet Global Protection Enable).

8. To view the current status of worksheet settings, use /WS (Worksheet Status).

QUIZ

1. To change the contents of a cell on the worksheet, you press which key?
   a. F1
   b. F2
   c. F3
   d. F4

2. When editing the contents of a cell, which key turns the *insert mode* on and off?
   a. Del
   b. End
   c. Home
   d. Ins

3. Which commands let you insert new rows into the worksheet?
   a. /WGR (Worksheet Global Row)
   b. /RIN (Range Insert Row)
   c. /WR (Worksheet Row)
   d. /WIR (Worksheet Insert Row)

4. Which commands allow you to erase a cell, or group of cells?
   a. /RE (Range Erase)
   b. /WE (Worksheet Erase)
   c. /WRE (Worksheet Range Erase)
   d. /S (System)

5. Which command(s) lets you move cell contents about the worksheet?
   a. /C (Copy)
   b. /RM (Range Move)
   c. /M (Move)
   d. /WM (Worksheet Move)

6. To change the worksheet recalculation procedures, use the commands:
   a. /WGR (Worksheet Global Recalculation)
   b. /WR (Worksheet Recalculation)
   c. /RGR (Range Global Recalculation)
   d. /RC (Range Calc)

7. When the worksheet needs to be recalculated manually, what message appears at the bottom of the screen?
   a. ERR
   b. CIRC
   c. NA
   d. CALC

8. The /WGPE (Worksheet Global Protection Enable) commands protect all cells from accidental change *except* which?
   a. Cells protected with /RP (Range Protect)
   b. Cells unprotected with /RU (Range Unprotect)
   c. Cells designated as output with /RO (Range Output)
   d. None of the above

9. When viewing the status of the worksheet, Available Memory displays
   a. The amount of disk space available
   b. The amount of RAM memory available
   c. The memory available in extra memory boards only
   d. None of the above

10. A circular reference in a formula causes which message to appear at the bottom of the screen?
    a. CALC
    b. ERR
    c. REF
    d. CIRC

Chapter 7

DISPLAYING WORKSHEETS ON THE PRINTER

ABOUT THIS CHAPTER

If you have a printer, you will probably want to display your worksheets on paper (hardcopy) from time to time. 1-2-3 has many commands for sending worksheets to the printer, and many options for formatting the hardcopy of the worksheet. You can also send a worksheet to a special disk file, called a print file, which allows you to print the worksheet at a more convenient time, or even make some changes to the printed worksheet prior to printing it.

THE STANDARD PRINTED REPORT

The /PP (Print Printer) options bring you to the Print menu for printing worksheets.

To print a copy of a worksheet, you first need to have the worksheet displayed on the screen. Then select the /P (Print) command. A series of print options appears in the control panel. The first one looks like this:

Printer   File
Send print output directly to the printer

To immediately print an exact copy of the worksheet as it appears on the screen, select the Printer option. Selecting the File option stores a special copy of the worksheet on a disk file, which can be printed out at a later time. Once you've selected one of these options, another menu appears, which looks like this:

Range Line Page Options Clear Align Go Quit

To print a worksheet, first select the Range option, which will ask:

131

Enter Print Range: A1

Select Range from the Print menu to specify a range to print, then select Go.

Then you can type in or draw the range that you wish to print (usually the range of all cells in the worksheet). Then, select the Go option to send the worksheet to the printer.

If nothing happens, either (1) the printer is not on, (2) the printer is not on-line, (3) the printer is not physically connected to the computer with a cable or, (4) the printer is not properly configured. If any of either 1, 2, or 3 is the problem, then 1-2-3 will beep at you and display a message indicating that it cannot find the printer. Just press the Escape (Esc) key, and you will be returned to the print menu. Make sure the printer is properly hooked up, and try again.

Whenever you type in the /P command, you need to specify a range to print. However, 1-2-3 will remember the last range you used, and display it on the screen. If that range is still acceptable, you need not reenter the range. However, if you should ever select the Go option from the print menu, and only get a beep from 1-2-3, that could mean you have not yet specified the range. Select the Range option again, specify a range, then select the Go option again.

To stop printing before the job is done, press the BREAK key (Ctrl-Scroll Lock on IBM keyboards).

HEADINGS AND FOOTINGS ON PRINTED WORKSHEETS

If you want additional headings or footings on each page of your printed worksheet, you can select the Option choice from the print menu. When you select Options, the following menu appears on the screen:

Header Footer Margins Borders Setup Pg-Length Other Quit

Select the Header option to create a heading for a worksheet, select Footer to create a footing. When you do so, 1-2-3 will ask you to type in the heading or the footing. Headings are always printed two lines above the printed worksheet, footings two lines below.

To repeat a heading or footing on the printed worksheet, select the Options Header or Options Footer commands from the Print menu.

You can left-justify, center, or right-justify headings and footings. The symbol | is used to specify justification. Suppose you want your heading to be "Grades for Computer Science 101." You can enter in any one of three formats, with these results:

Typed in as...	Result
Grades for Computer Science 101	Since there is no	character, this heading will be left-justified.

| Grades for Computer Science 101   Since there is one |char-
                                          acter, this heading will be
                                          centered.

|| Grades for Computer Science 101   With two |characters, this
                                          heading will be right-jus-
                                          tified

You can get fancy and include page numbers and today's date in headings. Use the symbol # to stand for a page number and the symbol @to stand for today's date. For example, if we type in the heading as:

@ | **Grades for Computer Science 101**|#

it will appear with the date left-justified, the heading centered, and the page number right-justified as shown in Fig. 7-1.

```
03-Mar-84           Grades for Computer Science 101                    1


Name            Test 1          Test 2          Test 3          Test 4
...........................................................................
Adams             90              100             88              70
Bovee             80              90              78              100
Carlson           90              90              95              90
```

Fig. 7-1. Header on a printed worksheet.

If the printed worksheet is more than one page long, the heading (and footing) will be displayed on each page. And of course, the page number will be correct.

PRINTING THE ACTUAL CONTENTS

The Options Other Cell-Formulas options display actual cell contents on the printer.

The Printer commands generally display the worksheet as it appears on the screen. In some circumstances, however, you might prefer to see a printed copy of the worksheet's actual contents (including formulas) rather than its output. To do so, select Options from the Print menu of choices. From the next menu of options, select Other. This displays yet another menu of options:

As-Displayed Cell-Formulas Formatted Unformatted

Select Cell-Formulas. Then select Quit from the Other menu, and select Go from the Print Menu. The Printer will display a listing of all active cells in the worksheet and their contents, as shown in Fig. 7-2.

```
A1: U 'Principal
B1: U 60000
A2: U 'Interest
B2: U @.17
A5: U 'Term
B5: U 'Payment
A6: I 1
B6: @PMT($B$1,$B$2/12,A6*12)
A7: I 2
B7: @PMT($B$1,$B$2/12,A7*12)
A8: I 3
B8: @PMT($B$1,$B$2/12,A8*12)
A9: I 4
B9: @PMT($B$1,$B$2/12,A9*12)
A10: I 5
B10: @PMT($B$1,$B$2/12,A10*12)
```

Fig. 7-2. Worksheet Cell-Formulas.

This display shows the contents of the loan analysis worksheet we created earlier. Most of the cells have the letter U in front of them, indicating that these are "Unprotected" cells. The formula cells, however, do not have a U in front of them because the last time you used this worksheet in an example, you set up the worksheet so that the formula cells would be protected and unmodifiable. To return to normal worksheet printing, select Options Other As-Displayed from the Print menu.

Another way to view the actual contents of the worksheet rather than the output is to first use the /RFT (Range Format Text) commands to have the actual formulas rather than their outputs displayed on the screen. Then, select the /P option, specify the range of the entire worksheet, and print the file. The output will be displayed exactly as it appeared on the screen (Fig. 7-3).

```
Principal      60000
Interest        0.16

Term           Payment

  1            @PMT($B$1,$B$2/12,A6*12)
  2            @PMT($B$1,$B$2/12,A7*12)
  3            @PMT($B$1,$B$2/12,A8*12)
  4            @PMT($B$1,$B$2/12,A9*12)
  5            @PMT($B$1,$B$2/12,A10*12)
```

Fig. 7-3. Worksheet printed in Text format.

You may want to make such printouts of all the worksheets you create. If some minor disaster should ever destroy a prized worksheet, a printout such as this can help you key it back in from scratch. You may have to use the /WC (Worksheet Column-Width) command to make the columns extra wide to accommodate the formulas. Do so before you select the /P command.

COMPRESSED AND EXPANDED PRINT

Most dot matrix printers have commands for switching to compressed or expanded print. 1-2-3 can send special codes to such printers through the Options Setup commands. Of course, you must know what special characters to send to a particular printer to achieve a desired result. You'll need to check your printer manual for that.

Once you have determined what special characters your printer requires for various print sizes, select Options from the print menu. From the menu of subcommands, select Setup. 1-2-3 will ask that you:

Enter Setup String:

To send special printer codes to your printer, use the Options Setup commands from the Print menu.

Now you need to type in the appropriate code. The code is typically a number below 26 (the "control key" range of the ASCII standard character set used by most computers). It is necessary to precede the code with a backslash, and extend it to three characters. For example, the Epson printer uses ASCII character 15 to go into compressed print mode. So, the actual code you type onto the screen is:

＼015

After typing in the code, press RETURN. Select Quit from the menu of subcommands, then Go from the Print menu. The worksheet will be printed in compressed print.

When printing worksheets with compressed or expanded print, you will probably want to adjust the margins accordingly. The Option Margins option will allow you to adjust the left and right margins of your printed worksheet. To do so, select Options from the Print menu, and select Margins. This allows you to further select from the left, right, top, and bottom margins. If you are changing the print size, you probably want to alter the right margin accordingly.

Select R for right margin, and type in a new value for the right margin (the standard right margin is 76). You may have to experiment a bit to get just the report you want, since the printer may not always produce exactly what you had expected.

Changing the right-margin setting is also useful if you use wide paper in your printer. To take advantage of the full width of the paper, set the right margin to 120 or so.

You can also change the number of lines printed on each page by adjusting the page length. 1-2-3 assumes a standard 8 1/2 by 11 inch page size, and prints 66 lines to a page. If you are using other than standard size paper, or you set your printer to print 8 lines to the inch (rather than the standard 6 lines), you can change the page length. Type in the /P command, select Options from the Print menu, select Page-length from the next menu. 1-2-3 will ask that you:

Enter Lines per Page: 66

Type in the new page length. For example, if you are printing 8 lines to the inch, you'll want the page length to be 88 (8 lines times 11 inches). Type in 88 and press RETURN. Your worksheet will be formatted accordingly.

You can embed special printer codes directly in a worksheet using the | | characters.

Once you've set up your printer to print in compressed or expanded print, it will continue to do so until you either turn the printer off and back on again, or send it the special code for normal print using the Options Setup commands from the Print menu. If you opt to just turn the printer off and back on, be sure to use the Options Setup commands from the Print menu (and the Backspace key) to erase the previous Setup string. (Optionally, you can use the Clear Format options from the Print menu to reset the margin, page length, and setup options altogether.)

Table 7-1 shows printer settings for a number of printers. Notice that some require a *multicode sequence* of characters (more than a single \). For example, the Epson FX requires that you enter \027\087\049 for expanded print. Some manufacturers might change printer codes, so I can't guarantee that these will be accurate for all time. However, if you see your printer on the list, you might just want to give one a try.

If you cannot locate your printer in the table, check your printer manual for the appropriate codes. These may be displayed in character form. You can use the worksheet to help convert the characters to numbers. For example, if your printer uses Escape = (Escape key and equal sign) to enter compressed print, the code you need is \027\061. How would you know this? For one, the Escape key is *always* \027. You can use the @CODE function to find the code for any other character. Just put the cell pointer anywhere on the worksheet and enter the @CODE function, with the appropriate character in quotation marks. For example, the code for " = " can be found with @CODE(" = "). The function displays 61. Hence, Escape = converts to \027\061.

Numbers and letters also have ASCII codes. To find the ASCII code for 8, use @CODE("8"). To find the ASCII code for the letter Z, use @CODE("Z"). @CODE won't work to find the ASCII code for the quotation mark (e.g. @CODE("""")). The quotation mark does have an ASCII code, but it is \034. Hence, Esc" would be \027\034.

EMBEDDED PRINTER CODES

You can also embed special printer codes directly into your worksheet, which means you can print portions of the worksheet in expanded print, others in compressed print, and still others in normal print. If your printer allows, you can also add other features such as underlining, boldface, and italics (by using the appropriate \ codes).

Table 7-1. Attribute Codes for Various Printers

Manufac-turer	Printer Model	Normal (10 CPI)	Condensed Print	Expanded Print-On	Expanded Print-Off
BMC	PB101	\027\078	\027\081 \014		\015
Brother	HR-1	\027\080	\027\077		
C. Itoh	Prowriter I & II	\027\078	\027\081 \014		\015
	8510 or 1550	\027\078	\027\081 \014		\015
	Hot Dot	\027\078	\027\081 \014		\015
Comrex	CR-1	\027\080	\027\077		
Epson	RX or FX	\018	\015	\027\087\049	\027\087\050
	MX80 or MX100	\018	\015	\027\083	\027\084
	MX w/ Graftrax	\018	\015	\027\083	\027\084
	MX w/o Graftrax	\018	\015	\014	\020*
IBM	PC Printer	\018	\015	\014	\020*
IDS	Prism 80 & 132	\029	\031	\001	\002
	Microprism	\029	\031	\001	\002
NEC	PC-8023-A \027\078	\027\081 \014	\015		
Okidata	82A, 83A, 84	\030	\029	\031	\030
	92,93	\030	\029	\031	\030
	2350, 3410	\027\054	\027\066	\027\067	\027\090
Panasonic	1090	\018	\015	\027\083	\027\084
	1091, 1092, 1093	\018	\015	\027\087\049	\027\087\050
PMC	DMP85	\027\078	\027\081 \014		\015
Star Micronics Gemini, Delta	\018	\015			
	Radix	\018	\015		
TEC	DMP85	\027\078	\027\081 \014		\015
Victor	6020	\018	\015	\014	\020*

* Double-widths turn off automatically at the end of the line.

Fig. 7-4 shows a worksheet printed with the heading in expanded print, and the data in compressed print. (Notice that all 12 columns fit across a single 8 1/2 by 11 inch sheet of paper, which would not be possible without compressed print.)

ABC Company
Monthly Sales

	Jan.	Feb.	March	April	May	June	July	Aug.	Sept.	Oct.	Nov.	Dec.
Apples	440.62	559.81	569.44	321.49	193.21	45.84	403.83	108.23	77.33	380.93	833.64	315.32
Bananas	686.47	670.03	816.28	906.69	196.07	258.82	504.87	42.11	32.18	499.47	671.91	360.41
Cherries	906.87	411.68	373.15	844.29	536.04	153.70	945.05	255.76	732.44	134.94	177.85	838.26
	2033.96	1641.58	1758.86	2072.47	925.32	458.36	1859.75	406.10	841.95	1015.34	1683.40	1513.99

Fig. 7-4. Worksheet printed with expanded and compressed print.

Embedded printer codes are placed directly in the worksheet, preceded by two ||characters (though only one |character will appear on the screen). Fig. 7-5 shows the sample worksheet on the screen. Only a portion of the worksheet fits on the screen. Cell A1 contains the code ||\031, which is expanded print for the Okidata 83A printer. Cell A4 contains the code ||\029, which sets the Okidata into compressed print. Cell A14 contains the code ||\030, for normal print.

```
A16:                                                              READY

         A        B        C        D        E        F        G        H
1   |\031                             <-- Expanded print on.
2            ABC Company
3            Monthly Sales
4   |\029                             <-- Compressed Print on.
5
6            Jan.     Feb.     March    April    May      June     July
7            ..............................................................
8   Apples   440.62   559.81   569.44   321.49   193.21    45.84   409.83
9   Bananas  686.47   670.09   816.28   906.69   196.07   258.82   504.87
10  Cherries 906.87   411.68   373.15   844.29   536.04   153.70   945.05
11           ===============================================================
12           2033.96  1641.58  1758.86  2072.47  925.32   458.36  1859.75
13
14  |\030                             <-- Normal print
15
16
17
18
19
20
```

Fig. 7-5. Printer codes embedded in a worksheet.

Notice that next to each code is an explanatory comment preceded by an arrow (e.g. ← Expanded print). It is important to keep in mind that rows containing the || codes do not print at all. Therefore, these comments do not appear on the printed worksheet. This also means that if you want a blank row between two rows on the printed worksheet, the row containing the code must have a blank row above or beneath it.

Even though you specify compressed print for a worksheet, the data might still be spread across several pages if you do not extend the right margin. In the sample printed worksheet in Fig. 7-4, the right margin was set to 140 using the Options Margins Right commands from the Print menu.

The codes used with the || symbols in the worksheet are the same codes used with the Setup option from the Print menu. Therefore, the codes in Table 7-1 will work as well for embedded || printer codes.

WORKSHEET BORDERS

1-2-3 will divide large worksheets onto separate pages, if necessary. For example, the ten-year projection worksheet shown in Fig. 7-6 extends to the year 1996, beyond the right edge of the screen. When printed, this worksheet displays the latter years 1991 through 1996 on a second page, as in Fig. 7-7.

The second page of the worksheet is a little difficult to interpret because the left column, which shows tenants and expense categories, isn't visible.

Using the Options Borders commands, you can have 1-2-3 repeat rows and columns on each printed page. Fig. 7-8 shows the second page of the Ten-Year projection worksheet, with columns A and B repeated. The repeated columns make the second page more legible because the titles are carried over from the first page.

To repeat rows or columns on the printed worksheet, first position the cell pointer to the row and/or column you want to repeat. Call up the Print menu and select the Options Borders commands. Select Columns to repeat columns, or Rows to repeat rows. 1-2-3 will then let you type in or highlight the rows and columns to repeat.

In the sample worksheet in Fig. 7-8, the Columns option was used, and A4 was specified as the column to repeat. (Since only the columns are repeated, the row number doesn't matter. For example, you could specify A1 or A1000.)

Next, you need to select Range to highlight the range to print. Do NOT include the Borders column or row. For example, in the sample worksheet, the range to print was specified as B1..M17, which is the entire worksheet excluding the repeat column A. Then, select Go to print the worksheet.

```
B6: (P2) [W10] 0.12                                                    READY

            A            B        C        D        E        F
 1  Ten Year Projection for Commercial Real Estate
 2
 3               Increase
 4  Description  Rate %      1986     1987     1988     1989
 5  ..............................................................
 6  Tenant 1      12.00%  $15,000  $16,800  $18,816  $21,074
 7  Tenant 2      15.00%  $10,000  $11,500  $13,225  $15,209
 8  Tenant 3      11.00%   $5,000   $5,550   $6,161   $6,838
 9  Tenant 4      11.00%   $5,000   $5,550   $6,161   $6,838
10  Tenant 5      15.00%  $12,500  $14,375  $16,531  $19,011
11  ..............................................................
12  Maintenance   13.00%   $9,000  $10,170  $11,492  $12,986
13  Insurance     13.00%   $8,000   $9,040  $10,215  $11,543
14  Debt Serv.     0.00%     $900     $900     $900     $900
15  Mgmt Fee      11.00%   $1,000   $1,110   $1,232   $1,368
16  ..............................................................
17  Cash Flow             $28,600  $32,555  $37,054  $42,173
18
19
20
```

Fig. 7-6. Portion of a very wide worksheet.

```
    1990     1991     1992     1993     1994     1995
 ..............................................................
 $23,603  $26,435  $29,607  $33,160  $37,139  $41,596
 $17,490  $20,114  $23,131  $26,600  $30,590  $35,179
  $7,590   $8,425   $9,352  $10,381  $11,523  $12,790
  $7,590   $8,425   $9,352  $10,381  $11,523  $12,790
 $21,863  $25,142  $28,913  $33,250  $38,238  $43,973
 ..............................................................
 $14,674  $16,582  $18,738  $21,173  $23,926  $27,036
 $13,044  $14,739  $16,656  $18,821  $21,268  $24,032
    $900     $900     $900     $900     $900     $900
  $1,518   $1,685   $1,870   $2,076   $2,305   $2,558
 ..............................................................
 $48,000  $54,635  $62,192  $70,802  $80,615  $91,802
```

Fig. 7-7. Printed second half of wide worksheet.

```
 Description   1990     1991     1992     1993     1994     1995
 ..............................................................
 Tenant 1   $23,603  $26,435  $29,607  $33,160  $37,139  $41,596
 Tenant 2   $17,490  $20,114  $23,131  $26,600  $30,590  $35,179
 Tenant 3    $7,590   $8,425   $9,352  $10,381  $11,523  $12,790
 Tenant 4    $7,590   $8,425   $9,352  $10,381  $11,523  $12,790
 Tenant 5   $21,863  $25,142  $28,913  $33,250  $38,238  $43,973
 ..............................................................
 Maintenance $14,674  $16,582  $18,738  $21,173  $23,926  $27,036
 Insurance  $13,044  $14,739  $16,656  $18,821  $21,268  $24,032
 Debt Serv.    $900     $900     $900     $900     $900     $900
 Mgmt Fee    $1,518   $1,685   $1,870   $2,076   $2,305   $2,558
 ..............................................................
 Cash Flow  $48,000  $54,635  $62,192  $70,802  $80,615  $91,802
```

Fig. 7-8. Printed second half of worksheet with repeated border.

OTHER PRINTING OPTIONS

The Print main menu displays the options:

Range Line Page Options Clear Align Go Quit

As mentioned, the Range command lets you specify a range to print, and the Options command provides options for headings, borders, and other formatting features. The Go command prints the specified range, and Quit returns to the READY mode.

The Line option moves the paper in the printer down a line. You can use this command to print one or more blank lines before selecting Go. The Page option moves the paper to the top of the next page. Use this option to ensure that the printed worksheet starts at the top of a new page.

The Align option tells 1-2-3 where the top of a new page begins. If you have trouble getting your worksheets to break evenly across pages, turn the printer off, manually crank the paper to the top of a new page, then turn the printer back on. Select Align from the Print menu to "tell" 1-2-3 that the printer is at the top of a new page, then select Go.

The Clear command displays the menu:

All Range Borders Format

Select All to reset all print settings back to their original (default) values. Select Range to "unselect" a previous range specification. Select Borders to clear any previous borders (repeated rows or columns). Select Format to clear only previous margin, page length, and printer setup strings back to their original (default) settings.

INTERFACING WORKSHEETS WITH WORD PROCESSORS

The /PF (Print File) commands let you store "printed" copies of worksheets on disk files.

We mentioned earlier that printed worksheets could be sent to disk files rather than directly to the printer. This allows you to send a worksheet to a disk file, then pull it into a word processor (such as the WordStar™ program) for additional editing or for inclusion in a formal document. You can use all of the various options described in this chapter with worksheets sent to disk files as well as with printed worksheets. To send worksheets to disk files for printing, you should:

1. Select File rather than Printer from the first /P menu.

2. Specify a file name to store the worksheet on when asked.

The file name can be up to eight characters in length, and may not include spaces, periods, or commas.

Your worksheet will be "printed" on the named disk file rather than on the printer. 1-2-3 will add the extension .PRN to your file name, so if you call your file LOANS, it will be stored on disk as LOANS.PRN. You can specify which disk drive to use by preceding the file name with the letter of the drive and a colon. Hence, if you name the file B:LOANS, the disk in drive B will have the LOANS.PRN file on it.

Now suppose you have a 10-page report that you've created with the WordStar™ program stored on a disk. You want to include the LOANS worksheet in the report, but you don't want to do any cut and paste (Heaven forbid!). You can read the disk-file version of the worksheet into your report by following these steps.

First you need to decide whether you want 1-2-3 to format the printed report, or if you want to format it yourself with the word processor. If you want to format the printed worksheet yourself, select the Options Other Unformatted commands from the Print menu. That way, you can add your own page breaks, headings, borders, and so forth later using your word processor.

To take advantage of the built-in formatting, select Options Other Formatted. (You may want to try both options with each worksheet that you export, since some may be easier to work with if already formatted.)

Next, you need to follow these steps to create the file and import it into your word processor:

1. Make sure to create your .PRN file using the /PF (Print File) options as mentioned above. Also, use /FS (File Save) to save your worksheet if necessary. Then use /QY (Quit Yes) to exit 1-2-3, and leave the ACCESS menu so the DOS A> prompt reappears. Remove the LOTUS 1-2-3 disk from drive A, and the data disk from drive B.

2. Put a copy of the .PRN file on the same disk that contains your WordStar document. To do so, put your WordStar document disk in drive B, and the 1-2-3 data disk containing the .PRN file in drive A. From the DOS A> prompt, use the COPY command to copy the .PRN file to the disk in drive B. For example, if the name of the .PRN file is LOANS, enter the command:

   COPY LOANS.PRN B:

   at the A> prompt. Press RETURN.

3. Now, remove the 1-2-3 data disk from drive A and put in the disk that has WordStar on it. Run WordStar (using the usual

WS command at the DOS A> prompt). Select D to edit a Document, and specify the name of the WordStar document (e.g. B:MyDOC.TXT). You should see your document appear on the screen.

4. Position the cursor to the place where you want to read in your 1-2-3 worksheet. Type ^KR (hold down the Ctrl key and type KR). When WordStar asks for the name of the document to read, enter the drive and name of the .PRN file (e.g. B:LOANS.PRN). Press RETURN. The 1-2-3 file will be inserted at the location of the cursor. (Don't forget to save the WordStar document after reading in the new file.)

5. When you go back to using 1-2-3, be sure to put your 1-2-3 data disk back in drive B, then run 1-2-3 in the usual fashion.

The procedure is basically the same for a hard disk system, only you won't need to juggle all those floppy disks around. You can just copy the .PRN file to the directory that has the WordStar document on it using the DOS COPY command.

Word processing systems other than WordStar™ may require different commands for reading in the worksheet file, but the procedures will be basically the same.

If the worksheet you are sending to a disk file is large, you may want to ensure that no extraneous "page breaks" or headings and footings get sent to the disk file. You can do so by selecting Options from the Print menu. From there, select Other, and then select Unformatted. When you select the Go option, the worksheet will be sent to the named disk file without any extraneous print characters (such as page breaks). This gives you more control over formatting the report through a word processing system.

In summary, 1-2-3 provides many options for displaying worksheets on paper through the /PP command. The same options are available for sending worksheets to special print files on disk. You can use print files on a disk as you would any standard word processing file.

In the next chapter, we'll discuss techniques for managing worksheet files on disk.

WHAT HAVE YOU LEARNED?

1. The /PP (Print Printer) commands bring up the Print menu for printing a worksheet.

2. Use the Range option under the Print menu to highlight the range of cells to print.

3. The Options command on the Print menu lets you add headers and footers to each page of the printed worksheet.

4. The Options Other Cell-Formulas commands from the Print menu will display the actual contents and formulas of the worksheet, instead of the results of calculations.

5. The Options Setup commands allow you to send special codes to your printer for special attributes such as under-lining, compressed, and expanded print.

6. The || symbols let you place special printer attribute codes directly into your worksheet.

7. The Options Borders commands let you repeat sections of a worksheet on each printed page.

8. The /PF (Print File) commands store a copy of the printed worksheet on a disk file.

QUIZ

1. All commands for printing worksheets are under which main menu option?
   a. Worksheet
   b. Range
   c. Print
   d. File

2. Before you select Go to print a worksheet, you must per-form which task?
   a. Select Range and highlight a range to print
   b. Select Other Borders and specify a border
   c. Select Align
   d. Select Page

3. In printed headings and footings, the @ symbol performs which task?
   a. Prints the page number
   b. Centers a heading or footing
   c. Right-aligns a heading or footing
   d. Prints the current date

4. A single | symbol in a heading or footing will do which of the following?
   a. Print the page number
   b. Center a heading or footing
   c. Right-align a heading or footing
   d. Print the current date

5. To display the actual contents of a worksheet, rather than the results of calculations in formulas, you select which commands from the Print menu?
   a. Options Other As-Displayed
   b. Options Other Cell-Formulas
   c. Options Other Formatted
   d. Options Other Unformatted

6. When entering special printer codes with the Options Setup commands, you must precede the code with which character?
   a. / (slash)
   b. \ (backslash)
   c. | (vertical bar)
   d. @ (at)

7. When embedding special codes directly in the worksheet, you must precede the code with which character(s)?
   a. | (vertical bar)
   b. || (two vertical bars)
   c. / (slash)
   d. @ (at)

8. Which 1-2-3 function can help you determine attribute codes for your printer?
   a. @ASC
   b. @CHAR
   c. @CODE
   d. @MOD

9. Once you've designed your printed worksheet using commands from the Print menu, which command do you select to begin printing?
   a. Page
   b. Align
   c. Go
   d. Quit

10. To store a copy of the "printed" worksheet on a disk file, you use which commands from the main menu?
    a. /PP (Print Printer)
    b. /PPOOC (Printer Printer Options Other Cell-Formulas)
    c. /PG (Print Go)
    d. /PF (Print File)

Chapter 8

MANAGING WORKSHEET FILES

ABOUT THIS CHAPTER

We have already discussed two basic commands for managing worksheets files; /FS (File Save) and /FR (File Retrieve). 1-2-3 has several additional commands for managing disk files. These allow you to extract parts of worksheets, combine worksheets, and create files that are compatible with other software systems. In this chapter, we will discuss the various file commands.

SAVING WORKSHEETS TO DISK FILES

Whenever you are creating a new worksheet or editing an existing one, it is a good idea to save the worksheet on a disk file from time to time. If you forget to save a worksheet before exiting 1-2-3, the worksheet is lost for good. Also, a sudden power shortage or accidentally typed command can wipe out a worksheet. This can be most unpleasant, especially if you've been working on the worksheet for several hours. If you remember to save a worksheet every fifteen minutes or so, the most you could possibly lose is fifteen minutes of labor. It only takes a few seconds to save a worksheet on disk. It could take much longer to recreate a lost one.

Use /FS (File Save) to save your work frequently.

To save a file, select the /FS (File Save) option. The names of all existing files on the presently logged disk drive will show on the screen as follows:

Enter save file name:
<u>LOANS.WK1</u>   **GRADES.WK1   STATS.WK1   TAXES.WK1**

If the worksheet you are currently saving has been saved previously, its name will appear along with the prompt, like this:

Enter save file name: TAXES.WK1
LOANS.WK1 GRADES.WK1 STATS.WK1 TAXES.WK1

If this is a new worksheet, then you'll need to come up with a new name for the file. (Remember, 8 letters maximum, no spaces or punctuation.) Type in the new file name and press the RETURN key. The file will be saved on disk, and will also remain on the screen for you to work with.

If this is not a new worksheet, you can just press RETURN to reuse the present file name. 1-2-3 asks:

Cancel Replace

If you select cancel, the present worksheet will not be saved. If you select replace, the worksheet currently displayed on the screen will replace the disk file that has this file name.

When you save a worksheet to a disk file, 1-2-3 also stores all the format characteristics of the worksheet. It remembers column widths, label prefixes, number displays, ranges, printer settings; anything that affects the way in which the worksheet is to be displayed. This is so that when you later retrieve the worksheet for future use, it looks exactly the same on the screen as it did when you saved it.

If you try to save a worksheet to a file, and there is not enough room on the disk to store the file, 1-2-3 will display the message "disk full." This unhappy message can create problems if you don't have any other formatted disk handy. If you do have another disk handy, you can press the Esc key when you see the error message, and put a new disk in drive B. Then use the /FS command again to save the worksheet on the new diskette. You can also erase some files on the existing disk to make room for the new worksheet. We discuss this under "Erasing Files" later in this chapter.

RETRIEVING FILES FROM DISK

The /FR (File Retrieve) commands retrieve previously saved worksheets from disk back onto the screen.

The /FR (File Retrieve) command pulls copies of worksheets from disk files onto the screen. To use it, simply select the /FR command. All existing worksheet files on the logged disk drive appear on the screen. Either type in the name of the file you want to work with, or highlight it with the menu pointer and press RETURN. The worksheet will appear on the screen, and completely erase the presently displayed worksheet from the screen.

Note that when you retrieve a file, you only bring up a copy of the worksheet. The disk file remains intact. Any changes you make to the worksheet on the screen do NOT affect the disk file. This can be both a curse and a blessing. For example, suppose you are editing a worksheet on the screen, and accidentally make a complete mess of it. If you just use the /FR command to retrieve the worksheet again, it will come back in its original form; so all you have lost is some editing time. You need not go back and try to "undo" the accidental mess you've created. On the other hand, if you spend a couple of hours editing a worksheet, and you make some great improvements, then you accidentally retrieve the same file again, the original comes onto the screen, and the newly edited version is lost for good.

Again, you can avoid risky situations by just remembering to save the worksheet from time to time. If you do so every fifteen minutes, the most you can lose is 15 minutes labor.

DISPLAYING FILES AND STORAGE SPACE

The /FL (File List) commands show the names and sizes of files currently stored on the data disk.

1-2-3 can display file names of all 1-2-3 files stored on disk. The /FL (File List) command shows all file names of a particular type, and also displays the amount of available space left on the disk. When you select the command, it asks which type of files you wish to see:

Worksheet Print Graph Other

Worksheet (.WK1) files are stored worksheets, Print (.PRN) files are those created with the /PF (Print File) command. Graph (.PIC) files, which we have not discussed yet, are special files for printing graphs. Select which types of files you want to display the names of. The file names will be displayed, and will temporarily overwrite any worksheet that is displayed on the screen, such as:

AMORT.WK1   04/18/86   06:15   11707

AMORT.WK1	**AUCHECK.WK1**	**BALSHEET.WK1**	**COMPRINT.WK1**
DATEFUNC.WK1	**GRADES.WK1**	**REGISTER.WK1**	**STOCKS.WK1**
TENYEAR1.WK1			

As you move the highlight from one file name to another the statistics at the top of the screen (date, time, and file size) will change to reflect the currently highlighted file name. Press the RETURN key to return to the worksheet.

If the screen does not display the files you were expecting, use the Directory option from the Files submenu to change the drive or directory specification. For example, if your worksheets are stored on the disk in drive B, change the Directory specification to B:. If your worksheets are stored under the directory named \123 on your hard disk, change the Directory setting to C:\123.

The Other option under the /FL (Files List) commands displays all files on the disk. You can also specify certain types of files using the Other option. To do so, select the /FLO (File List Other) commands to view all files. Then press the Backspace key to define the files you want to view. For example, if you enter *.COM, the directory will display the names of all files ending with the extension .COM. If you enter LOANS.*, the directory will display all files that have the file name LOANS, regardless of the extension. If there are no files of the type you've selected to display on the disk, then 1-2-3 beeps and displays a message. Press RETURN or the Esc key to return to the Ready mode.

ERASING FILES

The /FE (File Erase) commands permanently erase files previously saved on disk.

It is not unusual to get a bit of junk cluttering up a disk. Old letters to friends, old backup (.BAK) files, and the like really don't need to be stored forever. 1-2-3 has a built-in command to erase a file from disk. This can come in handy when you try to save a worksheet and get an error message saying that the disk is full. Often, if you just erase an unwanted file or two, and try to save again, you'll have enough disk space. (The /FL command displays available disk space.)

To erase files, first select the /FE (File Erase) command. 1-2-3 will ask which type of file you want to erase, Worksheet, Print, or Graph. Select one of these, then indicate a file name and press RETURN. The file is erased permanently from the disk, and the space it was using up becomes available for storage.

You can also use "wild cards" in file names to erase entire groups of files. There are two wild card characters for file names. One is the question mark (?), which matches any single character in a file name. The other is an asterisk, which matches any group of characters in a file name. Hence, if you ask to erase file name GRADE?, you'll erase GRADE1, GRADE2, GRADE3, GRADE4, GRADE5, etc. If you elect to erase G*, you'll erase any file on the disk that begins with the letter G, such as GRADES, GOOSE, GENLEDGE, etc.

Do keep in mind that you are *permanently* erasing the files you select, so do be very careful with these wild cards. For example, if you select Worksheet from the File Erase menu, then type in *.* and you will erase *all* the files from the disk. This is one command you do not want to type in by accident. 1-2-3 always double-checks before erasing a file. When it asks for confirmation, always make sure you have typed in what you meant to prior to confirming the erase.

SAVING PARTS OF WORKSHEETS

The /FX (File Xtract) commands let you save a portion of a worksheet on a disk file.

At some point, you may create a worksheet that is too large to store on a single floppy diskette. When this happens, you will get the message "disk full" when you attempt to save the worksheet, even if the diskette has no previously saved files on it. When there are no existing files to erase to make more room, you'll need to break the worksheet into two or more parts, and store the separate pieces on separate diskettes. The /FX (File Xtract) option allows you to do this.

Suppose you have a gigantic worksheet that extends from cell A1 to cell HH500. You attempt to save it on an empty disk in drive B with the /FS command, but get a disk full error. You will need to split up the worksheet. Here's how to do it. Leave the blank disk in drive B, and select the /FX (File Xtract) command. This brings up two choices:

Formulas Values

Select Formulas. Then, provide a file name, such as GIANT1, and press RETURN. 1-2-3 will ask for the range to store. To store the top half of this worksheet type in the range A1..HH250 and press RE-TURN. The top half of the worksheet is stored on this diskette.

Now, remove the disk from drive B, and put in another blank, formatted diskette. Again, select the /FX option, select Formulas, and enter a file name. GIANT2 would be good in this example, because it reminds us that this is part two of the giant worksheet. When 1-2-3 asks for the range, specify the bottom half, A251..HH500, and press RETURN. At this point, the giant worksheet is safely stored on two separate diskettes, and is still on the screen.

One of the options that the /FX command allows is to store the partial worksheet either with the formula (Formula), or just the results of the formulas (Values). If you choose the latter option, Values, the formulas are lost forever in the stored file. Unless you are absolutely sure that results of calculations will not change in future use of the extracted portion of the worksheet, select the Formulas option from this menu.

COMBINING FILES INTO A SINGLE WORKSHEET

The /FC (File Combine) commands let you combine several files into a single worksheet.

Let's discuss methods for getting GIANT1 and GIANT2 back to the screen now. First, you want to load up 1-2-3 in the usual fashion, and put the disk with GIANT1 in drive B. Then use the /FR (File Retrieve) command to load B:GIANT1 onto the screen. Next, press the End and down-arrow keys to get down to the last cell in the worksheet, positioning the pointer to cell A256. Next, put the diskette with GIANT2 on it in drive B. Select the /FC (File Combine) command. 1-2-3 will ask if you wish to Copy, Add, or Subtract. Select Copy for this example. Next 1-2-3 will ask if you want to combine the Entire file, or a Named range. Select Entire, press RETURN, then type in the file name GIANT2 and press RETURN. The rest of the giant worksheet is displayed on the screen starting at the cell pointer's position.

In Chapter 15, we'll see how we can use the /FX and /FC commands to help with the task of managing year-to-date totals.

USING DOS TO MANAGE FILES

The DOS operating system includes many commands for managing files, including COPY, RENAME, and DIR. You should take the time to read up on these commands in your DOS manual if you plan on working with the computer regularly.

The /S (System) command lets you temporarily suspend 1-2-3 and return to the DOS prompt. Enter the command EXIT at the DOS prompt to return to 1-2-3.

You can temporarily "suspend" 1-2-3 and return to the DOS prompt without completely exiting 1-2-3. To do so, just select the System option from the main menu (/S). You'll see the DOS A>or C> prompt appear. At that point, you can use any DOS commands to manage your files.

To return to 1-2-3 after temporarily suspending 1-2-3, type in the command:

EXIT

at the DOS A> or C> prompt, and press RETURN. The worksheet will appear on the screen in exactly the state you left it. (NOTE: Just to play it safe, you should always use /FS (File Save) to save your current worksheet before using /S (System) to suspend 1-2-3.)

INTERFACING 1-2-3 WITH OTHER SOFTWARE SYSTEMS

You can transfer 1-2-3 data to and from other software systems using the Translate option from the Lotus ACCESS menu.

The Translate option from the ACCESS menu lets you interface with data from other popular microcomputer software systems.

To do so, first save the worksheet you're working on then Quit 1-2-3 (/QY) to return to the ACCESS menu. (From the DOS prompt, enter the command LOTUS as usual to get to the ACCESS menu.) Select Translate from the ACCESS menu. On a floppy disk system, you'll need to change disks according to instructions on your screen. Then you'll see options for translating a file FROM:

What do you want to translate FROM?

1-2-3, release 1A
1-2-3, release 2
dBase I
I dBase III
DIF
Jazz
SYMPHONY, release 1.0
SYMPHONY, release 1.1
VISICALC

Use the up- and down-arrow keys to highlight an option, then press RETURN to select it. The screen will then display options for translating the file TO:

What do you want to translate TO?
1-2-3, release 1A
dBase II
dBase III
DIF
SYMPHONY, release 1.0
SYMPHONY, release 1.1

Again, highlight an option and press RETURN to select it.

Depending on the particular translation you select, 1-2-3 will display instructions for proceeding with the translation, then allow you to select a file to translate. The procedure is quite easy and self explanatory, so we need not discuss these automated translations any more here. However, things are a little trickier when the translation does not fall into one of the categories in the Translate menu.

ASCII File Transfers

If you interface with mainframe computers or a software system that is not included in the Translate menu, you'll probably need to use *ASCII text files* for your transfers. These transfers are handled directly from the 1-2-3 menus, rather than from the Translate utility. If you do need to read (or create) an ASCII text file for a transfer, it will most likely be in either *structured* (random access) or *delimited* (sequential) format.

If you're not sure of the format of an ASCII text file, use the DOS TYPE command from the DOS A> or C> prompt to view its contents. For example, if the file you want to import is named Checks.TXT, enter the command:

TYPE Checks.TXT

or...

TYPE B:Checks.TXT

to specify the disk in drive B. We'll discuss the format and translation separately for each type of file below.

Reading Structured Data Files

A structured data file stores data in evenly spaced columns, as in the example below:

```
1001Joe Smith          −123.4519860601
   0Deposit            1000.0019860601
1002Rent               −1000.0019860601
1003Utilities          −98.0019860602
1003Car Payment        −300.0019860602
1004Cash               −100.0019860605
   0Deposit            −500.0019860606
1005Insurance          −300.0019860606
1006Credit Card        −100.0019860612
```

To read an ASCII text file into 1-2-3, start with a blank worksheet and the cell pointer in cell A1. Select the /FI (File Import) options from the menu. You'll be given the options to import Text or Numbers. The Numbers option will read in only numeric values from a structured file, so you'll want to select Text. Then, enter the name of the file to import (Checks.TXT in this example).

The file will appear on the worksheet. However, each line of data will be stored as a long label with an apostrophe label prefix, as below:

```
'1001Joe Smith             −123.4519860601
```

To break the data into worksheet columns, you need use the Data Parse commands.

Use /FIT (File Import Text) and /DP (Data Parse) to import structured ASCII text files.

To use Data Parse, type /DP (Data Parse) and select Format-line and Create options to create a format line. 1-2-3 will make a "best guess" as to how to divide the data into columns, as shown below:

	A	B	C	D	E	F
1	L>>>>>>*L>>>> ***********V>>>>>>>>>>>>>					
2	1001Joe Smith			−123.4519860601		
3	0Deposit			1000.0019860601		
4	1002Rent			−1000.0019860601		
5	1003Utilities			−98.0019860602		
6	1003Car Payment			−300.0019860602		
7	1004Cash			−100.0019860605		
8	0Deposit			−500.0019860606		

9	1005Insurance	−300.0019860606	
10	1006Credit Card	−100.0019860612	
11			

The symbols you can use in the format line at the top of the screen are listed below:

L	– first character of a Label column
V	– first character of a Value column
D	– first character of a Date column
T	– first character of a Time column
S	– Skip the character below
>	– continuation of this column
*	– undefined character

To improve the best-guess format line, select the Formatline and Edit options from the Data Parse menu. You'll be able to move the cursor with the arrow keys and change the format line. The improved format line below shows the data divided into Number, Label, and Date columns. Notice the use of the > symbol to define the length of each column, and the * symbol to ignore long strings of blank spaces:

	A	B	C	D	E
1	V>>>L>>>>>>>>>>>>> ****V>>>>>>>D>>>>>>				
2	1001Joe Smith		−123.4519860601		
3	0Deposit		1000.0019860601		
4	1002Rent		−1000.0019860601		
5	1003Utilities		−98.0019860602		
6	1003Car Payment		−300.0019860602		
7	1004Cash		−100.0019860605		
8	0Deposit		−500.0019860606		
9	1005Insurance		−300.0019860606		
10	1006Credit Card		−100.0019860612		

After you've edited the format line, you need to tell 1-2-3 which data to parse. Select the Input-column option from the Data Parse menu, and highlight the entire leftmost column of the imported file (A1..A10 in this example).

Next you need to tell 1-2-3 where to put the parsed data. Select the Output-range option from the menu, and specify any cell that has enough blank columns to the right, and enough blank rows beneath, to accommodate the size of the imported file. In this example, A12 will do nicely.

Finally, select Go from the Data Parse menu. 1-2-3 will divide up your data accordingly, and store the data beginning at the selected Output range. If you like, you can use /WDR (Worksheet Delete Row) to delete the unparsed imported file and the format line (rows 1 through 10 in this example).

Writing Structured Data Files

Use /PF (Print File) to create structured ASCII text files for exportation.

To create a structured ASCII text file data file from a 1-2-3 worksheet (or database), move the cell pointer to the upper left corner of the range of cells to be exported. Select the Print File options, and assign a name to the exported file. Select Range, and highlight the range of cells to export.

To control the format of the exported file, select Options from the Print menu, and set the Margin Left to 0. Set the Right margin to 240. Then use the Other and Unformatted options to remove page breaks, headings, and the like. Quit the submenus and select Go from the Print menu. Unless you specified an extension in the file name when requested, the exported file will have the name you assigned, along with the extension .PRN.

Reading Delimited Data Files

There is no easy way to create an ASCII delimited file from 1-2-3 data, although importing this data is usually fairly easy. Delimited data files usually have commas, rather than spaces, between individual fields (or columns), and quotation marks around strings (label data), as below:

```
1001,"Joe Smith",-123.45,19860601
0,"Deposit",1000.00,19860601
1002,"Rent",-1000.00,19860601
1003,"Utilities",-98.00,19860602
1003,"Car Payment",-300.00,19860602
1004,"Cash",-100.00,19860605
0,"Deposit",-500.00,19860606
1005,"Insurance",-300.00,19860606
1006,"Credit Card",-100.00,19860612
```

Use /FIN (File Import Numbers) to import delimited ASCII text files.

To read a delimited text file into 1-2-3, you can usually just use the /FIN (File Import Numbers) commands. More specifically, start with a blank worksheet and the cell pointer in cell A1. Select the File Import Number options from the menu, and specify the name of the file to import. (Be sure to include the file name extension, e.g. Checks.TXT.) More than likely, the imported data will be ready to work with.

Converting Imported Dates

When you import an ASCII text file into 1-2-3, the dates will most likely be stored as numbers (e.g. 19860612) or labels (e.g. '19860612) in YYYYMMDD format. To determine whether labels or numbers are used, move the cell pointer to the imported date and look at the control panel. An apostrophe label prefix will precede the imported date if it is stored as a label.

To convert imported dates to 1-2-3 serial dates, you'll need to use a pretty fancy formula. For numeric imported dates in YYYYMMDD format, you'll need to use the formula:

```
@DATE(@INT((D1-19000000)/10000),
      @INT(@MOD(D1,100000)/10000),
      @INT(@MOD(D1,100)))
```

To convert imported dates stored as labels in YYYYMMDD format, you'll need to use the formula:

```
@DATE(@VALUE(@MID(D1,2,2)),
      @VALUE(@MID(D1,4,2)),
      @VALUE(@RIGHT(D1,2)))
```

NOTE: The formulas are displayed broken into several lines of text to fit in the book. In actual practice, the formula must be entered into a single cell with no spaces. If you are not sure whether an imported date is a label or a number, just move the cell pointer to one of the imported dates. Look at the imported date in the control panel. If it has an apostrophe label prefix in front of it (such as '19861231), it's a label. Otherwise, it's a number.

To convert dates, first determine whether yours are stored as labels or numbers. Then enter the appropriate formula on the top row of the imported file. (If you used Data Parse, enter the formula on the appropriate row of the parsed copy of the imported file.) Use a column that has as many blank rows beneath it as there are rows in the imported file. Where the example formula shows D1 as the cell reference, substitute the appropriate cell containing the imported date on your worksheet. After entering the formula correctly, the cell should show a serial date (such as 31752).

Next, use /C to copy the conversion formula from the single cell down as many rows as the imported file is long. (If there are 20 rows in the imported file, copy the formula down 20 rows). The column should then show the serial date for each date in the imported file.

You can use the Range Values command to replace the imported numeric or label dates with serial dates. Move the cell pointer to the top row of the serial date formulas and type /RV (Range Values). Highlight the range of converted serial dates, then press RETURN. Next, move the cell pointer to the top row of the imported dates and press RETURN. Serial dates will replace the imported dates. Use /RFD (Range Format Date) to select a date format, and highlight the entire range of new serial dates. You may need to use /WCS (Worksheet Column Set-Width) to widen the column and display all the dates.

You can erase the formulas using /RE (Range Erase) used to convert the dates once you've completed the Range Values step. Don't forget to use /FS (File Save) to save your work.

WHAT HAVE YOU LEARNED?

1. Use the /FS (File Save) commands regularly to save your work.

2. Use the /FR (File Retrieve) commands to read a saved worksheet back into 1-2-3.

3. The /FL (File List) commands display the names and sizes of files stored on the data disk.

4. The /FE (File Erase) commands let you erase files from the data disk.

5. The /FX (File Xtract) commands allow you to save portions of worksheets on a disk.

6. The /FC (File Combine) commands allow you to combine separate files into a single worksheet.

7. The /S (System) command lets you temporarily suspend 1-2-3 and return to the DOS A> or C> prompt.

8. To return to 1-2-3 after temporarily suspending it, enter the command EXIT at the DOS prompt.

9. The Translate option from the ACCESS menu lets you share data between 1-2-3 and other popular software systems.

10. The /FI (File Import) option lets you read foreign "ASCII files" into the 1-2-3 worksheet.

QUIZ

1. Which commands let you save an entire worksheet file on disk?
   a. /FS (File Save)
   b. /FR (File Retrieve)
   c. /FI (File Import)
   d. /FL (File List)

2. Which commands display the names of files stored on disk?
   a. /FS (File Save)
   b. /FR (File Retrieve)
   c. /FI (File Import)
   d. /FL (File List)

3. Which commands bring previously saved worksheets from the disk back onto the screen?
   a. /FS (File Save)
   b. /FR (File Retrieve)
   c. /FI (File Import)
   d. /FL (File List)

4. Which commands let you erase files from the disk?
   a. /FX (File Xtract)
   b. /FE (File Erase)
   c. /FI (File Import)
   d. /FL (File List)

5. Which commands let you save a portion of a worksheet?
   a. /FX (File Xtract)
   b. /FE (File Erase)
   c. /FI (File Import)
   d. /FC (File Combine)

6. Which commands allow you to combine separate files into a single worksheet?
   a. /FX (File Xtract)
   b. /FE (File Erase)
   c. /FI (File Import)
   d. /FC (File Combine)

7. To temporarily suspend 1-2-3 and return to the DOS prompt, you must:
   a. Select /QY (Quit Yes) from the main menu
   b. Select /S (System) from the main menu
   c. Select /QS (Quit System) from the main menu
   d. Reboot the computer

8. To return to 1-2-3 after temporarily suspending it, you must:
   a. Reboot the computer
   b. Enter the command RESUME at the DOS prompt
   c. Press the BREAK key
   d. Enter the command EXIT at the DOS prompt

9. The /DP (Data Parse) commands allow you to rearrange which type of imported file?
   a. dBASE III PLUS
   b. ASCII delimited file

      c. ASCII structured file

      d. 1-2-3 Version 1A

10. To read an ASCII delimited file into the worksheet, you'd use which commands?

      a. /FIT (File Import Text)

      b. /FIN (File Import Numbers)

      c. /FX (File Xtract)

      d. /FC (File Combine)

Chapter 9

SOME PRACTICAL EXAMPLES

ABOUT THIS CHAPTER

In this chapter, you will develop several business worksheets using many of the techniques discussed so far. The worksheets demonstrate many techniques for managing business data including numbers, dates, and percentages.

CREATING THE SAMPLE WORKSHEETS

This chapter shows sample worksheets as they appear on the screen, as well as a listing of cell contents using the Cell-Formulas option from the Print menu.

The exact steps used in creating each worksheet are covered in detail. Furthermore, a copy of each worksheet, printed with the /PPOOC (Print Printer Options Other Cell-Formulas) options from the Print menu are provided. (To conserve space and avoid redundancy, worksheets that contain many copied formulas are displayed without the copied formulas.) These displays show the exact contents, width, and format of every cell in the worksheet. For example, a single line from one of these displays might show:

D21: U (C2) [W10] @SLN(C25,1000,5)

The leftmost portion, D21:, is the cell location. The letter U following the cell location means the cell is Unprotected, using /RU (Range Unprotect). The portion in parentheses, (C2) is the format set using the /RF (Range Format) commands. Examples of possible formats include:

(C2) Currency, 2 decimal places
(C0) Currency, 0 decimal places

(,2)   , (comma), 2 decimal places
(F2)   Fixed, 2 decimal places
(P3)   Percent, 3 decimal places
(D1)   Date 1
(D6)   Date Time 1

Time formats are offset by 5. Hence, Time 2 is displayed as Date 7 (D7); Time 4 is displayed as (D9). Cells set for General numeric format display show no format setting.

The section in brackets is the column width set using the /WCS (Worksheet Column Set-Width) commands. The symbol [W10] indicates a column width of ten. The rightmost portion is the label (with label prefix), number, or formula in the cell.

The step-by-step instructions will explain how to develop the worksheet quickly, taking full advantage of the Copy command and Absolute and Relative cell addressing.

THE CHECK REGISTER

The Check Register worksheet acts as an electronic check register and demonstrates a use of the @IF function.

The first example is a worksheet that acts as an electronic checkbook register. Like most check registers, you enter check and deposit amounts. This check register, however, keeps a running balance for you automatically.

Fig. 9-1 shows the check register with some sample data entered. Table 9-1 shows the contents of each cell in the register. To create the check register, follow the steps below.

```
A10: (D2) U [W7]                                                    READY

       A     B    C          D               E          F          G
 1                      Check Register
 2
 3   Date   No.        Description        Deposit      Check     Balance
 4   ===================================================================
 5                     Bal. Forward       $2,500.00              $2,500.00
 6   24-May 1001       House Payment                  $1,000.00  $1,500.00
 7   24-May 1002       Utilties                          $90.00  $1,410.00
 8   25-May 1003       Car payment                      $303.85  $1,106.15
 9   25-May            Deposit             $500.00              $1,606.15
10
11
12
13
14
15
16
17
```

Fig. 9-1. Check register worksheet with sample data.

Table 9-1. Check Register Worksheet Contents Before Copying Formulas

```
D1:   [W20]    ^Check Register
A3:   [W7]     ^Date
B3:   [W5]     ^No.
D3:   [W20]    ^Description
E3:   [W12]    ^Deposit
F3:   [W12]    ^Check
G3:   [W12]    ^Balance
A4:   [W7]      \ =
B4:   [W5]      \ =
C4:   [W3]      \ =
D4:   [W20]     \ =
E4:   [W12]     \ =
F4:   [W12]     \ =
G4:   [W12]     \ =
D5:   U [W20]  'Bal. Forward
G5:   (C2) [W12] + E5
G6:   (C2) [W12] @IF(E6>0#OR#F6>0,G5 + E6 —F6," ")
```

1. Use /WEY (Worksheet Erase Yes) to begin with a clean worksheet.

2. Use /WCS (Worksheet Column Set-Width) to set columns A through E as indicated below:

Column	Width
A	7
B	5
C	3
D	20
E	12
F	12
G	12

3. Enter the label ^Check Register in cell D1.

4. Enter labels across row 3. (Note that the narrow column C has no label, and is used only to put space between columns B and D.) Refer to Fig. 9-1 and Table 9-1 for the exact locations of labels.

5. Move the cell pointer to cell A3, and type /RLC (Range Label Center). Type in or highlight the range A3..G3 to center all the labels.

6. Move the cell pointer to cell A4 and type in the \ = symbol

to create and underline. Use /C to Copy the underline FROM A4..A4 to B4..G4.

7. Place the label "Bal. Forward" (without the quotation marks) in cell D5. Place an initial starting balance (such as 2500) in cell E5.

8. Place the formula + E5 in cell G5 to reflect the starting balance in cell E5.

9. Move the cell pointer to cell A5 and type /RFD2 (Range Format Date 2) to set up a date format for the column. Specify the range A5..A105 (you can press the PgDn key 5 times to do so). Press RETURN.

10. Move the cell pointer to cell G6 and type in the formula:

   @IF(E6>0#OR#F6>0,G5 + E6−F6," ")

   and press RETURN. Nothing will appear at first (we'll explain why in a moment).

11. Copy the formula down through row 105 by typing /C and specifying G6..G6 as the range to copy FROM, and G7..G105 as the range to copy TO. (Again, you won't see any immediate results).

12. Move the cell pointer to cell E5 and type /RFC2 (Range Format Currency 2 decimal places) and press RETURN. Press the End key, then the right-arrow key, then the End key and the down-arrow key to highlight the range E5..G105. Press RETURN.

13. Save the worksheet by typing /FS (File Save) and assigning a file name (such as Checks).

To test the worksheet, move the cell pointer to cell A6 and enter the @NOW function (or another date using the @DATE function). The date should appear in DD-Mmm format. Enter a check number in cell B6, a description in cell D6, and a check amount in cell F6. Cell G6 should show the proper balance immediately. Try a few more checks and deposits (real or hypothetical) in a few more rows.

Let's discuss the formula in column G which reads:

   @IF(E6>0#OR#F6>0,G5 + E6−F6," ")

In English this formula translates to "If either cell E6 (Deposit) or F6 (Check) is greater than zero, then calculate and display the balance by adding the deposit and subtracting the check amount from the balance immediately above. If neither a Check nor Deposit appear in this row, display nothing (a blank space " ")."

You can verify that the formulas were copied down to row 105 by putting the cell pointer in cell G5 and selecting the /RFT (Range Format Text) menu options. Specify G5..G105 as the range to format. You should see all the formulas in place. (If not, repeat step 11 above.) To return back to Currency format, use /RFC2 (Range Format Currency 2) and again specify G5..G105. Again, only rows in which there is a check or deposit will display a balance in this column.

If you use the worksheet and need more than the 105 rows allotted, just copy the formula in cell 105 down as many rows as necessary. Use /RFD2 (Range Format Date 2) to format column A below rows 105, and /RFC2 (Range Format Currency 2) to format columns E, F, and G below row 105.

Check Register Cell Protection

To protect the formulas and headings in the worksheet from accidental deletion, move the cell pointer to cell A5 and use the /RU (Range Unprotect) commands. Highlight (or type in) the range A5..F105. Then use /WGPE (Worksheet Global Protection Enable) to turn in the global cell protection.

Check Register Recalculation Procedures

If the electronic check register takes too long to recalculate, use /WGRM (Worksheet Global Recalculation Manual) to switch to manual recalculation.

If the check register takes a long time to recalculate after adding many transactions, use /WGRM (Worksheet Global Recalculation Manual) to turn off the automatic recalculation. Enter checks and deposits, then press the CALC key (F9) to calculate the balance.

Using the Electronic Check Register

When entering data into the check register, don't leave any rows blank. The formula for calculating the balance depends upon the balance in the row immediately above.

STOCK PORTFOLIO

Fig. 9-2 shows a worksheet that can help keep track of a stock portfolio. Enter the stock symbol in column A, the number of shares bought in column B, and the purchase price in column C. At anytime you can enter the current price of the stock in column D, and the worksheet will calculate the Market Value, Dollar gain (or loss) and Percent gain. The worksheet also calculates the total market value and dollar gain automatically.

The Stock Portfolio worksheet manages a stock portfolio, and also demonstrates some uses for the 1-2-3 @IF function.

Fig. 9-2 shows the Portfolio worksheet with some sample data entered. Table 9-2 shows the contents of each cell. The step-by-step instructions for creating the worksheet are listed below.

```
A2:                                                              READY

          A        B       C        D       E       F       G      H
  1  Stock Portfolio
  2
  3                    Purchase  Current  Market   Dollar  Percent
  4   Symbol   Shares   Price    Price    Value    Gain     Gain
  5  ...............................................................
  6   ABC        100    10.00    13.00   1300.00   300.00   30.00%
  7   IBM         40    22.55    25.00   1000.00    98.00   10.86%
  8   DEC        200     5.00     7.50   1500.00   500.00   50.00%
  9   RMR         10    10.00     5.00     50.00   -50.00  -50.00%
 10   ZYZ       1000     1.00     2.00   2000.00  1000.00  100.00%
 11                                      ====================
 12                                      5850.00  1848.00
 13
 14
 15
 16
 17
```

Fig. 9-2. Stock portfolio worksheet with sample data.

1. Use /WEY (Worksheet Erase Yes) to start with a clean work-sheet.

2. Type the label Stock Portfolio into cell A1.

3. Type in the labels in rows 3 and 4, using Fig. 9-2 and Table 9-2 as a guide.

4. Move the cell pointer to cell A3 and enter /RLC (Range Label Center). Highlight or specify the range A3..G4. (You can press the period, down-arrow, End, and right-arrow keys to highlight quickly). Press RETURN. The labels will all be centered.

5. Move the cell pointer to cell A5 and enter the ∖ − symbol to create underlines. Copy the underline (/C) FROM A5..A5 TO B5..G5, so all labels are underlined.

6. Move the cell pointer to cell E6, and calculate the Market Value by entering the formula:

   +B6∗D6

   (The Market value is the number of shares in column B times the current price in column D.)

Table 9-2. Contents of Stock Portfolio Worksheet Before Copying Formulas

```
A1:     'Stock Portfolio
C3:     ^Purchase
D3:     ^Current
E3:     ^Market
F3:     ^Dollar
G3:     ^Percent
A4:     ^Symbol
B4:     ^Shares
C4:     ^Price
D4:     ^Price
E4:     ^Value
F4:     ^Gain
G4:     ^Gain
A5:     \ —
B5:     \ —
C5:     \ —
D5:     \ —
E5:     \ —
F5:     \ —
G5:     \ —
E6:     (F2) + B6*D6
F6:     (F2) + E6—(B6*C6)
G6:     (P2) + F6/(C6*B6)
E11:    \ =
F11:    \ =
E12:    (F2) @SUM(E6..E10)
F12:    (F2) @SUM(F6..F10)
```

7. Move the cell pointer to cell F6 and enter the formula for calculating the Dollar Gain as below:

   + E6—(B6*C6)

   (In English, this formula translates to "The current market value minus the Purchase Price times the number of Shares", or in other words "What it's worth now minus what it was worth when I bought it.)"

8. Move the cell pointer to cell G6 and enter the formula for calculating the Percent Gain, shown below:

   @IF(B6 > 0, + F6/(B6*C6)," ")

   (The formula + F6/(B6*C6) means "The Dollar Gain divided by the Purchase Price times the number of Shares," or "The Dollar Gain divided by the original purchase value"). The

@IF function tells 1-2-3 to only perform the calculation if there are shares in cell B6. This keeps the formula from displaying ERR in rows where no shares have been entered. The formula will show nothing until you enter test data in cells B6, C6, and D6.

9. Copy the formulas down four rows (or more, depending on your portfolio) using the /C (Copy) command. Move the cell pointer to cell E6, type /C, enter E6..G6 as the range to copy FROM, and E7..E10 as the range to copy TO.

10. Format the currency numbers for two decimal places. Move the cell pointer to cell C6, type /RFF2 (Range Format Fixed 2). Specify the range C6..F12 as the range to format. Any numbers in the highlighted range will be displayed with two decimal places.

11. Move the cell pointer to cell G6. Use /RFP2 (Range Format Percent 2) to format the range G6..G10. Numbers in column G will appear as percentages when data is entered in the worksheet.

12. Enter the \ = symbol in cells E11 and F11 to create underlines.

13. Enter the formula @SUM(E6..E10) in cell E12 to calculate the sum of the Market Value.

14. Use /C (Copy) to copy the formula FROM cell E12 TO cell F12 to calculate the sum of the Dollar Gain.

Stock Portfolio Cell Protection

To protect the formulas in the worksheet, move the cell pointer to cell A6 and select the /RU (Range Unprotect) commands. Highlight or type in the range A6..D10 and press RETURN. Use /WGPE (Worksheet Global Protection Enable) to turn the global protection on.

Testing the Portfolio Worksheet

Try entering some sample data, as shown in Fig. 9-2, to test the worksheet. Use /FS (File Save) to save the worksheet with a file name (such as STOCKS) when you know all is working well.

Use /WIR (Worksheet Insert Row) and /C (Copy) to add new rows to the stock portfolio worksheet.

If at some time you need to add new rows to the Portfolio worksheet, just place the cell pointer above the totals in the last row and use /WIR (Worksheet Insert Row) to add a new row. Then use /C (copy) to copy the formulas in columns E, F, and G in the row immediately above down to the new row. All relative references will adjust automatically, so you can add as many new rows as you need to.

LOAN AMORTIZATION SCHEDULE

The Loan Amortization worksheet displays a schedule for a loan of up to 40 years, and demonstrates the use of the @IF, @PMT, and @PV functions.

Here is a very handy worksheet for anyone who deals in loans (which is just about everyone). It allows you to enter a principal, annual interest rate, and term (in years). It then displays the monthly payment, total payback, and a complete amortization schedule. Fig. 9-3 shows the worksheet with some sample data in it. Table 9-3 shows the cell-by-cell contents of the worksheet. Specific instructions for quickly creating the worksheet follow.

```
A1: [W5]                                                    READY

      A       B          C          D          E          F
1           Principal:  $50,000.00
2           Rate:        16.000%
3           Years:          10
4           Payment:     $837.57              Payback:   $100,507.87
5
6     Year  Beg. Bal.  End. Bal.  Total Pd.   Interest
7     ===================================================
8      1    50,000.00  47,791.93  10,050.79   7,842.72
9      2    47,791.93  45,203.48  10,050.79   7,462.33
10     3    45,203.48  42,169.11  10,050.79   7,016.42
11     4    42,169.11  38,612.01  10,050.79   6,493.69
12     5    38,612.01  34,442.13  10,050.79   5,880.90
13     6    34,442.13  29,553.89  10,050.79   5,162.55
14     7    29,553.89  23,823.56  10,050.79   4,320.45
15     8    23,823.56  17,106.05  10,050.79   3,333.28
16     9    17,106.05   9,231.32  10,050.79   2,176.05
17    10     9,231.32      0.00   10,050.79     819.47
18    11
19    12
20    13
```

Fig. 9-3. Loan amortization worksheet with sample data.

Table 9-3. Contents of Amortization Worksheet Before Copying Formulas

```
B1: [W12] 'Principal:
B2: [W12] 'Rate:
B3: [W12] 'Years:
B4: [W12] 'Payment:
C4: (C2) [W12] @PMT(C1,C2/12,C3*12)
E4: [W12] 'Payback:
F4: (C2) [W15] +C4*(C3*12)
A6: [W5] "Year
B6: [W12] "Beg. Bal.
C6: [W12] "End. Bal.
D6: [W12] "Total Pd.
```

Table 9-3 cont.

```
E6: [W12] "Interest
A7: [W5] \ =
B7: [W12] \ =
C7: [W12] \ =
D7: [W12] \ =
E7: [W12] \ =
A8: [W5] 1
B8: (,2) [W12]  + C1
C8: (,2) [W12]
@IF(A8< = $C$3,@PV($C$4,$C$2/12,12*($C$3−A8))," ")
D8: (,2) [W12] @IF(A8< = $C$3,$C$4*12," ")
E8: (,2) [W12] @IF(A8< = $C$3, + D8−(B8−C8)," ")
A9: [W5] 2
B9: (,2) [W12] @IF(A9< = $C$3,C8," ")
A10: [W5] 3
A11: [W5] 4
A12: [W5] 5
A13: [W5] 6
A14: [W5] 7
A15: [W5] 8
A16: [W5] 9
A17: [W5] 10
A18: [W5] 11
A19: [W5] 12
A20: [W5] 13
A21: [W5] 14
A22: [W5] 15
A23: [W5] 16
A24: [W5] 17
A25: [W5] 18
A26: [W5] 19
A27: [W5] 20
A28: [W5] 21
A29: [W5] 22
A30: [W5] 23
A31: [W5] 24
A32: [W5] 25
A33: [W5] 26
A34: [W5] 27
A35: [W5] 28
A36: [W5] 29
A37: [W5] 30
A38: [W5] 31
A39: [W5] 32
A40: [W5] 33
A41: [W5] 34
A42: [W5] 35
A43: [W5] 36
A44: [W5] 37
```

Table 9-3 cont.

```
A45: [W5] 38
A46: [W5] 39
A47: [W5] 40
```

1. Use /WEY to start with a blank worksheet.

2. Use /WGC (Worksheet Global Column-Width) to set all columns to 12 spaces wide.

3. Then use /WCS (Worksheet Column Set-Width) to make column A five spaces wide.

4. Enter the labels in column B, and the labels across row 6. Use Fig. 9-3 and Table 9-3 as a guide.

5. Enter some sample data to start with: Put 50000 in cell C1, 16% (or 0.16) in cell C2, and 10 in cell C3.

6. Move the cell pointer to cell C4 and enter the formula for calculating the monthly payment, as shown below:

   @PMT(C1,C2/12,C3∗12)

7. Use /RFC2 (Range Format Currency 2) to format cells C1 and C4.

8. Use /RFP3 (Range Format Percent 3) to format cell C2.

9. Move the cell pointer to cell A6. Use /RLR (Range Label Right) to right-justify labels in the range A6..E6.

10. Put the symbol ╲ = in cell A7, then copy the underline using /C (Copy). Specify A7..A7 as the range to copy FROM, and B7..E7 as the range to copy TO.

11. Move the cell pointer to cell A8. Use /DF (Data Fill) to fill in the years. Specify the A8..A47 as the range to fill. Enter 1, as the Start value, press RETURN, 1 as the Step value, press RETURN and 40 as the Stop value, press RETURN. Use the End key and down-arrow key to verify that the years in column A extend to 40.

12. Put the simple formula:

    +C1

    in cell B8. (The beginning balance for the first year is the same as the principal on the loan.)

13. Column C calculates the ending balance using the Present Value (@PV) function. Move the cell pointer to cell C8 and enter the formula:

@IF(A8< = $C$3,@PV($C$4,$C$2/12,12*($C$3−A8)),″ ″)

In English, this formula reads "If the year in column A is less than, or equal to, the term of the loan specified in cell C3, then calculate and display the ending balance (present value), otherwise display a blank cell (″ ″)". The absolute references are necessary for copying the formula, which you will do later.

14. Column D calculates the Total paid for the year, which is simply 12 times the monthly payment. In cell D8 enter the formula:

@IF(A8< = $C$3,$C$4*12,″ ″)

In English this formula means "If the year in column A is less than, or equal to, the term of the loan, then display the monthly payment multiplied by 12, otherwise display nothing."

15. Move the cell pointer to cell E8. Enter the formula for calculating the interest paid for the year, which is:

@IF(A8< = $C$3, + D8-(B8-C8),″ ″)

The formula calculates the interest paid as the total paid minus the beginning balance minus the ending balance. Once again, this formula checks the current year in column A against the term of the loan in cell C3.

16. Finally, to calculate the beginning balance beyond the first year, move the cell pointer to cell B9 and enter the formula

@IF(A9< = $C$3,C8,″ ″)

In English this formula means "If the year in column A is less than, or equal to, the term of the loan, display the ending balance from the previous year, otherwise display nothing."

17. With the cell pointer still in cell B9, use /C (Copy) to copy the formula FROM B9..B9 TO B10..B47. You'll see zeros in the first 10 rows for the time being.

18. Move the cell pointer to cell C8. Use /C (Copy) to copy formulas FROM C8..E8 down TO C9..E47. You should see the amortization data fill in, as in Fig. 9-1 (though not formatted yet).

19. Move the cell pointer to cell B8. Select /RF,2 (Range Format Comma 2) to format the numbers. Use the End, right-arrow, and End down-arrow keys to highlight the range B8..E47 for the formatting.

20. For the grand finale, move the cell pointer to cell E4 and

type in the label Payback:. Move the cell pointer to cell F4 and enter the formula for calculating the total payback on the loan, which is the monthly payment times the full term, or...

+ C4*(C3*12)

Since this is usually a whopping number, use /WCS (Worksheet Column Set-Width) to widen column F to 15 spaces. Then use /RFC2 (Range Format Currency 2) to display cell F4 in Currency format.

21. Use /FS (File Save) to save the worksheet with a valid file name such as Amort.

Testing the Amortization Worksheet

To test the worksheet, try entering different values in the Years cell (C3). With longer terms, more rows are needed to amortize the loan. Yet with shorter terms, fewer rows are needed and the rows beneath seem to disappear. The longest term for a loan in this worksheet is 40 years.

Of course, you can vary the Principal and Rate as well. (Needless to say, this is a very useful worksheet for trying "What-if" scenarios with various loan packages, and is even more interesting when you start graphing some of the data). When entering the interest rate, be sure to use an annual percentage rate and the percent sign (e.g. 16% or 9.375%). DON'T enter data in the payment cell (C4), since this is a calculation and other cells depend on its data for accuracy.

Loan Worksheet Cell Protection

You can use /RU (Range Unprotect) to unprotect C1..C3, then use /WGPE (Worksheet Global Protection Enable) to protect the many formulas in this worksheet.

Shorter Term Loans

You can easily modify the Loan Amortization worksheet to schedule shorter term loans on a monthly basis.

To create a similar worksheet for shorter term loans and a monthly (rather than yearly) schedule, you can modify the existing worksheet and save it under a new name. Remember to use /WGPD (Worksheet Global Protection Disable) to unprotect the cells if you have already protected them.

First, enter the label 'Months in cell B3. Enter the label 'Month in cell A6.

Since the term will be entered in months, there is no longer any need to multiply the term by 12 in any of the formulas. Therefore, move the cell pointer to cell C4 and type in (or edit) the formula to read:

@PMT(C1,C2/12,C3)

Change the formula in cell F4 to

+C4*C3.

Change the formula in cell C8 to:

@IF(A8< = $C$3,@PV($C$4,$C$2/12,($C$3−A8)),'' '')

Move the cell pointer to cell D8 and enter the formula:

@IF(A8< = $C$3,$C$4,'' '')

Copy all the new formulas using the techniques in step 18 above. You might want to extend the months in column A to 48, and Copy the formulas all the way down to row 55 rather than row 47.

Save the worksheet using /FS (File Save) and a new file name, such as Amort2. When using the worksheet, enter the annual interest rate as a percentage in cell C2 (3.g. 12.5%), and the term in months (e.g. 36 for a three-year loan).

TEN YEAR PROJECTION FOR REAL ESTATE

In this exercise you will develop a worksheet that can project cash flow on a commercial real estate investment. You can vary the increase rates and initial values on such factors as rent (as income), maintenance, insurance, debt service, and management fee (as expenses). The worksheet will instantly calculate and display the cash flow for ten years.

The Ten Year Projection worksheet demonstrates a general format for projection worksheets, as well as advanced techniques for copying formulas.

Fig. 9-4 shows a portion of the projection worksheet with some data entered. The figure shows only a portion of the worksheet. You can scroll to the right to view the projection out to the year 1996. We'll discuss a technique later in this chapter for splitting the screen so that you can see both the early and later years simultaneously).

Table 9-4 shows the cell-by-cell contents of the worksheet. The steps for producing the worksheet quickly are listed below.

1. Use /WEY (Worksheet Erase Yes) to start with a blank worksheet.

2. Use /WGC (Worksheet Global Column-Width) to set the default column width to 10.

3. Use /WCS (Worksheet Column Set-Width) to widen column A to 15 spaces.

```
A1: [W15]                                                              READY

            A            B         C          D          E          F
   1                  Ten Year Projection for Commercial Real Estate
   2
   3                  Increase
   4   Description    Rate %       1986       1987       1988       1989
   5   ................................................................
   6   Tenant 1       12.50%    $15,000    $16,875    $18,984    $21,357
   7   Tenant 2       12.50%    $10,000    $11,250    $12,656    $14,238
   8   Tenant 3       12.50%     $5,000     $5,625     $6,328     $7,119
   9   Tenant 4       12.50%     $5,000     $5,625     $6,328     $7,119
  10   Tenant 5       12.50%     $7,500     $8,438     $9,492    $10,679
  11   ................................................................
  12   Maintenance    13.00%    $11,000    $12,430    $14,046    $15,872
  13   Insurance      13.00%     $7,500     $8,475     $9,577    $10,822
  14   Debt           10.00%    $10,000    $11,000    $12,100    $13,310
  15   Mgmt Fee       14.00%     $9,000    $10,260    $11,696    $13,334
  16   ................................................................
  17   Cash Flow                 $5,000     $5,648     $6,370     $7,175
  18
  19
  20
```

Fig. 9-4. Portion of the ten-year projection worksheet with sample data.

4. Enter the label "Ten Year Projection for Commercial Real Estate" (without the quotation marks) in cell B1.

5. Enter the label "Increase" (no quotation marks) in cell B3.

6. Enter the labels "Description" and "Rate %" in cells A4 and B4 respectively.

7. Move the cell pointer to cell C4. Type /DF to access Data Fill. Enter C4..M4 as the range to fill, 1986 as the Start value, 1 as the Step value, and 1996 as the Stop value. This will fill in the years across row 4.

8. Move the cell pointer to A5, and enter the formula:

   @REPEAT("−",135)

   to place the underline across row 5.

9. Copy the underline to row 11 by using /C (Copy), and specifying A5..A5 as the range to copy FROM, and A11 as the range to copy TO.

10. Copy the underline again by using /C (Copy) to copy FROM A5..A5 TO A16.

11. Enter the sample labels in the cells from A6 to A17 as shown in Fig. 9-4, and Table 9-4.

Table 9-4. Contents of the Projection Worksheet Before Copying Formulas

B1:	'Ten Year Projection for Commercial Real Estate
B3:	'Increase
A4:	[W15] 'Description
B4:	'Rate %
C4:	1986
D4:	1987
E4:	1988
F4:	1989
G4:	1990
H4:	1991
I4:	1992
J4:	1993
K4:	1994
L4:	1995
M4:	1996
A5:	[W15] @REPEAT("−",135)
D6:	(C0) +C6+($B$6*C6)
D7:	(C0) +C7+($B$7*C7)
D8:	(C0) +C8+($B$8*C8)
D9:	(C0) +C9+($B$9*C9)
D10:	(C0) +C10+($B$10*C10)
A11:	U [W15] @REPEAT("−",135)
D12:	(C0) +C12+($B$12*C12)
D13:	(C0) +C13+($B$13*C13)
D14:	(C0) +C14+($B$14*C14)
D15:	(C0) +C15+($B$15*C15)
A16:	[W15] @REPEAT("−",135)
A17:	[W15] 'Cash Flow
C17:	(C0) @SUM(C6..C10)−@SUM(C12..C15)
D17:	(C0) @SUM(D6..D10)−@SUM(D12..D15)

12. Enter the sample percentage rates in column B as shown in Fig. 9-4 and Table 9-4. You can use the percent sign rather than the decimal equivalents (e.g. 12%, 15%, an so on).

13. Enter the hypothetical initial values for 1986 in column C. (Don't use commas when entering the numbers, you'll format these later to display the commas).

14. Move the cell pointer to cell D6, and enter the formula:

+C6+(B6*C6)

to increase the dollar amount for 1986 by the increase amount in column B.

15. Use /C (Copy) to copy the formula FROM D6..D6 TO D7..D10.

16. Move the cell pointer to cell D10. Use /C (Copy) to copy the formula FROM D10..D10 TO D12..D15.

Now, we need to copy these formulas in column D out to the year 1996, but we have a little problem on our hands. We want each formula to refer to the dollar amount in the previous year, but we need to lock in on the cell containing the increase rate. In other words, the reference to the previous year's dollar amount needs to be a relative cell reference, but the increase rate needs to be an absolute cell reference.

There is no quick and easy way to change all the necessary references to absolute references, so you'll need to repeat the next step for every formula in column D. For each formula in column D, follow the next step to make the reference to the increase rate absolute.

17. Move the cell pointer to D6. Press the Edit key (F2), and move the cursor to the reference to cell B6, as below:

    +C6+(B6*C6)

    Press the ABS key (F4) so that the B6 turns to $B$6, as below:

    +C6+($B$6*C6)

    Press RETURN when done to put the edited formula back into its cell. Repeat this process for cells D7, D8, D9, D10, D12, D13, D14, and D15. The results displayed by these formulas will not change, but the formulas will be ready for copying. When you are done, column D will contain the formulas:

    +C6+($B$6*C6)
    +C7+($B$7*C7)
    +C8+($B$8*C8)
    +C9+($B$9*C9)
    +C10+($B$10*C10)

    +C12+($B$12*C12)
    +C13+($B$13*C13)
    +C14+($B$14*C14)
    +C15+($B$15*C15)

18. Move the cell pointer to cell C17, and enter the formula for subtracting the sum of the expenses from the sum of the income, as shown below:

    @SUM(C6..C10)-@SUM(C12..C15)

19. Use /C (Copy) to copy the formula FROM cell C17 TO cell D17.

20. To fill in all ten years of formulas, move the cell pointer to cell D6. Use /C (Copy) to copy FROM D6..D17 TO E6..M17. That will fill in the projection. All we need to do now is format the display.

21. Move the cell pointer to cell C6. Use /RFC0 (Range Format Currency 0) to format the range C6..M17.

22. To format column B, move the cell pointer to B6, type /RFP2 (Range Format Percent 2), and specify B6..B15 as the range to format.

Projection Worksheet Cell Protection

To protect the worksheet, move the cell pointer to cell A6, and use /RU (Range Unprotect) to unprotect cells in the range A6..C15. Then use /WGPE (Worksheet Global Protection Enable) to protect the many formulas in the worksheet.

Once entered, remember to save the file using /FS (File Save) and a valid file name like TenYear.

Using the Projection Worksheet

When entering the increase rate in column B, remember to use the % sign (e.g. 15% or 12.66%). You can modify any of the data in columns A, B, and C. Any change to the initial dollar amounts in column C, or the increased rates in column B will, of course, affect the cash flow all the way out to column M.

Splitting the Screen

The /WW (Worksheet Window) commands let you divide the screen so that you can view two sections of the worksheet simultaneously.

On a wide worksheet such as this, you need to scroll back and forth as you try out new assumptions in columns B and C. As an alternative, you can divide the screen into *windows*, and view two separate areas of the screen at once. The /WW (Worksheet Window) commands let you create vertical, horizontal, synchronized, and unsynchronized windows. Here are the steps to divide the Ten Year Projection worksheet vertically into two windows.

1. Move the cell pointer to column E.

2. Type /WWV (Worksheet Window Vertical)

3. Press the WINDOW key (F6) to move to the window on the right

4. Press the Home key.

5. Press GoTo (F5) and enter L1 as the cell to go to, and press RETURN.

6. Press WINDOW (F6) to move the cell pointer back into the window on the left.

Now you can change assumptions in columns B and C, and see their effects in 1986 immediately, as shown in Fig. 9-5.

```
A1: [W15]                                                                    READY

              A          B         C          D            L        M
 1                    Ten Year Projection for Commer1
 2                                                   2
 3                     Increase                      3
 4    Description     Rate %      1986      1987 4       1995     1996
 5    ...........................................5  ......................
 6    Tenant 1        12.50%   $15,000   $16,875 6     $43,298  $48,710
 7    Tenant 2        12.50%   $10,000   $11,250 7     $28,865  $32,473
 8    Tenant 3        12.50%    $5,000    $5,625 8     $14,433  $16,237
 9    Tenant 4        12.50%    $5,000    $5,625 9     $14,433  $16,237
10    Tenant 5        12.50%    $7,500    $8,438 10    $21,649  $24,355
11    ...........................................11 ......................
12    Maintenance     13.00%   $11,000   $12,430 12    $33,044  $37,340
13    Insurance       13.00%    $7,500    $8,475 13    $22,530  $25,459
14    Debt            10.00%   $10,000   $11,000 14    $23,579  $25,937
15    Mgmt Fee        14.00%    $9,000   $10,260 15    $29,268  $33,365
16    ...........................................16 ......................
17    Cash Flow                 $5,000    $5,648 17    $14,255  $15,909
18                                               18
19                                               19
20                                               20
```

Fig. 9-5. Projection worksheet with two windows.

You may want to take some time to experiment with the /WW (Worksheet Window) commands, and try out some window combinations on your own. The options for creating (and deleting) windows are all under the /WW commands, and are summarized below:

Horizontal: Splits the screen horizontally at the currently highlighted row.

Vertical: Splits the screen vertically at the currently highlighted column.

Sync: Synchronizes scrolling in all windows, so that any movement through one window causes the same movement through the other window.

Unsync: Unsynchronizes scrolling so that you can scroll through the windows independently.

Press the WINDOW key (F6) to move the cell pointer from one

window to another. /WWC (Worksheet Window Clear) will remove any windows and return to the normal screen.

Printing the Worksheet

If you have a dot matrix printer that can use compressed print, you might be able to display this worksheet on a single sheet of paper. Optionally, use /POB (Print Options Borders) to repeat the information in the left column on each page. See Chapter 7 for details.

ACCOUNTS RECEIVABLE AGING REPORT

The Accounts Receivable worksheet demonstrates techniques for manipulating and comparing dates in 1-2-3.

The accounts receivable aging report will give us an opportunity to do some 1-2-3 *date arithmetic* and to work with ranges of dates as well. When loaded, the worksheet immediately compares all the due dates on the loans to the current system date. It then places the loan amount in the proper column (Current, Over 30, Over 60, Over 90), as shown in Fig. 9-6. The worksheet also sums the total amount, and the amount owed per period, in the bottom row. You enter a loan due date, customer name, and loan amount in the left three columns. 1-2-3 does the rest.

The worksheet is shown in Fig. 9-6. Notice that the current date on the worksheet is July 29, 1986. This is the date that the loan amounts are compared against. The cell-by-cell contents of the worksheet are listed in Table 9-5. Step-by-step instructions from creating the worksheet follow:

```
D3: (D1) [W15] @NOW                                          READY

     A B C      D           E        F        G        H        I
 1  Accounts Receivable Aging Report
 2
 3  Date:          29-Jul-86
 4
 5  Due Date
 6  MM DD YY Customer      Amount   Current  Over 30  Over 60  Over 90
 7  ===================================================================
 8    1  1 86 Adam Jones    100.00    0.00     0.00     0.00   100.00
 9    2  1 86 Bobby Smith   200.00    0.00     0.00     0.00   200.00
10    3  1 86 Cat Co        300.00    0.00     0.00     0.00   300.00
11    4  1 86 David May     400.00    0.00     0.00     0.00   400.00
12    5  1 86 Eddie Tide    500.00    0.00     0.00   500.00     0.00
13    6  1 86 Frankly Gross 600.00    0.00   600.00     0.00     0.00
14                          ========================================
15                         2100.00    0.00   600.00   500.00  1000.00
16
17
18
```

Fig. 9-6. Accounts receivable worksheet with sample data.

Table 9-5. Contents of the AR Worksheet Before Copying Formulas

```
A1:     [W3] 'Accounts Receivable Aging Report
A3:     [W3] 'Date:
D3:     (D1) [W15krt@ @NOW
A5:     [W3] 'Due Date
A6:     [W3] 'MM
B6:     [W3] 'DD
C6:     [W3krt@ 'YY
D6:     [W15] 'Customer
E6:     'Amount
F6:     'Current
G6:     'Over 30
H6:     'Over 60
I6:     'Over 90
A7:     [W3] \ =
B7:     [W3] \ =
C7:     [W3] \ =
D7:     [W15] \ =
E7:     \ =
F7:     \ =
G7:     \ =
H7:     \ =
I7:     \ =
F8:     (F2) @IF(@NOW-@DATE($C8,$A8,$B8)< =30,$E8,0)
G8:     (F2) @IF(@NOW-@DATE($C8,$A8,$B8)>30#AND#@NOW-@DATE
        ($C8,$A8,$B8)< =60,$E8,0)
H8:     (F2)@IF(@NOW-@DATE($C8,$A8,$B8)>60#AND#@NOW-@DATE
        ($C8,$A8,$B8)< =90,$E8,0)
I8:     (F2) @IF(@NOW-@DATE($C8,$A8,$B8)>90,$E8,0)
E14:    (F2) \ =
F14:    (F2) \ =
G14:    (F2) \ =
H14:    (F2) \ =
I14:    (F2) \ =
E15:    (F2) @SUM(E8..E13)
F15:    (F2) @SUM(F8..F13)
G15:    (F2) @SUM(G8..G13)
H15:    (F2) @SUM(H8..H13)
I15:    (F2) @SUM(I8..I13)
```

1. Use /WEY (Worksheet Erase Yes) to start with a blank worksheet.

2. Use /WCS (Worksheet Column Set-Width) to set columns A, B, and C to three spaces wide each. Set column D to 15 spaces wide.

3. Enter the label "Accounts Receivable Aging Report" (without the quotation marks) in cell A1.

4. Enter the label "Date:" (without the quotation marks) in cell A3.

5. Enter the function @NOW in cell D3.

6. Use /RFD1 (Range Format Date 1) to format cell D3.

7. Enter the label "Due Date" (no quotation marks) in cell A5.

8. Enter the labels MM, DD, YY in cells A6, B6, and C6, respectively.

9. Enter other labels across row six, as shown in Fig. 9-6.

10. Enter the \ = symbol in cell A7. Use /C (Copy) to copy FROM A7..A7 TO B7..I7.

11. Enter some hypothetical dates, customers, and loan amounts in columns A, B, C, D, and E, as shown in Fig. 9-6. Note that column A stores a month (1-12), column B a day (1-31), and column C a year (e.g. 86).

12. Move the cell pointer to cell F8 and enter the formula:

    @IF(@NOW−@DATE($C8,$A8,$B8)< = 30,$E8,0)

    In English, this formula means "If today's date minus the Due Date is less than, or equal to, 30 days, display the loan amount. Otherwise display zero." Absolute references in the formula are for copying later.

13. Move the cell pointer to cell G8 and enter the formula:

    @IF(@NOW-@DATE($C8,$A8,$B8)>30
    #AND#@NOW-@DATE($C8,$A8,$B8)< = 60,$E8,0)

    (NOTE: The formula is split only to fit in the book. You must type it into a single cell with no spaces or breaks). In English this formula means "If today's date minus the due date is more than 30 days, AND today's date minus the due date is less than, or equal to, 60 days, then display the loan amount in this column, otherwise display zero."

14. Use /C (Copy to copy the formula FROM cell G8 TO cell H8. Move the cell pointer to cell H8, press the EDIT key. Use the arrow keys and Del keys to change the 30 to 60, and the 60 to 90, so the formula in cell H8 reads:

    @ @IF(@NOW−@DATE($C8,$A8,$B8)>60
    #AND#@NOW−@DATE($C8,$A8,$B8)< = 90,$E8,0)

    (Again, make sure to enter the formula in a single cell with no spaces or breaks.) It's not necessary to copy and change the formula; you can just type the formula directly into cell H8 if you prefer. This formula displays the loan amount in the Over 60 column if the loan date is at least 61 days, but not more than 90 days, past due.

15. Use /C (Copy) to Copy the formula FROM cell F8 TO cell I8. Move the cell pointer to cell I8 and press the EDIT (F2). Change the reference to < =30 to >90 as shown below:

    @IF(@NOW− @DATE($C8,$A8,$B8)>90,$E8,0)

    This formula displays the loan amount in the Over 90 column if it is more than 90 days past due.

16. Copy all the formulas downward by using /C (Copy) and specifying F8..I8 as the range to copy FROM, and F9..I13 as the range to copy TO.

17. Put the symbol \ = in cell E14.

18. Put the formula @SUM(E8..E13) in cell E15.

19. Use /C (Copy) to copy FROM cells E14..E15 TO cells F14..I15.

20. Move the cell pointer to cell E8. Use /RFF2 (Range Format Fixed 2) to format the range E8..I15.

21. Use /FS (File Save) to save the file with a name such as AR.

Accounts Receivable Cell Protection

To protect the formulas, use /RU (Range Unprotect) to unprotect the range A8..E13. Use /WGPE (Worksheet Global Protection Enable) to turn on the global protection.

Testing the Accounts Receivable Worksheet

Try changing the months in column A to see the effect the date has on the worksheet. (Note: Use dates that are near the actual date that you are using the worksheet while experimenting.) Obviously, all the loan amounts in Fig. 9-5 will be over 90 days past due if you create this worksheet in December of 1986.)

To temporarily leave 1-2-3 to change the system date, use the /S (System) command from the 1-2-3 menu, and the DATE and EXIT commands at the DOS prompt.

On most computers you can quickly change the current date shown in cell D3. Enter /S (System) to temporarily leave 1-2-3 and return to the DOS prompt. At the DOS prompt, enter the command DATE and press RETURN. Fill in a new date. Then, from the DOS prompt, enter the command EXIT and press RETURN to return to 1-2-3. When you get back to the 1-2-3 worksheet, press CALC (F9) to update the worksheet to the new system date.

This worksheet has given us an opportunity to perform some date arithmetic in 1-2-3. By subtracting the loan due date from the current date (@NOW), the worksheet was able to calculate whether or not a loan was overdue, and by how much. Using the @IF clause, and the #AND# operator in some cases, you could place loan amounts within very specific "past due" ranges within specific columns. Note the use of the #AND# operator in the formulas in columns G and H to pinpoint a range of dates. In English, the formula in column G says "If the loan is more than 30 days old and the loan is less than 60 days old, then display the loan amount here, otherwise display zero." The formula in column H makes the same decision for loans that are between 60 and 90 days past due.

This worksheet works with ranges of dates using @IF and #AND# operators. Table lookups can work with ranges of data as well. Refer to the tax table worksheet back in Chapter 2 for an example of a worksheet that can figure taxes for salaries that fall within various ranges.

Hiding the Zeros

Use /WGZY (Worksheet Global Zero Yes) to display blank spaces instead of zeros in a worksheet.

If you like, you can select the commands /WGZY (Worksheet Global Zero Yes) to suppress the display of zeros in the columns. Fig. 9-7 shows how the Accounts Receivable worksheet looks with the zeros suppressed.

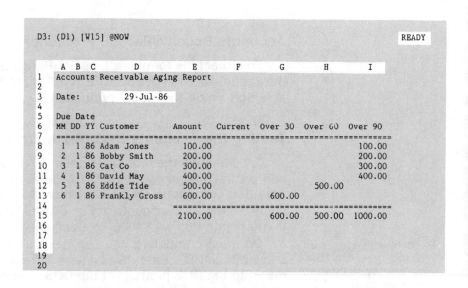

Fig. 9-7. Accounts Receivable worksheet with zero suppression.

BALANCE SHEET

The Balance Sheet worksheet shows a general format for setting up a balance sheet with calculated depreciations.

It seems that there are as many different balance sheets as there are businesses in the world, so this example is indeed very general. Nonetheless, the basic techniques described in this example should give you some ideas for putting together your own electronic balance sheet. Fig. 9-8 shows the entire balance sheet, though only a portion of it will fit on your screen at any given time. Of course, you can use the PgDn and PgUp keys to scroll around the balance sheet. Table 9-6 shows the exact contents of each cell in the balance sheet.

Instructions for creating the worksheet are listed below. Since there are no tricky copying techniques that can help speed development of this worksheet, the instructions are somewhat general this time.

1. Use /WEY (Worksheet Erase Yes) to start with a blank worksheet.

2. Use /WCS (Worksheet Column Set-Width) to make column A two spaces wide, and column B 40 spaces wide. Columns C, D, and E are each the default 9 spaces wide.

3. Enter the labels in cells B1, B2, and B3, preceding each with the ^ symbol to center it (e.g. ^ABC Company).

4. Enter all labels and underlines in columns A and B. You'll need to use Fig. 9-8 and Table 9-6 to help with this step. Notice that some labels in column B are indented. To indent within a column, press the space bar several times before typing the first letter of the label (just as you would on a typewriter). The trailing dots are best entered by trial and error. That is, type in the label and a "best guess" number of trailing dots, then press RETURN. You'll be able to see right away if you have too few or too many. Press EDIT (F2), and use the backspace key to erase extra dots, or type in more dots. Repeat until just right (depending upon how much of a perfectionist you are).

5. Cell C20 contains the formula:

   @SLN(C19,500,5)

   which calculates the depreciation allowance on the amount in C19 using the straight line method, a salvage value of $500.00, and a life of five years. Similarly, cell C23 contains the formula

   @SLN(C22,1000,5)

	A	B	C	D	E
1		ABC Company			
2		Balance Sheet			
3		December 31, 1986			
4					
5		Assets			
6	Current Assets:				
7	------------------------				
8	Cash			1400.00	
9	Notes Receivable....................................			290.00	
10	Accounts Receivable...............................			2780.00	
11	Merchandise Inventory			9671.00	
12	Prepaid Insurance...................................			300.00	
13	Office Supplies			200.00	
14	Store Supplies			169.00	
15	Total current assets			----------------	$14,810
16					
17	Plant and equipment:				
18	----------------------------------				
19	Office Equipment		2500.00		
20	Less depreciation...............................		400.00		
21			----------------	2100.00	
22	Store equipment		5000.00		
23	Less depreciation..		800.00		
24			----------------	4200.00	
25	Buildings		77125.00		
26	Less depreciation..		13425.00		
27			----------------	63700.00	
28	Land...			4200.00	
29	Total Land and Equipment			----------------	$74,200
30					----------------
31	Total assets				$89,010
32					= = = = = = =
33		Liabilities			
34					
35	Current Liabilities:				
36	------------------------------				
37	Notes payable..		10000.00		
38	Accounts payable		3031.00		
39	Wages payable		900.00		
40	Mortgage payable (current portion).................		2400.00		
41	Total current liabilities.............................		----------------	16331.00	
42					
43	Long-term liabilities:				
44	---------------------------------				
45	Secured first mortgage			18000.00	
46	Total liabilities			----------------	$34,331
47					
48		Owner's Equity			
49					
50	Oscar P. Bizowner capital, January 1			43679.00	
51	Net Income for the year......................................	31000.00			
52	Less withdrawals..	20000.00			
53	Excess income over withdrawals.......................	----------------		11000.00	
54				----------------	
55	Oscar P. Bizowner capital, December 31...............				$54,679
56					----------------
57	Total liabilities and owner's equity..................				$89,010
58					= = = = = = =
59					
60					

Fig. 9-8. Balance sheet.

(salvage value of $1000.00 and 5-year life). Cell C26 contains the formula:

@SLN(C25,10000,5)

(salvage value of $10,000.00 and 5-year life). Of course, these are merely examples. Every balance sheet will need its own unique formulas and calculations.

6. Cell D21 contains the formula:

   +C19-C20

   to subtract the depreciation allowance from the office equipment. Similarly, cell D24 contains the formula:

   +C22-C23

   and cell D27 contains the formula:

   +C25-C26

7. Formulas in column E calculate various subtotals and totals. Cell E15 contains the formula:

   @SUM(D8..D14)

   to sum the Current Assets. Cell E29 contains the formula:

   @SUM(D21..D28)

   to sum the building and equipment (less depreciation). Cell E31 contains the formula:

   +E15+E29

   to sum the total assets. Cell E46 contains the formula:

   +D41+D45

   to sum the long-term liabilities. Cell E55 sums the owner's capital using the formula:

   +D50+D53

   Cell E57 sums liability and equity using the formula:

   +E55+E46

8. In this example, the range C8..D57 is formatted for 2 decimal places using /RFF2 (Range Format Fixed 2). The range E8..E32 is Currency format using /RFC0 (Range Format Currency Zero).

Remember to save the worksheet using /FS (File Save) and a valid filename such as BalSheet.

Table 9-6. Contents of the Balance Sheet Worksheet

B1: U [W40] ^ABC Company
B2: U [W40] ^Balance Sheet
B3: U [W40] ^December 31, 1986
B5: U [W40] ^Assets
A6: U [W2] 'Current Assets:
A7: U [W2] \-
B7: U [W40] ' ----------------------------
B8: U [W40] 'Cash...
B9: U [W40] 'Notes Receivable ....
B10: U [W40] 'Accounts Receivable ....
B11: U [W40] 'Merchandise Inventory ....
B12: U [W40] 'Prepaid Insurance ....
B13: U [W40] 'Office Supplies..................................
B14: U [W40] 'Store Supplies ....
B15: U [W40] '   Total current assets ....
D15: (F2) U \-
E15: (C0) [W9] @SUM(D8..D14)
A17: U [W2] 'Plant and equipment:
A18: U [W2] '--
B18: U [W40] ' ----------------------------
B19: U [W40] 'Office Equipment..............................
B20: U [W40] '   Less depreciation..................................
C20: (F2) U @SLN(C19,500,5)
C21: (F2) U \-
D21: (F2) +C19 – C20
B22: U [W40] 'Store equipment................................
B23: U [W40] '   @Less depreciation ....
C23: (F2) U @SLN(C22,1000,5)
C24: (F2) U \-
D24: (F2) +C22 – C23
B25: U [W40] 'Buildings...
B26: U [W40] '   Less depreciation..................................
C26: (F2) U @SLN(C25,10000,5)
C27: (F2) U \-
D27: (F2) +C25 – C26@
B28: U [W40] 'Land ....
B29: U [W40]'   Total Land Equipment ....
D29: U (F2) U \-
E29: (C0) [W9] @SUM(D21..D28)
E30: (C0) U [W9] \-
B31: U [W40] '   Total assets ....
E31: (C0) [W9] +E15 + E29
E32: (C0) U [W9] \ =
B33: U [W40] ^Liabilities
A35: U [W2] 'Current Liabilities:
A36: U [W2] '--
B36: U [W40] ' ----------------------------
B37: U [W40] 'Notes payable ....

Table 9-6 cont.

```
B38: U [W40] 'Accounts payable ..........................................
B39: U [W40] 'Wages payable..........................................
B40: U [W40] 'Mortgage payable (current portion) ...............
B41: U [W40] '          Total current liabilities .....................
C41: (F2) U \-
D41: (F2) @SUM(C37..C40)
A43: U [W2] 'Long-term liabilities:
A44: U [W2] '--B44: U [W40] '----------------------------
B45: U [W40] 'Secured first mortgage...................................
B46: U [W40] '          Total liabilities ................................
D46: (F2) U \-
E46: (C0) [W9] + D41 + D45
B48: U [W40] ^Owner's Equity
A50: U [W2] 'Oscar P. Bizowner capital, January 1 ..............
B51: U [W40] 'Net Income for the year .................................
B52: U [W40] 'Less withdrawals ...........................................
B53: U [W40] 'Excess income over withdrawals ..................
C53: (F2) U \-
D53: (F2) + C51 − C52
D54: (F2) U \-
A55: U [W2] 'Oscar P. Bizowner capital, December 31........
E55: (C0) [W9] + D50 + D53
E56: (C0) U [W9] \-
B57: U [W40] 'Total liabilities and owner's equity ...............
E57: (C0) [W9] + E55 + E46
E58: U [W9] \ =
```

Balance Sheet Cell Protection

You might want to use /RU (Range Unprotect) to unprotect all the cells in the range A1..E58. Then use /RP (Range Protect) to individually protect the cells that compute totals and subtotals: E15, D21, D24, D27, E29, E31, D41, E46, D53, E55, and E57. Use /WGPE (Worksheet Global Protection Enable) to protect the cells after using the /RU and /RP commands.

WHAT HAVE YOU LEARNED?

In this chapter, you have used skills and techniques developed through preceding chapters to develop some practical worksheets. The examples demonstrate many techniques and formulas for managing business data, as well as techniques for managing dates.

The only new command that was discussed is /WW (Worksheet Window), which allows you to split the screen. Since the concepts that were discussed in this chapter are somewhat general, a quiz that usually ends each chapter is not presented here.

1-2-3 GRAPHICS

Chapter 10

CREATING GRAPHS

ABOUT THIS CHAPTER

In this chapter the discussion focuses on the commands and techniques to display 1-2-3 data on the various types of graphs. The techniques for plotting graphs vary somewhat from computer to computer, and are especially dependent upon which type of CRT (screen) your computer uses. Your computer may have any one of the three following screens: (1) monochrome, which is the standard screen used for general computing purposes, (2) graphics screen, which allows high-resolution graphics in black and white, and (3) RGB color monitor, which allows color graphics. 1-2-3 treats each somewhat differently, as summarized below:

1. **Monochrome Screen:** If you have only the monochrome display, 1-2-3 cannot display graphs on the screen at all. However, you can still print graphs on the printer.

2. **Graphics Monitor:** 1-2-3 can display graphs on both the screen and the printer. Where multiple sets of data are displayed in a graph, 1-2-3 will use various shadings (cross hatching) to identify various data items.

3. **Color Monitor:** If your computer has a color monitor, 1-2-3 can display graphs in black and white and two additional colors.

4. **Multiple Monitors:** If your computer happens to have both a standard monochrome screen and a graphics screen, 1-2-3 can dis-

play a worksheet and graph simultaneously. This is an especially powerful feature, as it allows you to try out various combinations of data on the worksheet in a "what-if" fashion, and see the results displayed immediately on the graph on the other screen.

WHAT IS "GRAPHABLE"?

You can graph any range of numbers, be it a row or a column on a worksheet. On some displays, such as stacked-bar, side-by-side bar, and line graphs, you can plot up to six entire ranges of numbers.

For exercises in this chapter, we'll use the sample worksheet shown in Fig. 10-1. To create the worksheet begin with /WEY (Worksheet Erase Yes) to clear the screen. Use /WCS (Worksheet Column Set-Width) to set column A to 16 spaces wide. Enter all the labels, numbers (except totals), and underlines, as shown in Fig. 10-1.

```
A16: [W16]                                                    READY

                A           B           C           D           E
 1                              ABC Company
 2                              Seasonal Sales
 3
 4   Product               Spring      Summer        Fall      Winter
 5   ........          ..........  ..........  ..........  ..........
 6   Golf                $42,000     $47,000     $37,000     $32,000
 7   Tennis              $47,000     $60,000     $45,000     $33,000
 8   Surfing             $30,000     $82,000     $44,000     $41,000
 9   Skiing              $29,000     $29,000     $41,000     $76,000
10   ........          ..........  ..........  ..........  ..........
11   Total              $148,000    $218,000    $167,000    $182,000
12
13
14
15
16
17
18
19
20
```

Fig. 10-1. Sample worksheet.

Position the cell pointer to cell B6. Type /RFC0 (Range Format Currency Zero) to format the numbers, and highlight the range

B6..E11. Press RETURN. Move the cell pointer to cell B4, and type /RLR (Range Labels Right). Highlight the range B4..E4 and press RETURN to right-align the labels in row 4.

Enter the formula @SUM(B6..B9) into cell B11. Then use /C (Copy) to copy the formula FROM B11..B11 TO C11..E11. Use /FS (File Save) to save the worksheet with a name such as ABCGraph. When complete, the worksheet should look like Fig. 10-1.

You can plot up to six ranges of data on a single graph using the graph ranges labeled A through F.

To plot the performance of a single product for a single season on a graph, you need to specify the range to plot. To plot the sales performance in Spring, you would need to specify B6..B9 as the graph's A range. To plot the performance of multiple products over all four seasons, such as with a stacked-bar graph, you would have to specify all four ranges. Range B6 to E6 would be range "A" for plotting purposes. Range B7 to E7 would be range B, and so forth.

DEFINING DATA TO BE PLOTTED

Suppose you just want to plot a simple graph of sales of golf supplies. This data is in the range of cells B6..E6. Here are the steps to assign these values as the first range to plot on the graph:

1. Move the cell pointer to the beginning of the range, cell B6.

2. Call up the Graph menu by typing /G.

3. Select A from the Graph menu.

4. When 1-2-3 asks that you:

   Enter first data range B6..B6

   highlight, or type in, the range B6..E6. If you highlight (by pressing the End key and right-arrow key), the highlighted range appears on the screen as in Fig. 10-2. Press RETURN after specifying the range.

Once you have done that, 1-2-3 returns to the Graph Menu. Now that you have named a range to plot, you need to tell 1-2-3 what Type of graph you want these data plotted on. So select Type from the Graph menu, and a submenu of graph types appears on the screen like this:

Line Bar XY Stacked-Bar Pie

Data can be plotted on Line, Bar, Stacked-Bar, Pie, or XY graphs.

For this example, select Pie. Again, the Graph menu reappears. Now to see the graph, select View from the Graph menu, and lo and behold, a pie chart appears on the screen, as shown in Fig. 10-3.

```
A4: [W16] 'Product                                                    READY

              A           B           C           D           E
 1                            ABC Company
 2                           Seasonal Sales
 3
 4    Product         Spring      Summer        Fall      Winter
 5    ........      ..........................................
 6    Golf            $42,000     $47,000     $37,000     $32,000
 7    Tennis          $47,000     $60,000     $45,000     $33,000
 8    Surfing         $30,000     $82,000     $44,000     $41,000
 9    Skiing          $29,000     $29,000     $41,000     $76,000
10    ........      ..........................................
11    Total          $148,000    $218,000    $167,000    $182,000
12
13
14
15
16
```

Fig. 10-2. A- Range highlighted on the worksheet.

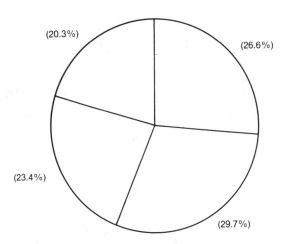

Fig. 10-3. Sample pie chart.

If you have only a monochrome display, you do not see any-thing. Instead, you hear only a beep. However, you can save the graph and print it later, as we discuss shortly. If you have two monitors hooked up, you still see the worksheet on the monocrhome display, and the pie chart on the graphics display. If you have a graphics screen (only) hooked up, the graph overwrites the worksheet on the screen.

When you have finished looking at the graph, simply press any key and the worksheet will be displayed on the screen, along with the Graph menu.

Take another look at this data in a bar graph form. You have already defined the A- range to plot, so now you just need to select another graph Type. So select option Type, and specify Bar. Next, select View, and voila!, the same data appears plotted on a bar graph, as shown in Fig. 10-4.

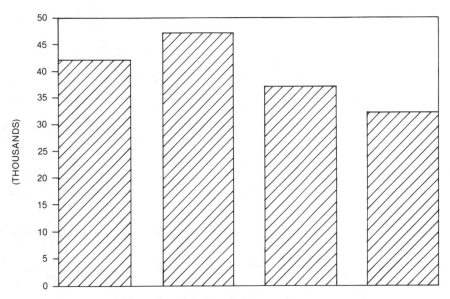

Fig. 10-4. Sample bar graph.

Press any key to clear the present graph and return to the Graph menu. This time select four ranges, A through D, to plot on the screen. Select B from the Graph menu, and define the range as B7..E7 and press RETURN. Select option C, and type in the range B8..D8 and press RETURN. Select option D, and type in the range B9..E9 and press RETURN. Now select the Type menu option, and specify Bar. Then select View, and watch a side-by-side bar graph appear on the screen, as in Fig. 10-5.

You can view this as a Stacked-bar bar chart by pressing any key to bring the worksheet and Graph menu back to the screen. Then, select graph Type again, and select Stacked-bar from the options. Select View again, and the data is displayed as in Fig. 10-6.

When displaying line graphs, the /GOF (Graph Options Format) commands let you specify Lines, Symbols, Both, or Neither method for plotting points.

To view the data on a Line Graph, press any key to redisplay the worksheet and Graph Menu. Select Type, and from its options, select Line. Now, select a format for the Line graph. From the Graph Menu, select the Options option. From its menu select Format. From the next menu, select Graph (to specify a format for the entire graph or certain ranges). The next menu to appear looks like this:

<u>Lines</u> Symbols Both Neither

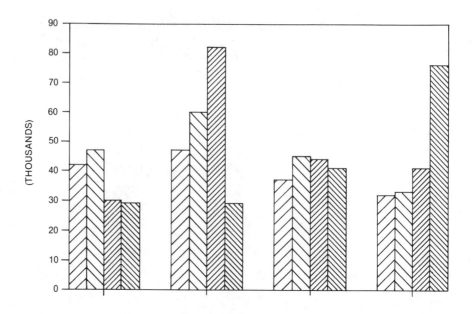

Fig. 10-5. Bar graph of four ranges.

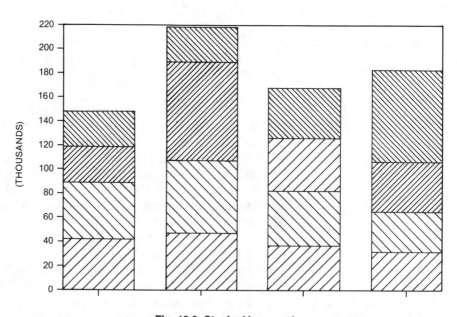

Fig. 10-6. Stacked-bar graph.

For this example, select B for both lines and symbols. Once you have defined an option for the line graph, select Quit from the two submenus to get back to the Graph menu. Select View once again, and the data is plotted accordingly. Fig. 10-7 shows the data displayed with both symbols and lines.

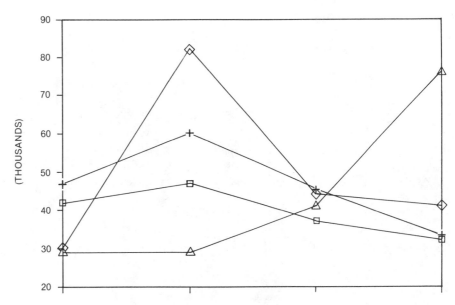

Fig. 10-7. Line graph with lines and symbols.

As you can see, displaying various types of graphs is an easy process. However, none of these graphs has very descriptive labels. You need to use some other options to put labels into the graphs.

PUTTING LABELS ON GRAPHS

1-2-3 allows three types of labels for graphs: (1) Axis labels which are displayed beneath the each column on the graph, or alongside pie slices. (2) Overall labels, which are actually titles or headings for the graph, and (3) Legends, which tell what set of data various shadings or colors in the graph refer to.

X-Axis Titles

Let's begin with some X-axis titles. Note in Fig. 10-8 that a range of titles is built right into the worksheet. Range B4..E4 contains the titles Winter, Spring, Summer, Fall.

The X-Range on a graph appears as labels across the X-axis.

To include these on the graph itself, select the X option from the Graph menu. Type in the range of labels, B4..E4 and press RETURN. Since you have already defined all other aspects of the graph, just select VIEW, and the graph is redisplayed as in Fig. 10-9.

On the pie chart, these labels are printed next to the individual slices. If we keep all these parameters the same, and select Pie from the Type options, and view the graph again, we see the graph displayed in Fig. 10-10.

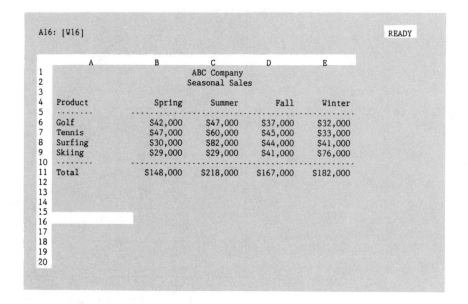

Fig. 10-8. Sample worksheets.

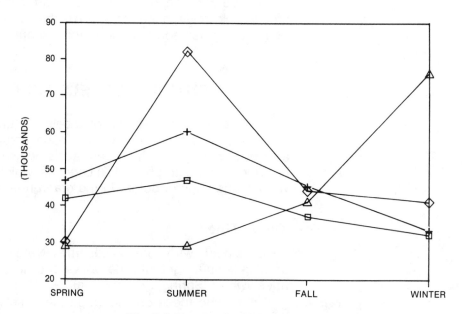

Fig. 10-9. Line graph with X-Range titles.

Notice that only the A-range is displayed in the pie chart. Since the pie chart is only capable of plotting one range of figures, it always plots range A, regardless of what other ranges have already been defined.

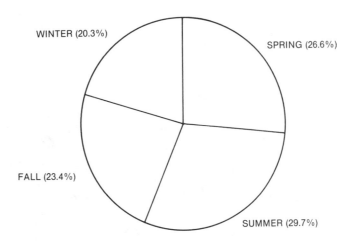

Fig. 10-10. Pie chart with X-Range titles.

Graph Titles

You can also display overall titles in any graph. The Options Titles command provides many options for this. When you select

The /GOT (Graph Options Titles) commands let you place titles on a graph.

Options, this menu appears:

Legend **Format** **Titles** **Grid** **Scale** **Color** **B&W** **Data-Labels** **Quit**

Select Titles. Another menu appears on the screen:

First **Second** **X-Axis** **Y-Axis**

From here you can select a First and/or Second line title, as well as titles for the X and Y axes. Select option First, and type in the title "ABC Company Product Sales" (leave out the quotation marks) and press RETURN. Next, select Titles again, then Second. Type in "By Season" and press RETURN. Next select Titles again and choose X for an X-axis title. Type in "Season" and press RETURN. Finally, select Titles Y-Axis, type in the title "Sales" and press RETURN. Whenever you type in a title, 1-2-3 goes into Edit mode, so you can backspace to make corrections or use the Esc key to erase a title. When you are finished creating titles, select Quit from the options menu to get back to the Graph menu.

Select Type from the Graph menu, and Bar from the submenu. Then select View to see the data. The result is displayed in Fig. 10-11. The First line title is displayed at the top of the graph. The Second line title is centered beneath the first title. The X axis title appears below the X axis, centered, and the Y axis title is printed sideways next to the Y axis.

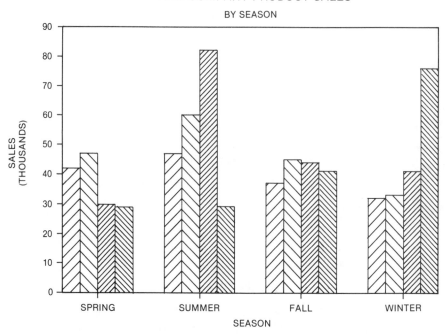

Fig. 10-11. Bar graph with titles.

Legends

Use /GOL (Graph Options Legend) to add legends to a graph.

For the finishing touches, add some legends that describe which bar goes with what product. The one catch with legend names is that they have to be brief. For example, if six ranges are displayed on the graph, then each legend name can only be one character long. 1-2-3 allows you to use legend names that are up to 19 characters long. But for neatness' sake, keep them abbreviated.

First, select Options, and from the options menu select Legend. It displays a menu of data ranges for creating legends:

A B C D E F

Our example bar graph contains ranges A-D. So select A, type in the legend name Golf, and press RETURN. Select legend again, then select B, type in the abbreviated legend name Tenn, and press RETURN. Type in names Surf and Ski for ranges C and D using the same procedure. Then Quit the options menu to return to the Graph menu. Select View. The graph appears with the legends shown at the bottom of the graph as shown in Fig. 10-12.

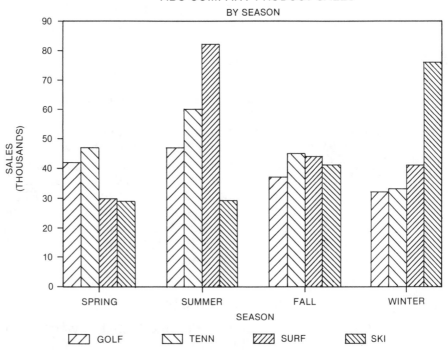

Fig. 10-12. Bar graph with legends.

FORMATTING GRAPHS

1-2-3 allows even more options for formatting graphs. These are also displayed on the Options menu. Rather than go into elaborate detail in their use, we'll just summarize them here.

Grid

The /GOG (Graph Options Grid) commands let you control the background grid on a graph.

The Grid option provides choices for displaying grid lines on graphs. Its menu asks if you want Horizontal, Vertical, Both, or to Clear grid lines displayed on the graph. If you select Both, then a graph is displayed, as seen in Fig. 10-13.

This option, of course, has no effect on pie charts. Selecting Horizontal will place horizontal grid lines on the graph, Vertical prints only vertical grid lines. The Clear option clears grid lines from the graph.

Scales

The Scale option allows you to manually set both the X and Y axis range. If you don't specify a scale, 1-2-3 automatically figures out the best scale and plots accordingly. The Scale command allows you to override the automatic settings and put in your own. When selected, it gives these options:

Y Scale   **X Scale**   **Skip**

The graph displayed in Fig. 10-13 uses a Y-axis range of 20 to 90,000.

The /GOS (Graph Options Scale) commands let you control aspects of the X- and Y-axis scales.

You can change this by selecting the Y option from this menu, and selecting Manual from the two options displayed. Next, you need to type in a new Y-axis range, such as 0 to 120,000. So, select Lower scale limit, type in 0 and press RETURN. Then, select Upper scale limit, type in 120000 and press RETURN. When you are done changing these options, select Quit to return to the Graph menu.

Next, select View to once again look at the graph, and it will appear as in Fig. 10-14. You can see that the Y-axis range has indeed changed.

Number Formats

The /GOSF (Graph Option Scale Format) commands let you control the formats of numbers on the graph axes, just as /RF (Range Format) lets you control number formats on the worksheet.

You can alter the format in which the numbers are displayed along the axes. For example, the Y-axis values in the graph in Fig. 10-14 are dollar amounts. You can switch these to the currency format using the Format option from the Options menu. From the Graph menu, select Options Scale. From the next submenu to appear, select Y scale. From the next menu, select Format. Specify a format from the options provided:

Fixed, Scientific, Currency, ,(comma), General, Percent, Date

These formats were discussed in Chapter 3. For our present example, select the Currency option. When you View the graph, the values along the Y axis will be in currency format, as shown in Fig. 10-15.

Color

The /GOC (Graph Options Color) and /GOB (Graph Options B&W) let you specify either color or black and white for graphs displayed on the screen.

Finally, you can specify that the graph be displayed in color using the Color choice from the Options menu. If you have a black-and-white monitor, graphs will be displayed in different shadings rather than with hatch marks.

If you have a color monitor, the data ranges are displayed in three different colors. Only graph bars, lines, and symbols are displayed in color; the titles, scale numbers, axes, and any grid lines are still displayed in white (on the screen). The ranges displayed are in these colors on the screen:

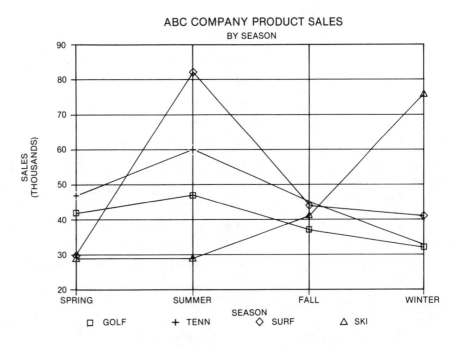

Fig. 10-13. Line graph with background grid.

A Red
B Blue
C White
D Red
E Blue
F Blue

These do not necessarily affect the way in which the graphs will be displayed on the printer. We'll deal with that in the next chapter.

NAMING GRAPHS

Any given worksheet can have any number of graphs associated with it. You need not constantly change a single graph to get different "views" of your data.

You can save several graphs with a worksheet by assigning names to the graphs with /GNC (Graph Name Create).

To have several graphs associated with a single worksheet, you need to assign each graph a unique name (up to 14 characters long) using the /GNC (Graph Name Create) commands. Later, you can use the /GNU (Graph Name Use) commands to view a menu of all your named graphs, and select a particular graph to view or

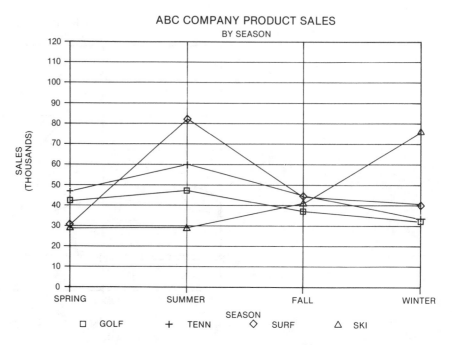

Fig. 10-14. Line graph with manual Y-axis.

change. Let's try out these new commands using the ABC Graph worksheet.

1. Bring the current graph into view using the View option from the Graph menu, or by pressing the GRAPH (F10) key.

2. If you are satisfied with the appearance of the graph, press any key to return to the worksheet.

3. From the Graph menu, select NC (Name Create) and assign a graph name (such as Products), then press RETURN.

4. Select Reset Graph to cancel all current settings on the graph.

5. Select A to draw an A-range, and specify B11..E11 as the range to plot, then press RETURN.

6. Select TB (Type Bar) to make a bar graph.

7. Select X, and specify B4..E4 as the X-range of labels.

8. Select OTF (Options Titles First) and enter the title "Total Sales" (without the quotation marks) and press RETURN.

9. Select Quit to leave the Options menu, then select View. You'll see the new graph as in Fig. 10-16. (You may want to fix this graph up a bit more.)

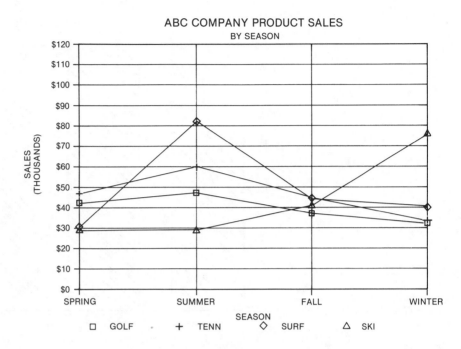

Fig. 10-15. Graph with formatted Y-range values.

10. Press any key to leave the new graph and return to the graph menu.

11. Select NC (Name Create) and assign a new graph name, such as Totals, and press RETURN.

Now you have two graphs associated with the worksheet. However, you must still use /FS (File Save) to save the worksheet so the graphs will be saved too. Do so now... Quit the graph menu, and save the worksheet with its graphs using /FS and the ABCGraph filename.

Select a Graph to View

To view a named graph, use the commands /GNU (Graph Name Use), highlight the graph name, and press RETURN.

To select a graph to view, enter /GNU (Graph Name Use), and select a graph by name (highlight the name and press Enter). The graph you selected will appear on the screen. Press any key to return to the worksheet. To view another graph, select NU (Name Use), then highlight the graph name and press RETURN. The graph will appear on the screen.

You can modify the graph being viewed at anytime. 1-2-3 re-members the changes you've made to the named graph, so long as

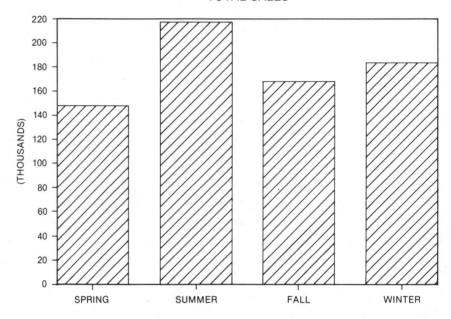

Fig. 10-16. Graph of quarterly totals.

you remember to save the entire worksheet (/FS) after making the changes.

Let's add one more graph to the collection. Rather than resetting any ranges as in the last example, you can just create a pie chart of the totals, using the A-Range from the Totals graph.

1. Select Name Use from the Graph menu, and specify the Totals graph.

2. After viewing the bar graph, press any key to return to the graph menu.

3. Select the Type and Pie options to specify a pie chart.

4. Select View to view the pie chart.

5. Press any key to return to the menu.

6. Select Name Create, and assign the name TotPie to the new pie chart.

Now you have three graphs in this worksheet:

Products: A graph of all product sales.

Totals: A bar graph of total sales.

TotPie: A Pie chart of total sales.

Remember to Quit the Graph menu and save the entire worksheet (/FS) after creating the new pie chart so it will be saved along with the worksheet.

The Delete option under the Graph Name menu allows you to delete a named graph from the list. The Reset option deletes all named graphs. (Use this option with caution!)

EXPLODED PIE SLICES

You can make your pie charts a bit fancier by using exploded slices and hatch marks. There are eight different hatch mark patterns, numbered 0 through 7, as shown in Fig. 10-17.

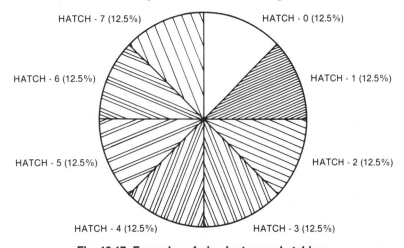

Fig. 10-17. Examples of pie chart cross-hatchings.

To explode a pie slice in a pie chart, add 100 to its hatch code in the graph B- Range.

To explode a pie slice, add the number 100 to its hatch code.

Generally, you'll want to put these codes in some out-of-the-way place on the worksheet, since they serve no other purpose than to format the pie chart. Then, assign these numbers to a graph B-Range. Let's give it a try using the ABCGraph worksheet.

1. With the ABCGraph worksheet on the screen, first Quit the graph menu if necessary.

2. Move the cell pointer to cell R1 (press F5, then enter R1 and press RETURN).

3. Put the numbers 1, 102, 4, and 7 in cells R1, R2, R3, and R4 respectively (one atop the other). Note that the second slice (102) will be exploded.

4. Enter /GNU (Graph Name Use) and select TotPie. After viewing the pie chart, press any key to return to the Graph menu.

5. Select B, and highlight (or enter) the range R1..R4.

6. Select View to view the modified Pie Chart, as shown in Fig. 10-18.

7. Press any key to return to the Graph menu, then Quit the Graph menu.

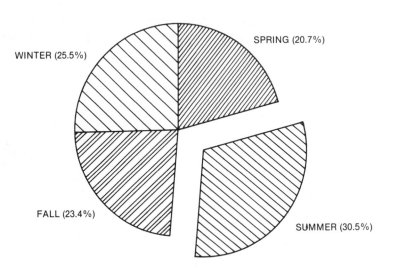

Fig. 10-18. Pie chart with exploded slice.

To view the worksheet data, press Home. Then once again, use /FS (File Save) to save the modified pie chart with the worksheet. Whenever you use the worksheet in the future, you'll have all three graphs available from the /GNU (Graph Name Use) menu.

PLOTTING DATA FROM NONCONTIGUOUS CELLS

Graphs are easy to create when the data to be plotted is right next to each other (contiguous) in rows, or is in contiguous rows. However, plotting noncontiguous data is a little different. For example, look at the worksheet in Fig. 10-19.

Suppose you want to plot the Sales totals in on the graph range,

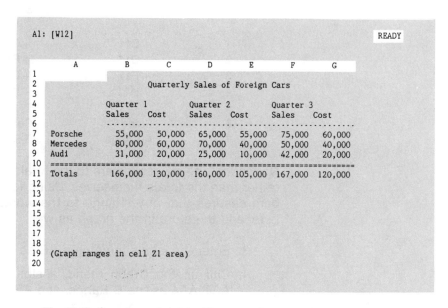

Fig. 10-19. Sample worksheet with noncontiguous sales and cost data.

and the Cost totals in another range. What's the dilemma? The sales and cost totals are not each in contiguous columns. Each sales total has a Cost total in between. There is no direct way to tell 1-2-3 to "Plot the sales in the A-Range, but skip over the Costs and put those in the B-range".

However, by using simple formulas that duplicate the totals in the worksheet, you can set up a rearranged version of the actual data to be plotted in a far away place on the worksheet. Then you can plot the A-Range and B-Range from the rearranged duplicate data.

To plot data in noncontiguous cells, use formulas that refer to the data to be plotted, and assign graph ranges to the formulas.

Using the example worksheet of quarterly costs and sales of foreign cars, you would follow these steps to set up the rearranged data for graphing.

1. Use the GoTo key to move the cell pointer to an out-of-the-way cell such as Z1.

2. Enter formulas in the range Z1..AA1 to reflect the totals in row 11.

Note that the formulas for sales totals (B11, D11, F11, and H11) are in one column, and totals for Costs (C11, E11, G11, I11) are in another row. (When you enter the formulas, the totals from the worksheet will appear in the cells, not the formulas.)

	Z	AA	AB
1	+ B11	+ C11	Quarter 1
2	+ D11	+ E11	Quarter 2
3	+ F11	+ G11	Quarter 3
4	+ H11	+ I11	Quarter 4
5			
6	Sales	Costs	
7	A-Range	B-Range	X-Range

Notice that the references are to the totals in the actual worksheet, rather than the totals themselves. Using formulas rather than numbers ensures that any change to the worksheet will be reflected here, and therefore in the graph as well.

3. Enter the labels in column AB as shown above.

4. Call up the Graph menu, assign Z1..Z4 as the A-Range, AA1..AA4 as the B Range, and AB1..AB4 as the X-Range.

5. Select Options Legend from the Graph menu. Enter the "Sales" (without the quotation marks) as the A-legend. Select Legend again, and enter "Cost" as the B-legend.

6. Select Titles from the Options menu, and enter the First title as:

Quarterly Sales and Costs

for the Second title enter:

(Totals)

7. Quit the submenu, and select V to view the graph. The graph appears on the screen with sales and costs separated, as shown in Fig. 10-20.

"WHAT-IF" ANALYSES WITH GRAPHS

Once you have created a graph, you can quickly jump back and forth between the worksheet and the graph using the Graph (F10) key. This is very helpful if you want to get an immediate visual display of the effects of a change in assumptions on the worksheet. For example, Fig. 10-21 shows a Real Estate projection worksheet like the one you developed in Chapter 9.

Plotting the cash flow on a bar graph produces the graph shown in Fig. 10-22. Pressing any key after viewing the graph redisplays the worksheet on the screen. Now you can change an assumption. In Fig. 10-23 change the − .05 increase rate for the debt service to + .05. The quantities adjust accordingly on the worksheet.

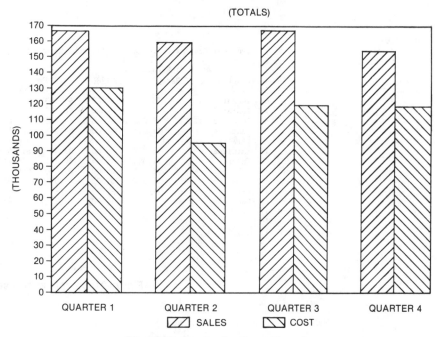

Fig. 10-20. Graph of sales and costs.

Pressing the F10 key redisplays the graph on the screen, and it too has adjusted to the new assumption, as in Fig. 10-24.

This easy to use feature is one of 1-2-3's best. If you are used to using other spreadsheets for "What-if" modeling, but have never had this immediate graphics capability, you'll soon wonder how you ever got along without it.

WHAT HAVE YOU LEARNED?

1. Any set of numbers on the worksheet can be plotted on a graph.

2. You can plot up to six ranges of data on a graph, using the option A through F on the Graph menu.

3. Graph types include Line, Bar, Pie, Stacked-Bar, and XY.

4. The X-Range option on the Graph menu lets you place titles along the X-axis of the graph (or next to pie slices).

5. The /GOT (Graph Options Titles) commands let you add titles to your graphs.

A17: [W15]   READY

```
                A          B        C        D        E        F
1   Ten Year Projection for Commercial Real Estate
2
3                     Increase
4   Description       Rate %       1986     1987     1988     1989
5   ...................................................................
6   Tenant 1          15.00%     $8,000   $9,200  $10,580  $12,167
7   Tenant 2          11.00%     $7,500   $8,325   $9,241  $10,257
8   Tenant 3           9.00%     $8,500   $9,265  $10,099  $11,008
9   Tenant 4          11.00%     $4,500   $4,995   $5,544   $6,154
10  ...................................................................
11  Maintenance       11.00%     $9,000   $9,990  $11,089  $12,309
12  Insurance         11.00%     $7,500   $8,325   $9,241  $10,257
13  Debt Service      -5.00%    $10,000   $9,500   $9,025   $8,574
14  Mgmt Fee          15.00%     $3,500   $4,025   $4,629   $5,323
15  ...................................................................
16  Cash Flow                   ($1,500)    ($55)  $1,481   $3,124
17
18
19
20
```

Fig. 10-21. Sample worksheet.

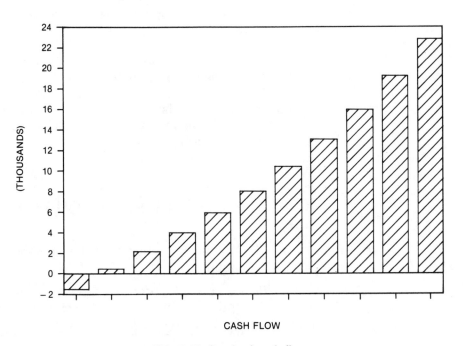

CASH FLOW

Fig. 10-22. Graph of cash flows.

B14: (P2) 0.15   READY

```
            A           B          C          D          E          F
1   Ten Year Projection for Commercial Real Estate
2
3                       Increase
4   Description         Rate %       1986       1987       1988       1989
5   ..................................................................................
6   Tenant 1            15.00%     $8,000     $9,200    $10,580    $12,167
7   Tenant 2            11.00%     $7,500     $8,325     $9,241    $10,257
8   Tenant 3             9.00%     $8,500     $9,265    $10,099    $11,008
9   Tenant 4            11.00%     $4,500     $4,995     $5,544     $6,154
10  ..................................................................................
11  Maintenance         11.00%     $9,000     $9,990    $11,089    $12,309
12  Insurance           11.00%     $7,500     $8,325     $9,241    $10,257
13  Debt Service         5.00%    $10,000    $10,500    $11,025    $11,576
14  Mgmt Fee            15.00%     $3,500     $4,025     $4,629     $5,323
15  ..................................................................................
16  Cash Flow                    ($1,500)   ($1,055)    ($519)      $121
17
18
19
20
```

Fig. 10-23. Data modified in row 13.

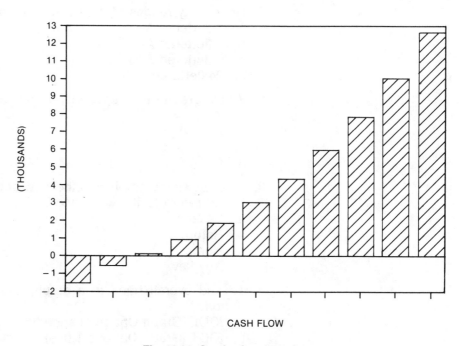

CASH FLOW

Fig. 10-24. Graph after data change.

6. The /GOL (Graph Options Legend) commands allow you to add legends to your graphs.

7. Other options under the /GO (Graph Options) menus let you control background grid, X- and Y-axis scales, numeric formats, and colors.

8. The /GNC (Graph Name Create) and /GNU (Graph Name Use) commands let you name and manage multiple graphs in a single worksheet.

9. Using the hatch codes 0-7 and the exploded codes 100-107 as the B-Range lets you design fancier pie charts.

10. To plot noncontiguous data in a graph, set up simple formulas in contiguous rows or columns in an out-of-the-way range of cells, and use this data for the graph ranges.

11. To quickly view a graph after changing data on the worksheet, press the Graph (F10) key.

QUIZ

1. How many ranges of data can you plot on a single graph?
   a. 1 (lettered A)
   b. 3 (lettered A-C)
   c. 6 (lettered A-F)
   d. 24 (lettered A-X)

2. Which graph range appears as titles along the X axis?
   a. X
   b. A
   c. B
   d. F

3. After viewing a graph with the view option, you press which key to return to the worksheet?
   a. Escape
   b. Return
   c. Home
   d. Any key

4. To add overall titles to a graph, you select which menu options?
   a. /GOL (Graph Options Legend)
   b. /GOT (Graph Options Titles)
   c. /GOG (Graph Options Grid)
   d. /GOS (Graph Options Scale)

5. To name a graph, use the commands:
   a. /GNU (Graph Name Use)

b. /GNC (Graph Name Create)
c. /GND (Graph Name Delete)
d. /GNR (Graph Name Reset)

6. Suppose you create a graph and name it, and then want to create a new graph for the worksheet. Which commands will clear out all the graph settings from the previously named graph?
   a. RA (Reset A)
   b. RG (Reset Graph)
   c. RQ (Reset Quit)
   d. RR (Reset Ranges)

7. Assigning a name to a graph ensures that the graph will be part of the worksheet *only* if:
   a. You remember to use /FS to save the worksheet after naming the graph.
   b. You use /GS (Graph Save) to save the graph as a separate file.
   c. You assign a name to only one graph on the worksheet.
   d. You use /GNR (Graph Name Reset) after naming the graphs.

8. To select a graph for viewing from a collection of named graphs, you use the commands:
   a. /GNU (Graph Name Use)
   b. /GNC (Graph Name Create)
   c. /GND (Graph Name Delete)
   d. /GNR (Graph Name Reset)

9. To explode a pie slice in a pie chart, you must:
   a. Add 100 to its hatch-mark code in the B-Range
   b. Add 100 to the formula that calculates its value
   c. Select /GES (Graph Explode Slice) from the menu
   d. All of the above

10. To quickly switch from the worksheet to the currently active graph, you press which key?
    a. F7
    b. F8
    c. F9
    d. F10

CHAPTER 11

PRINTING GRAPHS

ABOUT THIS CHAPTER

In this chapter the techniques for printing graphs using the Lotus PrintGraph program are discussed. There are several steps to printing a graph: (1) Use the Save option from the Graph menu to save a printable copy of the graph, (2) Select PrintGraph settings for your printer/plotter, (3) Design the printed graph, and (4) Select graphs for printing.

SAVING GRAPHS FOR PRINTING

To print a graph you must first save it using the Save option from the Graph menu.

Before you can print a graph, you need to save a special copy of the graph on disk using the Save option from the 1-2-3 Graph menu. This is a simple procedure (though one that's easy to forget to perform). Let's look at some examples using the ABCGraph work-sheet developed in the last chapter. If the worksheet is not on your screen now, use /FR (File Retrieve) to load the worksheet into 1-2-3.

To save a graph for printing, first view the graph. You can save several graphs for printing by using the following procedure:

1. Type /GNU (Graph Name Use), and select the Products graph. After the graph appears on the screen, press any key to return to the Graph menu. Select Save from the menu, and enter a valid file name for the saved graph. Type in GRAPH1 for this graph (remember, eight letters maximum length, no spaces or punctuation).

2. Select NU (Name Use), and the Totals graph. Press any key after viewing the graph, and select Save from the graph menu. Assign the file name GRAPH2.

3. Select NU once again, and specify the TotPie graph this time. Press any key after viewing the graph, select Save from the graph menu, and enter the file name GRAPH3.

4. Select Quit to leave the Graph menu.

You've just save three graph files, named GRAPH1.PIC, GRAPH2.PIC, and GRAPH3.PIC (yes, 1-2-3 automatically adds the .PIC extension to the file name). If you had made any changes to your worksheet or graphs during this step, you'd first want to use /FS (File Save) to save the worksheet. In this example, we made no changes, so it is not necessary to save. Therefore, you can just leave 1-2-3 by selecting /QY (Quit Yes).

THE PRINTGRAPH PROGRAM

To print saved graphs, exit 1-2-3 and run the PrintGraph program.

When you exit 1-2-3, you should see the Access menu appear. (If it does not appear, you can just enter the LOTUS command at the DOS A> or C> prompt, using the usual method for starting 1-2-3.) The Access menu offers the options:

1-2-3 PrintGraph Translate Install View Exit

Select PrintGraph. (On a floppy disk system, you'll need to remove the 1-2-3 disk from drive A, and put in the PrintGraph disk. Follow the instructions on your screen.)

When PrintGraph appears you'll see a new menu at the top of the screen and a lot of graphics settings, as shown in Fig. 11-1.

```
Select graphs for printing
Image-Select  Settings  Go  Align  Page  Exit
==================================================================

GRAPH       IMAGE OPTIONS                       HARDWARE SETUP
IMAGES      Size                  Range Colors  Graphs Directory:
SELECTED    Top          .395     X Black          C:\123
            Left         .750     A Black       Fonts Directory:
            Width       6.500     B Black          C:\123
            Height      4.691     C Black       Interface:
            Rotate       .000     D Black          Parallel 1
                                  E Black       Printer Type:
            Font                  F Black          Okidata 82,83
            1  BLOCK1                           Paper Size
            2  BLOCK1                              Width    8.500
                                                  Length  11.000

                                                ACTION OPTIONS
                                                Pause: No
                                                Eject: No
```

Fig. 11-1. Main PrintGraph screen.

HARDWARE SETUP

The options in the column labeled HARDWARE SETUP (on the right) need to be set up only once for your computer configuration. You need to do this first though, so PrintGraph can do its job correctly.

Graphs Directory

The Hardware Setup options in PrintGraph let you designate computer and printer configurations.

The first listed option under HARDWARE SETUP is the Graphs Directory, which tells PrintGraph where to look for the .PIC graph files. On a system with two floppy disk drives, this should be B:. On a hard disk system, it should be C:, or C: with a directory name (such as C:\123). If this is not the case, change it following these steps:

1. Select Settings.
2. Select Hardware.
3. Select Graphs-Directory.

PrintGraph asks where to search for picture files. Type in a drive specification (usually B: for a system with two floppy drives, or C: on a computer with a hard disk). Press RETURN, then Quit the Hardware menu, and Quit the Settings menu.

Fonts Directory

Check the Fonts Directory section of the screen under the HARDWARE SETUP column. On a system with two floppy drives, it should be A:\. On a hard disk system, it would probably be C:, or C: with a directory name. If it is not, follow these steps to change it:

1. Select Settings.
2. Select Hardware.
3. Select Fonts-Directory.
4. Enter the drive for Fonts files (A: for system with two floppy drives, C: for hard disk system.) Press RETURN.
5. Quit the Hardware menu.
6. Quit the Settings menu.

Graphics Printer

Look at the Printer Type option in the HARDWARE SETUP column. If no printer name appears, or the name that appears does not match the printer or plotter you use, you'll need to change that too. Here are the steps:

1. Select Settings.

2. Select Hardware.

3. Select Printer.

A menu appears on the screen, as in Fig. 11-2. If one printer or plotter name appears on the screen, and it does not have a # symbol next to it, press the space bar once. The # symbol should appear next to the name. If several different printers and plotters appear on the screen, use the down-arrow or up-arrow key to move the highlighter to the name of the appropriate printer or plotter. When the printer you want is highlighted, press the space bar until a # symbol appears next to the highlighted name. When the appropriate printer or plotter has a # symbol next to it, press the RETURN key then Quit the Hardware menu and Quit the Settings menu.

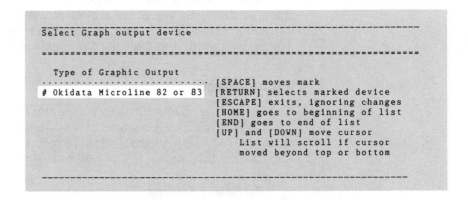

```
Select Graph output device
================================================================

   Type of Graphic Output
.......................... [SPACE] moves mark
# Okidata Microline 82 or 83  [RETURN] selects marked device
                              [ESCAPE] exits, ignoring changes
                              [HOME] goes to beginning of list
                              [END] goes to end of list
                              [UP] and [DOWN] move cursor
                                    List will scroll if cursor
                                    moved beyond top or bottom

----------------------------------------------------------------
```

Fig. 11-2. Menu and instructions for selecting graphics printer.

Printer Interface

The HARDWARE SETUP column also contains an option for Interface. Most microcomputers use a parallel interface, so you probably won't need to change this. If you do happen to know that the interface displayed is incorrect, select Settings Hardware Interface to select the appropriate interface. If you need additional information, check your printer or plotter manual, or ask your computer dealer.

Action Options

The Action Options let you determine how paper is handled in the printer or plotter.

If you are going to print several graphs at a time, and you want each graph to be printed on a separate page, make sure PrintGraph *ejects* each page from the printer when it finishes drawing each graph. To do so, change the Eject option to Yes by following these steps:

1. Select Settings.
2. Select Action.
3. Select Eject.
4. Select Yes.
5. Quit Action menu.
6. Quit Settings menu.

If you'd like your printer or plotter to pause between printing each graph, change the Pause option to Yes following these steps:

1. Select Settings.
2. Select Action.
3. Select Pause.
4. Select Yes.
5. Select Quit.
6. Select Quit.

Saving the Settings

After specifying Hardware Setup options, select Settings Save from the PrintGraph menu so you don't have to repeat the process in the future.

If during these steps you made any changes to the Graphs-Directory, Fonts-Directory, Interface, Printer Type, Pause, or Eject options, you can save these settings now so you do not have to repeat this procedure in the future. To save the new settings, follow these simple steps:

1. Select Settings.
2. Select Save.

PRINTING THE GRAPHS

Now, with that business out of the way, we can get back to the task of actually designing and printing some graphs. First, you need to select some fonts for the printed graphs.

Selecting Graph Fonts

The Settings Image Fonts options let you select fonts for your printed graph.

Select a font for the main title on the graph (Font 1). Here's how:

1. Select Settings.

2. Select Image.

3. Select Font.

4. Select 1.

A menu of font options appears, as in Fig. 11-3. Examples of the various fonts available are displayed in Fig. 11-4. Select a font by moving the highlighter with the UP and DOWN key. When the font you want is highlighted, press the space bar to mark it with the # symbol. Then, press RETURN. For example, to select BLOCK2 as the first font follow these steps:

1. Highlight BLOCK2.

2. Mark BLOCK2 (press space bar until # appears).

3. Press RETURN.

```
Select font 1
=================================================================
      FONT NAME        SIZE
      . . . . . . . . . . . . . . . . . . . . . .   [SPACE] moves mark
      BLOCK1           5737      [RETURN] selects marked device
      BLOCK2           9300      [ESCAPE] exits, ignoring changes
      BOLD             8624      [HOME] goes to beginning of list
      FORUM            9727      [END] goes to end of list
      ITALIC1          8949      [UP] and [DOWN] move cursor
      ITALIC2         11857          List will scroll if cursor
      LOTUS            8679          moved beyond top or bottom
      ROMAN1           6863
      ROMAN2          11847
      SCRIPT1          8132
      SCRIPT2         10367
```

Fig. 11-3. Menu and instructions for selecting a font.

Select a Font 2 for all remaining text on the graph. In this example, we'll use BLOCK1:

1. Select Font.

2. Select 2.

3. Press space bar until # appears next to BLOCK1.

ABCDEFGHIJKLM
NOPQRSTUVWXYZ
abcdefghijklm
nopqrstuvwxyz
1234567890
!@#$%^&*()
_-+={}[]:;'~
""?/<>,.|\

BLOCK1

ABCDEFGHIJKLM
NOPQRSTUVWXYZ
abcdefghijklm
nopqrstuvwxyz
1234567890
!@#$%^&*()
_-+={}[]:;'~
""?/<>,.|\

BLOCK2

ABCDEFGHIJKLM
NOPQRSTUVWXYZ
abcdefghijklm
nopqrstuvwxyz
1234567890
!@#$%^&()*
_-+={}[]:;'~
""?/<>,.

ITALIC1

ABCDEFGHIJKLM
NOPQRSTUVWXYZ
abcdefghijklm
nopqrstuvwxyz
1234567890
!@#$%^&()*
_-+={}[]:;'~
""?/<>,.|

ITALIC2

ABCDEFGHIJKLM
NOPQRSTUVWXYZ
abcdefghijklm
nopqrstuvwxyz
1234567890
!@#$%^&*()
_-+={}[]:;'~
""?/<>,.|\

ROMAN1

ABCDEFGHIJKLM
NOPQRSTUVWXYZ
abcdefghijklm
nopqrstuvwxyz
1234567890
!@#$%^&*()
_-+={}[]:;'~
""?/<>,.|\

ROMAN2

ABCDEFGHIJKLM
NOPQRSTUVWXYZ
abcdefghijklm
nopqrstuvwxyz
1234567890
!@#$%^&*()
_-+={}[]:;'~
""?/<>,.|\

SCRIPT1

ABCDEFGHIJKLM
NOPQRSTUVWXYZ
abcdefghijklm
nopqrstuvwxyz
1234567890
!@#$%^&*()*
_-+={}[]:;'~
""?/<>,.|\

SCRIPT2

Fig. 11-4. Examples of fonts for printed graphs.

Fig. 11-4—cont. Examples of fonts for printed graphs.

4. Finish selection (Press RETURN).

5. Quit the Font menu.

6. Quit the Settings menu.

The fonts you selected will be displayed near the bottom of the PrintGraph settings sheet, as below:

Font
1 BLOCK2
2 BLOCK1

If you like, you can save these fonts so that they automatically appear when when you load up the PrintGraph program. That way, you can avoid having to repeat this procedure in the future, until

you want to use other fonts for a graph. To save these fonts, select
Settings-Save.

Selecting Graphs to Print

The Image-Select option lets you select graphs to print.

Now you can tell PrintGraph which Graph (or Graphs) you want
to print. First you must select Image-Select from the PrintGraph
main menu. A menu for selecting graphs to print appears on the
screen, as shown in Fig. 11-5.

```
Select Graphs for output -----------------------------------------

==================================================================
PICTURE      DATE       TIME      SIZE
. . . . . . . . . . . . . . . . . . . . . .  [SPACE] moves mark
GRAPH1    01-01-86    1:40       4578    [RETURN] selects marked device
GRAPH2    01-01-86    1:42       1673    [ESCAPE] exits, ignoring changes
GRAPH3    01-01-86    1:44       1241    [HOME] goes to beginning of list
                                          [END] goes to end of list
                                          [UP] and [DOWN] move cursor
                                              List will scroll if cursor
                                                 moved beyond top or bottom
                                          [DRAW] displays highlighted graph


-------------------------------------------------------------------
```

Fig. 11-5. Menu and instructions for selecting graphs.

To preview a graph before printing, highlight its name on the menu and press F10.

As usual, you can use the up-arrow and down-arrow keys to
move the highlighter. You can take a quick look at a graph while its
name is highlighted on the menu by pressing the GRAPH (F10) key.
Press the space bar when done viewing.

Mark GRAPH1 by pressing the space bar so that the # symbol
appears. If you want to print other graphs, use the up-arrow and
down-arrow keys to highlight their names, and press the space bar
to mark the name. When you're done selecting graphs, press the
RETURN key.

The graph(s) you selected to print are displayed on the Print-
Graph settings menu under the GRAPH IMAGES SELECTED column, as below:

GRAPH
IMAGES
SELECTED

    GRAPH1
    GRAPH2
    GRAPH3

Now that you've specified the graph(s) to print, make sure the printer is on, and select Go from the menu to start printing. Be patient. It takes a couple of minutes to get a graph printed. If nothing at all happens, either the printer is not on or is not on-line, the Interface option is wrong, or the Printer Type option is wrong. If an error message appears on the screen stating that graphs or fonts were not found on the specified drive, the the Graphs-Directory or Fonts-Directory options are wrong. You'll need to reset these options according to your system's configuration.

Press the BREAK key to cancel graph printing.

If for some reason you need to interrupt the printer before all graphs are printed, just press the BREAK key (Ctrl-Scroll Lock on most keyboards). Then, press the Escape key.

Figs. 11-6 through 11-12 show some sample graphs printed by the PrintGraph program.

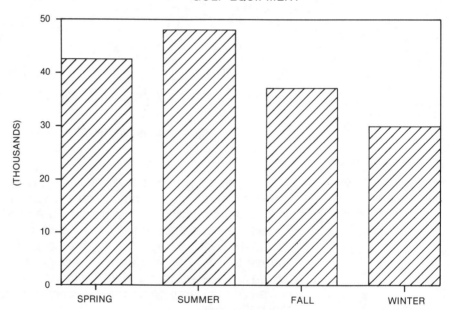

Fig. 11-6. Sample graph.

SIZING THE GRAPH

Unless you tell it otherwise, PrintGraph will display your graphs in half-page size (vertically on an 8 1/2 by 11 inch sheet of paper). You can specify other sizes by selecting the Settings

The Settings Image Size options let you determine the size of the printed graph.

Image Size options from the PrintGraph menu. You'll be given three new options:

SPORTS EQUIPMENT

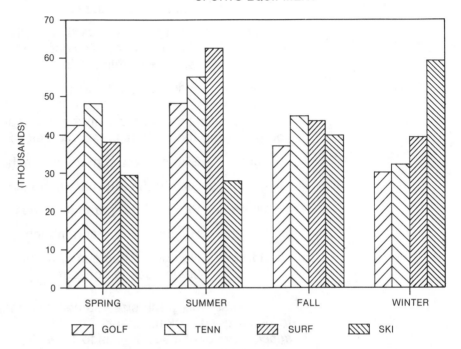

Fig. 11-7. Sample graph printed by PrintGraph program.

SPORTS EQUIPMENT

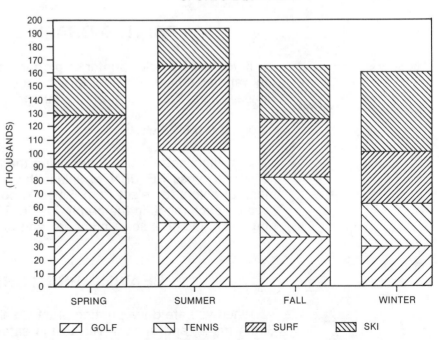

Fig. 11-8. Sample graph printed by PrintGraph program.

Full: Print the graph horizontally on an entire 8 1/2 by 11 inch sheet of paper.

Half: Print the graph vertically on half a sheet of 8 1/2 by 11 inch paper. (You can print two graphs on a single page with this setting.)

Manual: You select all size and margin variables.

If you select the Manual option, you can then size the graph yourself using the options presented below:

Top: Size of the top margin in inches.

Left: Size of the left margin in inches.

Width: Width of the graph in inches.

Height: Height of the graph in inches.

Rotate: Number of degrees of rotation: 0 degrees is vertical, 90 degrees is horizontal.

If you set the graph size yourself, you may need to experiment to get a good looking graph. The Full and Half settings use an *aspect ratio* of of 1.385 (X-axis) to 1 (Y-axis). Any deviation from this will make graphs that look taller or wider. Again, perhaps experimentation is your best bet when sizing a graph.

PRINTED GRAPH COLORS

The Settings Image Range-Colors options let you specify colors for the various ranges on your graphs.

If you have a color printer or plotter, you can select colors for the various ranges on your graph. Just select Settings Image Range-Colors. You'll be given the submenu:

X A B C D E F Quit

Just highlight a range letter using the left-arrow or right-arrow keys, and press RETURN to select the range. You'll be given a menu of colors to select from. Select a color, and repeat the process for each range in the graph. (NOTE: The X-Range color selection colors the grid, scale numbers, and titles.)

LEAVING PRINTGRAPH

When you are done printing graphs, select Exit from the Print-Graph menu, and answer Yes to the safety prompt. The Access System menu will reappear on the screen.

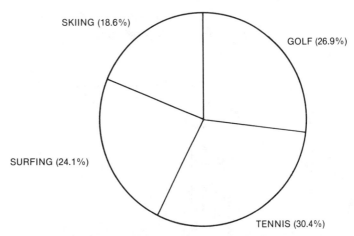

Fig. 11-9. Sample graph printed by PrintGraph program.

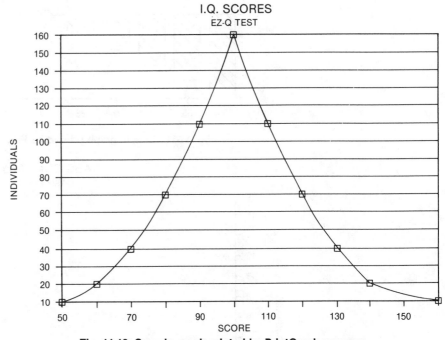

Fig. 11-10. Sample graph printed by PrintGraph program.

WHAT HAVE YOU LEARNED?

1. Before you can print a graph, you must save a copy of it using the Save option from the Graph menu.

2. To print saved graphs, you must exit 1-2-3 and run the Print-Graph program.

3. The PrintGraph program will run correctly only if the *Hardware Settings* are correct.

4. The PrintGraph Settings Save options save graph settings for future use.

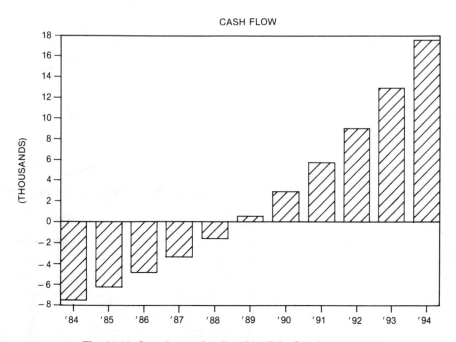

Fig. 11-11. Sample graph printed by PrintGraph program.

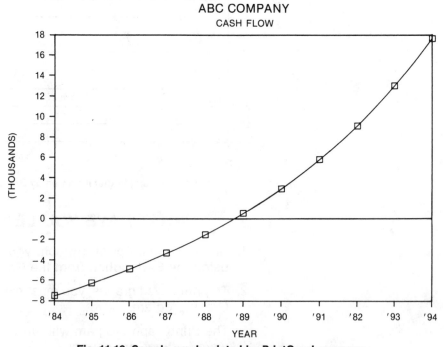

Fig. 11-12. Sample graph printed by PrintGraph program.

5. Use the Settings Image Font commands to select fonts for the printed graphs.

6. Use the Image-Select command to select graphs for printing.

7. While selecting graphs to print, you can press the GRAPH key (F10) to preview the graph.

8. Use the Go command to print selected graphs.

9. The Settings Image Size commands let you control the size of your printed graphs.

10. The Settings Image Range-Colors commands let you select colors for your graph, if you have a color printer or plotter.

QUIZ

1. When you Save a graph for printing, 1-2-3 automatically creates a file with which file name extension?
   a. .PRN
   b. .PIC
   c. .WK1
   d. .GRF

2. The Fonts-Directory option under the PrintGraph Hardware Setup options tells PrintGraph:
   a. Where to look for font (.FNT) files
   b. Where to look for worksheet (.WK1) files
   c. Where to look for named graphs
   d. Where to look for .PIC files

3. To save PrintGraph settings for future use, you use which commands from the PrintGraph menu?
   a. Settings Save
   b. Image Save
   c. Settings Image
   d. Settings Hardware

4. To print each graph on a separate page, you must do which of the following?
   a. Change the Eject Action Option to No
   b. Change the Eject Action Option to Yes
   c. Change the Pause Action Option to No
   d. Change the Pause Action Option to Yes

5. The Settings Image Font 1 commands select a font for which part of the graph?
   a. Grid and scale numbers
   b. Legends

c. First (main) title
d. All titles

6. To select graphs to print, you use which PrintGraph menu option?
    a. Settings
    b. Save
    c. Go
    d. Image-Select

7. To preview a graph while selecting graphs to print, you highlight its name then press which key?
    a. F2
    b. F7
    c. F9
    d. F10

8. After selecting graphs to print, which PrintGraph option prints the graph?
    a. Image
    b. Print
    c. Go
    d. Quit

9. To interrupt the printing of graphs, press which key?
    a. Escape
    b. Break
    c. F10
    d. End

10. When manually adjusting a graph's size, a rotation angle of 90 degrees prints the graph:
    a. Vertically
    b. Horizontally
    c. At an angle
    d. Upside down

DATABASE MANAGEMENT

Chapter 12

DATABASE MANAGEMENT

ABOUT THIS CHAPTER

As if the spreadsheet and graphics capabilities alone are not enough, 1-2-3 also includes a built-in database management system. A database management system is used to store and manage general information, such as a mailing list or inventory data. With 1-2-3's database capabilities, you can store, retrieve, sort, look up, and isolate important items of information quickly, and still perform all the standard worksheet operations with them!

WHAT IS A DATABASE?

Few people realize that they have probably worked with databases many times before they ever laid a finger on the computer keyboard. For example, a shoe box filled with index cards that have names and addresses on them is a database. Lists of sales leads, customers, phone numbers, library card catalogs, accounts receivable—just about anything that forms a list or a pile of index cards is actually a database.

A database is an organized collection of information.

Every time you look up information in your "shoe box" database, you are managing it. Most day to day database management is quite simple, such as looking up a phone number or a client's billing status. But some tasks are not so simple or pleasant. Sorting all the index cards into alphabetical order, then resorting them into zip code order for bulk mailing is tedious and time consuming with index cards. Or finding all the individuals who have outstanding invoices due, or making copies of certain individuals' cards takes a good deal of time. But with 1-2-3's database management capabilities, these tasks are a breeze.

237

Let's take a look at a shoe box filled with 5 × 7 inch index cards as an example of a database as shown in Fig. 12-1. Each index cards presumably has on it the name, address, city, state, and zip code of one individual, as in the card displayed in Fig. 12-1.

Andy Adams
123 Auburn St.
San Diego, Ca.
92222

MAIL LIST

Fig. 12-1. A "shoe box" database.

If you were to take all of the information from the shoe box, and type it onto a list, you may end up with a sheet of paper that looks like this:

LNAME	FNAME	ADDRESS	CITY	STATE	ZIP
Adams	Andy	123 A St.	San Diego	CA	92123
Smith	Sandy	234 B St.	Los Angeles	CA	91234
Jones	Janet	333 C St.	New York	NY	12345
Zeppo	Zeke	1142 Oak St.	Newark	NJ	01234
Kenney	Clark	007 Bond St.	Malibu	CA	91111

Of course there could be hundreds or even thousands of individuals on the list.

Computers store data on databases in exactly the same format as this list. There are some very specific terms that we use with computer databases, and it's a good idea to get familiar with these terms, since it will make matters much easier in the long run.

First, you can see that the above list has five individuals in it. In computer lingo, each one of these individuals occupies one *record*. Therefore, the list (or database) above has five records in it, one record for each individual.

In a database, information is stored in records (rows) and fields (columns).

Second, you can see that for each individual (or record), there are six items of information: Last name, first name, address, city, state, and zip code. Each of these individual items of information is called a *field* in computer argot. So the database above consists of five records, each record containing six fields.

In addition to the actual data in the database, there is also a line which describes what each column contains (LNAME, FNAME, ADDRESS, CITY, STATE, ZIP). These column headings are called *field names*, and are essential for database management. Each field must have a unique name associated with it, hence our database above has six field names.

Typically, managing a database such as this requires that you perform certain routine tasks from time to time. These tasks can be summarized as:

1. ADD new data to the database.

2. EDIT and DELETE data from the database.

3. SEARCH for an item or group of items.

4. SORT the data into some meaningful order.

How can 1-2-3 help with these tasks? In many ways which will probably make you throw away your index cards once and for all (though you may be wise to save them for a backup, just in case ...). But before you can manage a database with 1-2-3, you need to create one.

CREATING A 1-2-3 DATABASE

Creating a 1-2-3 database is essentially the same as creating a 1-2-3 worksheet. The only major difference is that you must make absolutely certain to include the field names. We'll use our mailing list example above to illustrate.

Your first step is to try to make the column widths reasonably wide, so that you can see the data in the cells. Technically speaking, the column widths really don't matter. However, from a practical point of view, you want to be able to see as much data as possible. For this example, follow these steps to adjust the column widths to 12 spaces wide each, with the State and Zip fields made a little smaller:

1. Use /WGC (Worksheet Global Column-Width) to set all columns to 12 spaces wide.

2. Move the cell pointer to column E, and use /WCS (Worksheet Column Set-Width) to make column E 5 spaces wide.

3. Move the cell pointer to column F, and use /WCS (Worksheet Column Set-Width) to make column F 10 spaces wide.

The top row of a database must consist of a unique field name for each column.

Next, you need to put the database field names across the first row. Put the field name LNAME in cell A1, the field name FNAME in cell B1, and so on until you put the field name Zip in cell F1. When done, your screen should look like Fig. 12-2.

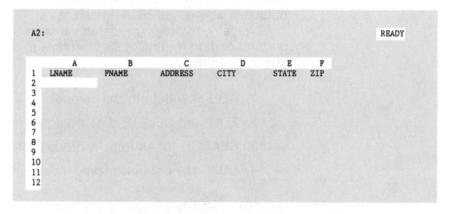

Fig. 12-2. Database field names on the worksheet.

ADDING DATA TO THE DATABASE

Enter data into a database using the same techniques you use to enter data in a worksheet.

Adding data to the database is the same as filling cells in the worksheet. The simplest method for entering a record is to position the cell pointer to the next record to be filled in the database (the first blank record at the bottom), and type in the new data in the usual fashion, following each entry with a right-arrow key to move the cell pointer to the next field. You will have to precede the address field's data with a label prefix (such as the apostrophe), since 1-2-3 will not be sure whether to make this a label or a number (i.e., 124 A St.). If you plan on using hyphenated zip codes (e.g. 92038-2802) or foreign zip codes with letters, you will have to precede all the zip codes with label prefixes.

To add the first record to the database, follow these steps:

1. Move the cell pointer to cell A2, type in the name Adams, and then press the right-arrow key.

2. In cell B2 type in the name Andy and press the right-arrow key.

3. In cell C2 type in the address '123 A St. (be sure to include the apostrophe label prefix, since this label begins with a number). Press the right-arrow key.

4. In cell D2 type in the city San Diego and press the right-arrow key.

5. In cell E2 type in the state CA and press the right-arrow key.

6. In cell F2 type in the zip code 92122 and press RETURN.

7. Press the down-arrow key, then press the End key and left-arrow key to move the cell pointer to cell A3.

You should be able to type in a few more records on your own now. Here is some sample data to enter.

Smith	Jane	'234 B St.	San Diego	CA	91235
Eggo	Sandy	'333 C St.	Los Angeles	CA	01234
Fredrex	Franny	'444 J St.	New York	NY	12345
Smith	Bob	'1101 Fig St.	Glendora	CA	91740

When you are done entering the records, use /FS (File Save) to save the database using MAIL as the file name.

EDITING DATA IN THE DATABASE

Use the EDIT (F2) key to make changes to data in a database.

Editing a field in the database is the same as editing a cell in the worksheet. You simply position the cell pointer to the field that needs to be changed, and type in the new data. Or, use the Edit key (F2) to modify the existing data.

To delete data from the database, use the /WDR (Worksheet Delete Row) command, or the database delete command described in Chapter 14.

Use /WDR (Worksheet Delete Row) to delete a record from the database.

Once in a while you need to do a different kind of database edit, where you actually need to add an entirely new field to the database. For example, suppose you decide to include phone numbers in the database. In this case, just position the cell pointer to column G1 (the top of the seventh column) and define its width with the /WCS command. You might want to be pretty liberal with your phone field width. For example, a phone number could actually look like this:

H:(619) 555-1212   W:(619) 555-111

That phone number is 35 characters wide. If you want to be able to include extensions, you have to allow for even more characters. Then be sure to type in the new field name, PHONE, in the first row of the column. Then adding phone numbers is simply a straightforward editing task of filling in a phone number for each individual in the database. If the phone field extends beyond the right edge of the screen so that you can't see the LNAME and PHONE fields at the same time, you can use the split-screen commands (/WWV) to divide up the worksheet so that the two fields are displayed simultaneously on the screen.

You can use /WIC (Worksheet Insert Column) to add new fields to a database.

In some cases, you might want to insert a field between existing fields. For instance, suppose you decide to include a field for middle initial, and want to place it between LNAME and FNAME. Use the /WIC (Worksheet Insert Column) command to add the new field. Simply position the cell pointer to cell B1. Enter the /WIC command so that all columns to the right get pushed over a notch. Then, use the /WCS command to format the column to an appropriate width, and be sure to put the field name (perhaps MI for middle initial) at the top of the column. Then, fill in the middle initials for the existing names on the list.

As you have probably surmised, you can use any of the worksheet commands to add to and edit data on the database. In fact, the database is just a worksheet with the data organized into columns (fields) and rows (records). There are, however, some capabilities that are unique to this highly structured database, as you will see in the next couple of chapters.

WHAT HAVE YOU LEARNED?

1. A database consists of records (rows) and fields (columns) of data.

2. When creating a database, you must remember to put field names on the top row.

3. Enter data into a database using the same techniques for entering data in a worksheet.

4. Edit data on a database using the same techniques for editing data in a worksheet.

5. You can use /WIC (Worksheet Insert Column) to add new fields to a database.

6. You can use /WDR (Worksheet Delete Row) to delete records from a database.

QUIZ

Use the sample database below to answer questions one and two.

NAME	TITLE	DEPARTMENT	EXTENSION
J. Jones	Vice President	Planning	1234
B. Smith	Manager	Finance	3434
K. Jones	Personnel Director	Personnel	5555
Z. Zackry	Manager	Finance	0302
S. Shumack	President	Sales	8928

1. The sample database contains how many *fields*?
   a. Six
   b. Five
   c. Four
   d. Three

2. The sample database contains how many *records*?
   a. Six
   b. Five
   c. Four
   d. Three

3. When entering an address such as 123 A St., or a foreign zip code like 1K5 VJS into a database, you must remember to:
   a. Press the EDIT (F2) key first
   b. Precede the item with an apostrophe label prefix
   c. Precede the item with an @ sign
   d. Press Home after entering the item

4. To delete a record from a database, you could use which commands?
   a. /WDR (Worksheet Delete Row)
   b. /WDC (Worksheet Delete Column)
   c. /WE (Worksheet Erase)
   d. /DE (Data Empty)

5. To insert a new field into a database, you could use which commands?
   a. /WIR (Worksheet Insert Row)
   b. /WIC (Worksheet Insert Column)
   c. /WCI (Worksheet Column Insert)
   d. /DF (Data Fill)

Chapter 13

SORTING THE DATABASE

ABOUT THIS CHAPTER

To *sort* the records in a database means to put them into some meaningful order, such as alphabetically by name, or in zip code order for bulk mailing. This chapter discusses the techniques for sorting a 1-2-3 database, using as an example the MAIL database developed in the last chapter.

THE KEY FIELD

Whenever you wish to sort a database, you need to specify a key field. That is, you need to specify which field you wish to sort by.

The field used to determine the order of a database is called the *key field*.

If you want to sort by zip code, use ZIP as the key field. If you want the records sorted alphabetically by last name, specify LNAME as the key field. Sometimes you might use multiple key fields. For the moment, it is important to discuss key fields in relation to how one goes about designing a database.

You may be wondering why we used two fields for each individual's names on the database, LNAME and FNAME. Why not just NAME? The reason is that the computers cannot recognize data based upon context as we can, For example look at these names:

John Smith
Andy Williams
Ruth Ashley
Clark Kenny
Pat Enscoe

If asked to sort these names into alphabetical order, you would probably put them into this order (unless you happen to be a computer programmer):

> Ruth Ashley
> Pat Enscoe
> Clark Kenney
> John Smith
> Andy Williams

The names are properly alphabetized by last name, the way we usually sort people's names. However, if we were to ask the computer to sort these names, we'd get this list:

> Andy Williams
> Clark Kenney
> John Smith
> Pat Enscoe
> Ruth Ashley

The names are sorted by first name. Why? Because the computer does not understand the concept of first and last name. It does not know that these are names and are, therefore, to be sorted by last name. You and I know this, because we understand this rule, and furthermore, we can spot the last name by its context and order. That is, chances are that Smith is the last name and John is the first name. Computers do not think this way. In fact, they don't think at all.

In view of this, you must think about all possible key fields in a database before you design it. If you know that you will be sorting by last name sometimes in the future, then the last name should be in a field all its own so it can be used as a key field for sorting. Of course, you could use a single NAME field, and enter the names in last, first format, as below:

> Smith, John
> Williams, Andy
> Ashley, Ruth
> Kenney, Clark
> Enscoe, Pat

These would sort properly because the last name is out in front. But this creates a new problem. Suppose you want to print a form letter from this database? You could not get at the first name to print salutations and the like. All your letters would start out with a salutation such as "Dear Smith, John." The moral of the story is; break out all your records to as many meaningful fields as you can, and keep the key fields in mind while you're determining how to structure each record in database.

GETTING THINGS IN ORDER

To sort a database, use the 1-2-3 /DS (Data Sort) command. Let's step through an example using our mailing system, which is displayed in Fig. 13-1.

```
A1: 'LNAME                                                              READY

        A            B            C            D            E      F
1   LNAME        FNAME        ADDRESS      CITY         STATE  ZIP
2   Adams        Andy         123 A St.    San Diego    CA     92122
3   Smith        Jane         234 B St.    San Diego    CA     91235
4   Eggo         Sandy        333 C St.    Los Angeles  CA     91234
5   Fredrex      Franny       444 J St.    New York     NY     12345
6   Smith        Bob          1101 Fig St. Glendora     CA     91740
7
8
9
10
```

Fig. 13-1. Sample database.

The records are in random order. (Actually, they are in the order in which we originally entered them.) To sort them by last name, enter the /DS command, which brings up a number of options in the control panel:

Data-Range **Primary-Key, Secondary-Key Reset Go Quit**

When specifying records to sort with Data-Range, do NOT include the row of field names.

First, you must specify the range of data to sort. Usually you want to sort the entire database, so select the Data-Range option on the menu, and type in the upper left and lower right cell addresses (NOT including the Field Names!). In this example, the data range would be entered as A2..F6. You can either type in or draw the range, as usual. Press RETURN.

The next step is to specify the key field to sort on. In this example, you will sort the records alphabetically by last name (LNAME), so select the Primary-Key option, and select A1 as the field to sort on. 1-2-3 will ask if you want the data sorted in ascending (smallest-to-largest) or descending (largest-to-smallest) order. Typically we list things from A to Z, so select Ascending. Now, to perform the actual sort, simply select the Go menu option. Instantly, the records appear on the screen in sorted order, as shown in Fig. 13-2.

To put these into zip code order, simply specify cell address F1 as the key field by selecting the Primary-Key option from the sort menu. Select Go again, and the records will be instantly sorted into

```
A1: 'LNAME                                                          READY

          A              B           C            D           E       F
  1   LNAME          FNAME       ADDRESS      CITY         STATE    ZIP
  2   Adams          Andy        123 A St.    San Diego    CA       92122
  3   Eggo           Sandy       333 C St.    Los Angeles  CA       91234
  4   Fredrex        Franny      444 J St.    New York     NY       12345
  5   Smith          Jane        234 B St.    San Diego    CA       91235
  6   Smith          Bob         1101 Fig St. Glendora     CA       91740
  7
  8
  9
```

Fig. 13-2. Database sorted by last name.

zip code order. 1-2-3 always remembers the last specified data range, so there is no need to respecify on the second sort.

Sorting is a pretty easy task in 1-2-3. Once in a while you may forget to specify a range or a primary field. If you do, 1-2-3 will beep to remind you. Select the Data-Range and Primary key options from the Sort Menu, and specify the ranges.

SORTS-WITHIN-SORTS

On large databases, sometimes a simple sort like this is not sufficient. For example, suppose you sort a database by zip code, but there are 500 people in the 92122 zip code area. In this case, you might want everyone in the 92122 zip code order to be listed alphabetically by last name. That is, within common zip codes, list last names alphabetically. Another example is sorting by last name. If you have 50 Smiths on your database, it would be helpful if these were listed alphabetically by first name rather than in haphazard order. It would certainly help us to pinpoint John Smith among a group of 50 Smiths. The telephone book sorts names this way for the obvious purpose of making names easier to locate in the book.

Specify a Secondary key to perform a sort-within-a-sort.

In everyday language, we typically call this a sort-within-a-sort, because the items appear to be sorted by one criterion first (LNAME), then sorted again by the second criterion (FNAME) without affecting the first sort. In computer argot, we call this "sorting by primary and secondary keys." The Primary key is the "major" sort order (such as LNAME), the Secondary key is the "minor" (within-sort) order. 1-2-3 can perform sorts-within-sorts if you select both a primary and secondary key from the sort menu of options).

To perform the sort-within-sort with the sample database, follow these steps:

1. Select the /DS (Data Sort) commands.

2. Select Data-Range, and specify A2..F6 as the range of data to sort.

3. Select Primary key.

4. Specify A1 as the Primary key, and Ascending as the order.

5. Select Secondary key.

6. Specify B1 as the Secondary key, and Ascending as the order.

7. Select Go.

Instantly, 1-2-3 will sort the data into alphabetical order by last name, with first names alphabetized within identical last names, as shown in Fig. 13-3. (Notice that Bob Smith is now listed before Jane Smith.)

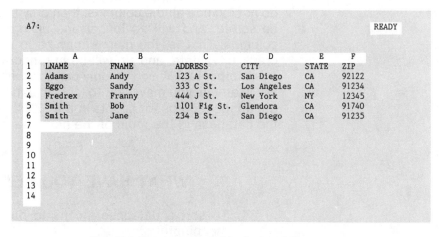

A7:   READY

	A	B	C	D	E	F
1	LNAME	FNAME	ADDRESS	CITY	STATE	ZIP
2	Adams	Andy	123 A St.	San Diego	CA	92122
3	Eggo	Sandy	333 C St.	Los Angeles	CA	91234
4	Fredrex	Franny	444 J St.	New York	NY	12345
5	Smith	Bob	1101 Fig St.	Glendora	CA	91740
6	Smith	Jane	234 B St.	San Diego	CA	91235
7						
8						
9						
10						
11						
12						
13						
14						

Fig. 13-3. Database sorted by last and first name.

WHEN THE UNEXPECTED HAPPENS

Blank records, and records with leading blank spaces, will appear at the top of a database sorted in ascending order.

Once in a while, the sort command does not produce quite what we had expected. One of the most common surprises is that things often appear at the top of the list which don't belong there. This is most often caused by the fact that a blank space is considered to be "less than" any letter in the alphabet by the computer. Therefore, if some of the last names in a database had (seemingly) invisible blank spaces in front of them, they would all appear at the very top of the list. That is, if we had these names in a list (I've put in quotation marks only to make the blank space stand out):

"Smith"
"Jones"
"Adams"
" Zeppo"

they'd come out in this order when sorted:

" Zeppo"
"Adams"
"Jones"
"Smith"

The leading blank in Zeppo's last name was considered to be "less than" the A at the start of Adam's name. Of course, any last names that were all blanks would appear at the very top of the list.

Also, make sure you always specify the entire database (with the field names) when selecting the data range. If you do not include all the rows, then only some of the rows will be sorted. If you do not include all the columns, then only the specified columns will be sorted, and will no longer line up properly with the unsorted columns. That is, the names may be in proper order, but the address, city, state, and zip will be in random order!

Another task we commonly perform with database is *searching*. For example, you may want to look up Jane Smith's address, or pull out all the records for people in the 92122 zip code area. Searching the database is the topic of the next chapter.

WHAT HAVE YOU LEARNED?

1. To sort a database means to put the records into some meaningful order.

2. The field that a database is sorted by is called the *key field* or the *sort key*.

3. Commands for sorting a database are under the /DS (Data Sort) menu options.

4. When specifying a range of data to sort using the Data-Range command, do not include the field names in the range.

5. The Primary-key option under Data Sort specifies the field to sort on.

6. When selecting sort fields, you can specify Ascending (smallest to largest), or Descending (largest to smallest) order.

7. To perform sorts-within-sorts, specify a Secondary key under the Data Sort menu.

8. Any blank records in the database will appear at the top of the database after an ascending sort.

QUIZ

1. The field use to determine the sort order in a database is called the:
   a. Sorting Criterion
   b. Multikey
   c. Key Field
   d. Sorting Field

2. Names are usually broken into at least two fields (such as the LName and FName fields) so that:
   a. The records can be properly sorted by last name
   b. The records will be sorted by first name
   c. The data is easier to read
   d. Commas do not interfere with the sort order

3. Which commands do you use to begin a database sort?
   a. /DQ (Data Query)
   b. /DO (Data Organize)
   c. /DS (Data Sort)
   d. /RS (Record Sort)

4. When using the Data-Range command to highlight the data to be sorted, you should:
   a. Exclude columns outside the key field
   b. Include field names at the top of the database
   c. Exclude rows beneath the field names
   d. Exclude the field names

5. To sort a list of names in Z to A order (as opposed to A to Z order), you would use which sorting option:
   a. Ascending
   b. Descending
   c. Backwards
   d. Forward

6. If you select Zip as a Primary key, and LName as a Secondary key when sorting a database, what order will the records be listed in?
   a. Alphabetically by last name, and in zip code order within identical last names
   b. In zip code order, with names listed alphabetically by last name within identical zip codes

c. In zip code order only

d. In last name order only

7. If you sorted a database using State as the Primary key, and City as the Secondary key, what order would the records be listed in?

a. In alphabetical order by City, and in alphabetical order by State within each City

b. In alphabetical order by State, and in alphabetical order by City within each state

c. In alphabetical order by City only

d. In alphabetical order by State only

8. If you sort a database in *descending* order, and the database contains blank records, where will the blank records appear?

a. At the top of the database

b. At the bottom of the database

c. In the middle of the database

d. In their original positions

```
┌─────────────────────────────────────────┐
│                                           │
│           SEARCHING THE                   │
│           DATABASE                        │
│                                           │
└─────────────────────────────────────────┘
```

ABOUT THIS CHAPTER

Searching a database involves asking the computer to display all the records that meet a specific criterion or several criteria. For example, using the mailing list as an example, you may want the computer to carry out any of the following searches:

Display everyone in the 12345 zip code area.
Display everyone with the last name Smith.
Display everyone in California with the last name Jones.
Find John Smith.
Display everyone who lives in either San Diego or Los Angeles.
Display everyone in the 90000 to 99999 zip code area.

In computer jargon, we often use the "query" rather than "search," but it means the same thing.

QUERY RANGES

Searching requires an Input Range, a Criterion Range, and in some cases, an Output Range.

The /DQ (Data Query) command is used to search for records in a database. The /DQ command requires that you first create some special search ranges:

INPUT RANGE: The Input Range is usually the entire database itself.

CRITERION RANGE: The Criterion Range is the field name(s) and the value(s) to search for. For example, to find all the people in the 92122 zip code area, ZIP is the field to search on, and 92122 is the value to search for. Both of these items need to be specified in the Criterion Range.

OUTPUT RANGE: If you want to create a new database from the selections made by a database search, you must specify this range as the location for placing the results of the search.

The Output Range is only necessary for searches that use the Extract or Unique options, which will be discussed shortly.

You need to set up these ranges while the worksheet is in the Ready mode, prior to selecting any menu options. Let's work through an example using a search on the small database shown in Fig. 14-1.

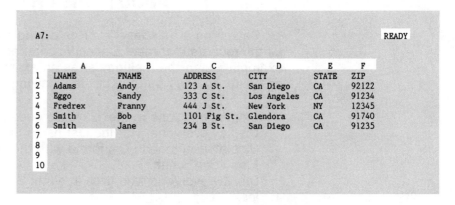

Fig. 14-1. Sample database.

The Criterion Range

The first step is always to create the Criterion Range. The easiest way to do this is to make a copy of either all the field names, or a few field names, using the Copy command. In this example, type in the /C command, specify A1..F1 as the range to copy FROM, and A9..F9 as the range to copy to. This places a list of field names outside the existing database, as shown in Fig. 14-2.

The actual location of the criterion range is unimportant, just as long as it is outside of the database. Also, the Criterion Range need not have all the field names in it, only those you wish to search on. I have included all the field names here because you will be doing several searches in this chapter, and you can just use the same criterion range over several times.

To quickly set up a Criterion Range, just use /C (Copy) to copy the row of field names to a new place on the worksheet.

Next, you must specify the search criterion (the value to search

```
A9: 'LNAME                                                          READY

         A          B          C          D          E      F
1   LNAME      FNAME      ADDRESS      CITY        STATE   ZIP
2   Adams      Andy       123 A St.    San Diego   CA      92122
3   Eggo       Sandy      333 C St.    Los Angeles CA      91234
4   Fredrex    Franny     444 J St.    New York    NY      12345
5   Smith      Bob        1101 Fig St. Glendora    CA      91740
6   Smith      Jane       234 B St.    San Diego   CA      91235
7
8
9   LNAME      FNAME      ADDRESS      CITY        STATE   ZIP
10
11
12
13
14
15
16
```

Fig. 14-2. Criterion range field names in row 9.

for). Do this by typing in the characteristic you wish to search for in the cell below the field to search on. For example, to search for all Smiths on the sample database, type the name Smith directly beneath the LNAME cell in the Criterion Range, as shown in Fig. 14-3.

```
A11:                                                               READY

         A          B          C          D          E      F
1   LNAME      FNAME      ADDRESS      CITY        STATE   ZIP
2   Adams      Andy       123 A St.    San Diego   CA      92122
3   Eggo       Sandy      333 C St.    Los Angeles CA      91234
4   Fredrex    Franny     444 J St.    New York    NY      12345
5   Smith      Bob        1101 Fig St. Glendora    CA      91740
6   Smith      Jane       234 B St.    San Diego   CA      91235
7
8
9   LNAME      FNAME      ADDRESS      CITY        STATE   ZIP
10  Smith
11
12
13
14
15
16
```

Fig. 14-3. Smith entered into criterion range.

Once the Criterion range exists and the value you wish to search for is placed under the field name you wish to search, you can use the /DQ (Data Query) command to perform the search.

FINDING RECORDS ON THE DATABASE

To begin the search, type in the command /DQ (Data Query). This brings up a menu of searching options:

Input Criterion Output Find Extract Unique Delete Reset Quit

The Input range must consist of the row of field names, and all the records and fields in the database.

First you need to specify the Input Range, so select Input from the menu of options. Specify the Input Range, which must include the field names. The Input Range is usually the entire database, so in this example it is (A1..F6). As usual, you can either type in the cell addresses for the range, or draw the range by pointing.

For simple searches, define the copied row of field names and the row beneath it as the Criterion Range.

Next you must tell 1-2-3 where the Criterion Range is, so select the Criterion option from the menu of choices. 1-2-3 will ask for the cell coordinates for the Criterion Range. In this example, the range is A9..F10. (You really only need to specify the smaller A9..A10 here, but if you include all the field names now, you won't have to redefine the Criterion range for other types of searches later.)

Now to perform the search, select the Find option from the menu. 1-2-3 will highlight the first Smith in the database, as shown in Fig. 14-4.

```
A5: 'Smith                                                            FIND

              A              B              C              D          E        F
   1  LNAME         FNAME          ADDRESS        CITY           STATE    ZIP
   2  Adams         Andy           123 A St.      San Diego      CA       92122
   3  Eggo          Sandy          333 C St.      Los Angeles    CA       91234
   4  Fredrex       Franny         444 J St.      New York       NY       12345
   5  Smith         Bob            1101 Fig St.   Glendora       CA       91740
   6  Smith         Jane           234 B St.      San Diego      CA       91235
   7
   8
   9  LNAME         FNAME          ADDRESS        CITY           STATE    ZIP
  10  Smith
  11
  12
  13
  14
  15
  16
  17
  18
  19
  20
```

Fig. 14-4. Smith located in database.

You can use the up-arrow and down-arrow keys to move to other Smiths in the database. If there are no Smiths above or below the Smith that the pointer is highlighting, then 1-2-3 will beep at you when you try to move in that direction.

/DQF (Data Query Find) positions the highlighter to the first record in the database that matches the Criterion Range Specifications.

Notice that nothing else seems to work right now. That's because the Find mode (as indicated by the mode indicator, upper right of screen) only finds. It can't do anything else. Press the Esc key to return to the Data menu.

You can be more specific in your search criteria and have 1-2-3 find Jane Smith rather than Smith. In this case you need to search on two fields: LNAME and FNAME. The values to search for would be Smith and Jane, respectively. The criterion range would have to be set up to handle both criteria, as in rows 9 and 10 in Fig. 14-5.

```
B11:                                                              READY

           A              B              C              D          E       F
1    LNAME          FNAME          ADDRESS        CITY         STATE   ZIP
2    .Adams         Andy           123 A St.      San Diego    CA      92122
3    .Eggo          Sandy          333 C St.      Los Angeles  CA      91234
4    Fredrex        Franny         444 J St.      New York     NY      12345
5    Smith          Bob            1101 Fig St.   Glendora     CA      91740
6    Smith          Jane           234 B St.      San Diego    CA      91235
7
8
9    LNAME          FNAME          ADDRESS        CITY         STATE   ZIP
10   Smith          Jane
11
12
13
14
15
16
17
18
19
20
```

Fig. 14-5. Search for Jane Smith specified in the Criterion Range.

In this example the first record highlighted by the Find command will be the one that has Smith as the LNAME *and* Jane as the FNAME. The database only has one Jane Smith, so only her record would be highlighted by the search.

COPYING SIMILAR RECORDS

Sometimes you may wish to make copies of records from the database which have some characteristic in common, such as all the people who live in San Diego. Before copying records, you need to have a place to put them. That is, you need to specify an Output Range. This you must do in the Ready mode. The easiest method is to copy the row with the field names in it to another location on the worksheet. Make sure that the location you copy to has plenty of blank rows under it, because 1-2-3 will fill these with the records extracted from the database in the search.

The Output Range

You can use /C (Copy) to quickly copy the row of field names to an Output Range.

To create the Output Range by copying, select /C and specify the top row (A1..F1) as the field to copy from, and A14 to F14 as the range to copy to. The field names will move to row 14, as shown in Fig. 14-6.

```
D10: 'San Diego                                              READY

        A              B              C           D          E      F
 1   LNAME          FNAME          ADDRESS      CITY        STATE   ZIP
 2   Adams          Andy           123 A St.    San Diego   CA      92122
 3   Eggo           Sandy          333 C St.    Los Angeles CA      91234
 4   Fredrex        Franny         444 J St.    New York    NY      12345
 5   Smith          Bob            1101 Fig St. Glendora    CA      91740
 6   Smith          Jane           234 B St.    San Diego   CA      91235
 7
 8
 9   LNAME          FNAME          ADDRESS      CITY        STATE   ZIP
10                                              San Diego
11
12
13
14   LNAME          FNAME          ADDRESS      CITY        STATE   ZIP
15
16
17
18
19
20
```

Fig. 14-6. Search for San Diego residents specified in the Criterion Range.

Notice also that the Criterion Range now has San Diego under the City range. For this example, you will pull out all the individuals who live in San Diego.

Follow these steps to rearrange the criterion range to copy records for all San Diego residents:

1. Move the cell pointer to cell A10 (in the criterion range).

2. Use /RE to erase A10..B10 (the existing criteria).

3. Move the cell pointer to cell D10.

4. Type in the new criterion, San Diego and press RETURN.

The criterion range should contain only the city San Diego, as in Fig. 14-6.

The /DQE (Data Query Extract) options copy all records that meet a search criterion to an Output Range.

Now select the /DQ command to bring up the Data Query menu, and from there select Output. 1-2-3 will ask for the coordinates of the Output Range. In this example, A14..F14 is the Output range. (If you specify only the Output Range's field names, 1-2-3 assumes that the Output Range extends to the bottom of the worksheet.)

Next, select the Extract option from the menu, and 1-2-3 copies all the records that meet the search criterion to the Output Range, as shown in Fig. 14-7. Notice that all the records in the Output Range have San Diego as their city.

```
D10: 'San Diego                                                    READY

          A              B            C            D          E       F
 1    LNAME          FNAME        ADDRESS      CITY        STATE   ZIP
 2    Adams          Andy         123 A St.    San Diego   CA      92122
 3    Eggo           Sandy        333 C St.    Los Angeles CA      91234
 4    Fredrex        Franny       444 J St.    New York    NY      12345
 5    Smith          Bob          1101 Fig St. Glendora    CA      91740
 6    Smith          Jane         234 B St.    San Diego   CA      91235
 7
 8
 9    LNAME          FNAME        ADDRESS      CITY        STATE   ZIP
10                                             San Diego
11
12
13
14    LNAME          FNAME        ADDRESS      CITY        STATE   ZIP
15    Adams          Andy         123 A St.    San Diego   CA      92122
16    Smith          Jane         234 B St.    San Diego   CA      91235
17
18
19
20
```

Fig. 14-7. San Diego residents extracted from the database.

If you change the search criteria in the Criterion Range, and perform another Extract search, the records meeting the new criteria will be pulled from the database and overwrite the records presently in the Output Range. To create a database of only the records selected from the search, use the /FX (File Xtract) command, as discussed in Chapter 8.

AND'S AND OR'S

To perform an "AND" search, place the criteria on the same row in the Criterion Range.

When you search on two fields at the same time, you may want records that match both criteria. At other times, you may want records that match either criterion. For example, suppose you want a listing of all the people whose last name is Smith and who live in California. In this case, you need to search on two fields, LNAME and STATE. And you would need two searching criteria: Smith and CA. To do so, set up the Criterion Range with the two field names at the top, and the two criteria directly beneath the field names, as illustrated in Fig. 14-8. In English, this Criterion range says, "display the records that have Smith as the LNAME *and* CA as the state."

```
A5: 'Smith                                                        FIND

              A          B          C           D          E      F
    1  LNAME      FNAME      ADDRESS      CITY        STATE  ZIP
    2  Adams      Andy       123 A St.    San Diego   CA     92122
    3  Eggo       Sandy      333 C St.    Los Angeles CA     91234
    4  Fredrex    Franny     444 J St.    New York    NY     12345
    5  Smith      Bob        1101 Fig St. Glendora    CA     91740
    6  Smith      Jane       234 B St.    San Diego   CA     91235
    7
    8
    9  LNAME      FNAME      ADDRESS      CITY        STATE  ZIP
   10  Smith                                          CA
   11
   12
   13
   14  LNAME      FNAME      ADDRESS      CITY        STATE  ZIP
   15
   16
   17
   18
   19
   20
```

Fig. 14-8. Search for Smiths in California.

To perform an ''OR'' search, stagger the search criteria across two or more rows, and extend the Criterion Range to include all the rows.

Some searches with multiple fields require an "or" type of logic. For example, suppose you want a listing of all the people who live in New York or in California. In this case, there is only one field to search on (STATE), but two criteria to consider (New York and California). To set up a criterion range that has an "or" capability for a single field like this, put the criteria to search for in the same column, one above the other, as shown in Fig. 14-9. In English, this Criterion Range says, "List all the people in the database who live in either New York or California."

As soon as you have two levels of criteria like this, you need to redefine the Criterion Range to include the new level. This is important to remember but easy to forget. If you forget, you won't get an error. Instead, everything will seem to work just fine, but the records that come out of the search will not be what you asked for. In this example, the Criterion range *must* be changed to A9..F11. Use the Criterion option from the Data Query menu to redefine the Criterion Range.

To search on two fields with an "or" relationship, stagger the two search criteria in this same fashion. For example, suppose you wanted a listing of all the people who live in either Los Angeles (proper) or the 92122 zip code area. In this case, you have two fields to search on, STATE and ZIP, and two search criteria, so the Criterion Range would look like the one in Fig. 14-10. Notice how the search criteria is staggered onto two separate lines.

Once again, since there are two rows of criteria in the criterion range, you must be sure to use the Criterion option under the /DQ

```
E12: [W8]                                                              READY

              A              B              C              D         E        F
    1   LNAME          FNAME          ADDRESS        CITY         STATE    ZIP
    2   Adams          Andy           123 A St.      San Diego    CA       92122
    3   Eggo           Sandy          333 C St.      Los Angeles  CA       91234
    4   Fredrex        Franny         444 J St.      New York     NY       12345
    5   Smith          Bob            1101 Fig St.   Glendora     CA       91740
    6   Smith          Jane           234 B St.      San Diego    CA       91235
    7
    8
    9   LNAME          FNAME          ADDRESS        CITY         STATE    ZIP
   10                                                             CA
   11                                                             NY
   12
   13
   14   LNAME          FNAME          ADDRESS        CITY         STATE    ZIP
   15
   16
   17
   18
   19
   20
```

Fig. 14-9. Search for residents in California or New York.

```
F11: [W6] 92122                                                        READY

              A              B              C              D         E        F
    1   LNAME          FNAME          ADDRESS        CITY         STATE    ZIP
    2   Adams          Andy           123 A St.      San Diego    CA       92122
    3   Eggo           Sandy          333 C St.      Los Angeles  CA       91234
    4   Fredrex        Franny         444 J St.      New York     NY       12345
    5   Smith          Bob            1101 Fig St.   Glendora     CA       91740
    6   Smith          Jane           234 B St.      San Diego    CA       91235
    7
    8
    9   LNAME          FNAME          ADDRESS        CITY         STATE    ZIP
   10                                                Los Angeles
   11                                                                      92122
   12
   13
   14   LNAME          FNAME          ADDRESS        CITY         STATE    ZIP
   15
   16
   17
   18
   19
   20
```

Fig. 14-10. Search for residents for Los Angeles or 92122 zip code area.

(Data Query) option to specify A9..F11 as the criterion range, so the field names and two rows of criteria are included.

You can even combine "and" and "or" type searches if you wish to have three factors in the search. For example, suppose you want a listing of all the Smiths who live in either Los Angeles or San Diego. In this case, you are searching on two fields, LNAME and CITY. However, there are three search criteria involved, Smith, Los Angeles, and San Diego. The Criterion Range capable of finding all the Smiths in either Los Angeles or San Diego would look like Fig. 14-11. In English, this says: "In order to be listed, a person must have the last name Smith and live in Los Angeles, OR have the last name Smith and live in San Diego."

```
A12:                                                                      READY

         A           B            C            D            E      F
  1  LNAME       FNAME        ADDRESS      CITY         STATE  ZIP
  2  Adams       Andy         123 A St.    San Diego    CA     92122
  3  Eggo        Sandy        333 C St.    Los Angeles  CA     91234
  4  Fredrex     Franny       444 J St.    New York     NY     12345
  5  Smith       Bob          1101 Fig St. Glendora     CA     91740
  6  Smith       Jane         234 B St.    San Diego    CA     91235
  7
  8
  9  LNAME       FNAME        ADDRESS      CITY         STATE  ZIP
 10  Smith                                 Los Angeles
 11  Smith                                 San Diego
 12
 13
 14  LNAME       FNAME        ADDRESS      CITY         STATE  ZIP
 15
 16
 17
 18
 19
 20
```

Fig. 14-11. Search for Smiths in Los Angeles or San Diego.

SEARCHING FOR RECORDS WITHIN A RANGE OF VALUES

Sometimes you may need to perform searches on ranges of values. For example, suppose you want a listing of all the people in the 92111 to 92117 zip code area. (e.g., 9211, 92112, 92113, to 92117). You certainly would not want to do all those searches one at a time. Rather, you need to specify a range of values to search for in the Criterion range. The Criterion Range in Fig. 14-12 sets up a search for all people in the desired zip code area.

You can use formulas with the #AND# operator to search for data that falls within some range.

The search criterion, +F2> =92111#AND#F2< =92999, is actually a formula. The cell reference in the formula must refer to the first record of the database. F2 is the first zip code in this database example, so F2 is the cell reference in the formula. When you ask 1-2-3 to Find or Extract, it will test every zip code in the database to see if it fits into the criteria specified by the formula. If the zip code

```
D11:                                                           READY

          A             B            C            D          E       F
 1   LNAME         FNAME        ADDRESS      CITY       STATE   ZIP
 2   Adams         Andy         123 A St.    San Diego  CA      92122
 3   Eggo          Sandy        333 C St.    Los Angeles CA     91234
 4   Fredrex       Franny       444 J St.    New York   NY      12345
 5   Smith         Bob          1101 Fig St. Glendora   CA      91740
 6   Smith         Jane         234 B St.    San Diego  CA      91235
 7
 8
 9                                           ZIP
10                                           +F2>=92111#AND#F2<=92999
11
12
13
```

Fig. 14-12. Search for all people in the desired zip code area.

meets the criterion, it is selected as a match, otherwise, it is ig-
nored.

You have to be careful with specifying ranges of numbers like
this. For example, the criterion +F2>92199#OR#F2<93000 will
match every record on the database. Why? The "or" condition won't
knock any records out of the range. After all, 01234 is less than
92300, and therefore 1-2-3 selects it. The formula says that the zip
code has to be *either* less than 92300 *or* greater than 92199, and so
since only one of the conditions need be true for the or statement
to find a match, this one will match. 01234 will be rejected by the
+F2>92199#AND#F2<93000 formula, however, because even
though it is less than 92300, it is not greater than 92199.

Also, since only one row of the Criterion Range is in use now,
be sure to redefine the Criterion Range as A9..F10.

SEARCHING WITH WILD CARDS

There are a number of symbols that you can use in the Criterion
Range to control the logic of a search in other ways. These symbols
are often called "wild cards," because they can be used to represent any character, just as a wild card in a card game can be
used to act as any other card.

The wild card characters are:

?   **Matches any character.**   A database search for
FNAME = J??N will find
*Joh*n, *Jea*n, and *Joa*n, but
not *Jane*t, or Bob.

*   Matches any group of characters.   A database search for John* will find John, Johnson, and Johnathan, but not UpJohn.

~   Does not match characters.   Finds records that have any group of characters *except* those in the Criterion Range. Therefore, ~John will find Isaac, Betty, Joe, and Andy, but not John.

The ~ also ignores empty cells. That is, a search for ~John (not John) will display everybody except John *and* empty fields.

AUTOMATIC ELIMINATION OF DUPLICATES

In some situations you may wish to see only the unique items of information in a database. For example, you might want to see what unique states are in the mailing list. (In this database, you can see at a glance. But, given a database with 5000 records, you'll need some extra help.)

The /DQU (Data Query Unique) commands let you view the unique values in a field.   The Unique option under the /DQ (Data Query) menu can help with this task. We'll demonstrate with the small MAIL database. Here are the steps:

1. First, erase data from the Output range. Use /RE (Range Erase) to erase A15..F20.

2. Erase any existing criterion by using /RE (Range Erase) to erase the range A10..F11.

3. If you have not set up the input range, use /DQI (Data Query Input) to specify A1..F6 as the Input Range.

4. Select Criterion to specify a criterion range, and enter E9..E10 as the criterion range. (When using Unique, you cannot use the larger Criterion Range with all the field names in it. Furthermore, the cell beneath the field name in the criterion range MUST be blank).

5. Select Output, and specify E14 as the Output Range. (When using Unique, your Output Range should use only the field being analyzed.)

6. Select Unique.

The Output range will display only the names of states in the database. (In this example, CA and NY, as in Fig. 14-13.)

```
E14: [W8] 'STATE                                                    READY

            A            B            C            D           E      F
 1   LNAME        FNAME        ADDRESS      CITY        STATE  ZIP
 2   Adams        Andy         123 A St.    San Diego   CA     92122
 3   Eggo         Sandy        333 C St.    Los Angeles CA     91234
 4   Fredrex      Franny       444 J St.    New York    NY     12345
 5   Smith        Bob          1101 Fig St. Glendora    CA     91740
 6   Smith        Jane         234 B St.    San Diego   CA     91235
 7
 8
 9   LNAME        FNAME        ADDRESS      CITY        STATE  ZIP
10
11
12
13
14   LNAME        FNAME        ADDRESS      CITY        STATE  ZIP
15                                                      NY
16                                                      CA
17
18
19
20
```

Fig. 14-13. Unique states listed in the Output Range.

DELETING RECORDS FROM THE DATABASE

The /DQD (Data Query Delete) commands let you delete from a database all records that meet some criterion.

The procedure for deleting records from the database is similar to all the procedures mentioned above. Suppose the big earthquake finally hits California, and you wish to eliminate all these people from your database. You would merely need to specify CA under the field name STATE in the Criterion Range, and select Delete from the Data Query options. All records that match the criterion are eliminated from the database, and all records below deleted records move up a notch to fill in the blanks left by the deletions. The Delete option does not require an Output Range, because it does not extract any records.

OTHER OPTIONS

The /DQR (Data Query Reset) commands cancel all previous Input, Criterion, and Output Range settings.

You have probably noticed two other options on the /DQ menu: Reset and Quit. The Quit option simply returns you to the 1-2-3 ready mode. The Reset option "undoes" the parameters of the previous search. 1-2-3 always remembers the parameter of the last search, and this is the option you can choose to make it forget. This is useful if you use the F7 function key rather than the /DQ command (though the two are identical). The F7 key will enter the /DQ command and immediately redo the last search.

WHAT HAVE YOU LEARNED?

1. To search, or *query*, a database means to locate records that meet some criterion, such as all Smiths, or all California residents.

2. Queries require an Input Range, Criterion Range, and in some cases, an Output Range.

3. An Input Range consists of the field names and all the fields and records in the database.

4. The Criterion Range consists of all the field names, and criteria to search for.

5. /DQF (Data Query Find) will highlight the first record in a database that matches the search criteria.

6. To terminate the Find mode, you need to press the Escape key.

7. To copy records in a database that meet some criteria, you need to create an Output Range, and use /DQE (Data Query Extract).

8. To perform an "AND" search, place the criteria on the same row in the Criterion range.

9. To perform an "OR" search, stagger the search criteria across two or more rows, and extend the Criterion Range to include all the rows.

10. You can use formulas with the #AND# operator to search for data that falls within some range.

11. The /DQU (Data Query Unique) commands let you view the unique values in a field.

12. The /DQD (Data Query Delete) commands let you delete from a database all records that meet some criterion.

13. The /DQR (Data Query Reset) commands cancel all previous Input, Criterion, and Output Range settings.

QUIZ

1. When specifying an Input Range for a database query, you should:

a. Include all rows and records, but not the field names
b. Include all rows and records, and the field names as well
c. Include only the field names
d. Include all records, but only fields you want to search on

2. Which commands will highlight the first record that matches the query criteria?
a. /DQU (Data Query Unique)
b. /DQR (Data Query Reset)
c. /DQE (Data Query Extract)
d. /DQF (Data Query Find)

3. Which commands will make a copy of all the records that meet the query criteria to an Output Range?
a. /DQU (Data Query Unique)
b. /DQR (Data Query Reset)
c. /DQE (Data Query Extract)
d. /DQF (Data Query Find)

4. What happens if you specify only the row of field names in an Output Range?
a. No records will appear after a query
b. An error occurs and 1-2-3 beeps
c. 1-2-3 treats the Output Range as though it extends to the bottom of the worksheet
d. None of the above

5. To specify an "AND" relationship between two criteria in a Criterion Range, you must:
a. Place the criteria on the same row
b. Place the criteria on separate rows
c. Use an #AND# operator and numeric data only
d. Extend the Criterion range two rows beneath the field names

6. To specify an "OR" relationship between two criteria in a Criterion Range, you must:
a. Place the criteria on the same row
b. Place the criteria on separate rows
c. Use an #OR# operator and numeric data only
d. Extend the Criterion range one row beneath the field names

7. When searching for data that falls within a range of data, such as zip codes in the range 90000–99999, you would most likely use a formula with which operator?
a. #OR#
b. #AND#

c. #NOT#
d. #XOR#

8. If you place the search criterion Sm?th in a criterion range, the query will match all records *except*:
   a. Smith
   b. Smyth
   c. Smitty
   d. Smeth

9. When using /DQU (Date Query Unique) to view unique values in a field, the criterion range:
   a. Can contain all field names
   b. Must contain only the field name of interest with a formula in the cell beneath it.
   c. Must contain only the field name of interest with a blank cell beneath it.
   d. Exactly the same fields as the Input Range.

10. Which key reperforms the last /DQ (Data Query) command?
    a. F6
    b. F7
    c. F9
    d. F10

Chapter 15

"WHAT-IF" TABLES AND STATISTICS

ABOUT THIS CHAPTER

One of the greatest assets of any spreadsheet program is that it allows you to set up a model, financial or otherwise, and experiment with "what if" possibilities. Usually you do this by developing the model, then substituting different values into the model and observing their effects. 1-2-3 has added a whole new twist to the "what if" type of analysis by providing the /DT (Data Table) commands. These commands let us build our model on the worksheet, then 1-2-3 tries out the various "what-if?" questions automatically.

PROJECTING NET INCOME WITH A DATA TABLE 1

Let's look at an example of the Data Table 1 command by determining the net income for a company. For this example, assume that ABC Company has a fixed overhead cost of $300,00 per year, and an additional variable cost of about 50% of gross sales. So the net income for any given amount of sales for ABC Co. can be expressed as: NET INCOME = GROSS SALES − (50% * GROSS SALES) − 300,000. ABC Company would like to find out what their net income for the year will be assuming gross sales of between two and three million dollars, in increments of $100,000. This problem can be solved by setting up a Data Table, as shown in Fig. 15-1.

The Data Table 1 commands perform "what-if" analyses with a single variable.

Notice that in cell B3, we've entered the formula:

$+A3 - 300000 - (.50*A3)$

A3 refers to the cell which contains gross sales, minus 300,000 (for

```
B14:                                                                   READY

             A          B        C        D        E        F        G
   1    Gross     Net
   2    Sales     Income
   3              +A3-300000-(0.5*A3)
   4    $2,000,000
   5    $2,100,000
   6    $2,200,000
   7    $2,300,000
   8    $2,400,000
   9    $2,500,000
  10    $2,600,000
  11    $2,700,000
  12    $2,800,000
  13    $2,900,000
  14    $3,000,000
  15
  16
  17
```

Fig. 15-1. Data table with formula exposed.

fixed costs) and 50% times gross sales. Cells A4 to A14 contain the projected gross sales, two to three million dollars in increments of 100,000. Cell A3 is currently empty. This is the proper format for a data table. That is, the table should look like this:

[BLANK CELL] [FORMULA FOR TEST]
[TEST 1]
[TEST 2]
[TEST 3]
[TEST 4]
etc.

In the example, cell A3 is the blank cell, cells A4 to A14 contain the values to test, and cell B3 contains the test formula for net income. To perform the automated "what if," type in the /DT1 (Data Table 1) command. 1-2-3 will ask for the *table range*. The table range should extend from the blank cell in the table to the bottom right cell in the formula column. So if we were to draw the table range by pointing on the screen, it would look like Fig. 15-2. If we were to type in the table range, it would be A3..B14.

The Input Cell in a Data Table is a blank cell referred to by the table formula.

Next, 1-2-3 will ask for the *Input Cell*. The input cell is the blank one referred to in the formula; in this example, it is cell A3. Fill in the value A3, and press RETURN. And that's all there is to it.

1-2-3 will substitute each of the gross sales figures below the Input Cell into the Input Cell, and will calculate the net income for all 11 gross sales figures. It will display its results in the column to the right of each sales figure, as in Fig. 15-3.

Now review what you (and 1-2-3) have just done. First, you set

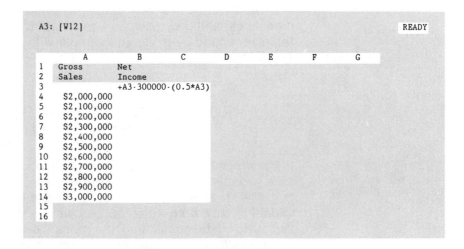

Fig. 15-2. Table range highlighted.

```
A3: [W12]                                                    READY

          A           B          C       D       E       F       G
  1   Gross       Net
  2   Sales       Income
  3               +A3·300000·(0.5*A3)
  4   $2,000,000
  5   $2,100,000
  6   $2,200,000
  7   $2,300,000
  8   $2,400,000
  9   $2,500,000
 10   $2,600,000
 11   $2,700,000
 12   $2,800,000
 13   $2,900,000
 14   $3,000,000
 15
 16
```

Fig. 15-2. Table range highlighted.

```
A3: [W12]                                                    READY

          A           B          C       D       E       F       G
  1   Gross       Net
  2   Sales       Income
  3               ($300,000)
  4   $2,000,000    $700,000
  5   $2,100,000    $750,000
  6   $2,200,000    $800,000
  7   $2,300,000    $850,000
  8   $2,400,000    $900,000
  9   $2,500,000    $950,000
 10   $2,600,000  $1,000,000
 11   $2,700,000  $1,050,000
 12   $2,800,000  $1,100,000
 13   $2,900,000  $1,150,000
 14   $3,000,000  $1,200,000
 15
 16
```

Fig. 15-3. Completed "what-if" table.

up a data table by providing a column of "what if" data below a blank cell. Then, you created a column for calculating the "what ifs" next to the blank cell. Next, you selected the /DT1 command, and showed 1-2-3 where the data table was on the screen, and where the Input cell was. 1-2-3 then took over, and substituted 2,000,000 into the input cell, calculated the net income, and placed it next to the figure 2,000,000. Then it substituted the value 2,000,000, calculated the net income, and placed it in the cell to the right of the figure 2,100,000, and so forth, until it reached the last value, 3,000,000 in the left column of the data table.

This is actually a very simple example of the Data Table command's capabilities. You can appreciate the true power of the data table command by using an example with two variables /DT2 (Data Table 2) command.

PROJECTING NET INCOME WITH TWO VARIABLES

Data Table 2 lets you perform "what-if" analyses with two variables.

In the preceding example, you considered the 50% of cost of sales as a variable cost; however, you treated it as a constant. ABC Co. might wish to test the various gross sales with a variety of cost variables, say from 40 to 55 percent. In this case, there are two "what ifs" to be considered, the gross sales and the percent of cost of sales. When two "what ifs" are involved in an equation, you need to use the /DT2 (Data Table 2) command. The rules here are a little different.

Fig. 15-4 shows the basic skeleton for analyzing the effects of gross sales and the variable cost of sales percentage figure in a data table.

```
B4: (C0)                                                          READY

              A              B          C          D          E
 1   Sales:                        Percent:
 2
 3   +B1-300000-(D1*B1)    40.00%     45.00%     50.00%     55.00%
 4            $2,000,000
 5            $2,100,000
 6            $2,200,000
 7            $2,300,000
 8            $2,400,000
 9            $2,500,000
10            $2,600,000
11            $2,700,000
12            $2,800,000
13            $2,900,000
14            $3,000,000
15
16
```

Fig. 15-4. Data Table 2 with formula exposed.

As before, the assumed gross sales figures are listed down the lefthand column of the data table. The various percentage figures for the test are in the top row. The /DT2 command requires that the formula be in the upper-left corner of the table. In this example, the formula in cell A3 is:

$$+ B1 - 300,000 - (D*B1)$$

The data table is set up such that each gross sales amount is substituted into cell B1, and each of the percentage figures is substituted into cell D1. So the formula still calculates net income from gross sales minus the $300,000 fixed cost and minus the variable cost figure. The structure of the table looks like this:

```
                        [INPUT CELL]              [INPUT CELL]
         [FORMULA]      [TEST 1]     [TEST2]      [TEST 3]     [TEST 4] etc. . .
         [TEST 1]
         [TEST 2]
         [TEST 3]
         [TEST 4]
         etc. . .
```

The two Input cells can be placed anywhere in the worksheet, but the table itself must adhere to this structure.

You're ready to have 1-2-3 answer the many "what ifs." Type in the command /DT2 (Data Table 2). 1-2-3 asks for the table range. The table range must extend from the upper left corner of the table (the one with the formula in it) to the lower right corner of the table. So in this example, the range must be defined as cells A3..E14, as shown in Fig. 15-5.

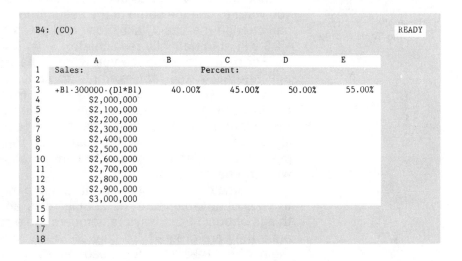

Fig. 15-5. Table range highlighted.

In Data Table 2. Input Cell 1 refers to column values, and Input Cell 2 refers to row values.

1-2-3 will also ask for the Input Cells. These are the ones specified in the formula, cells B1 and D1. Note that Input Cell 1 is for the column values, and Input Cell 2 is for the row values.

Once you specify the Input Cells, press RETURN, and 1-2-3 will calculate the net income gross sales amount and each percentage figure, as shown in Fig. 15-6.

```
B1:                                                                    READY

            A           B           C           D           E
 1   Sales:                      Percent:
 2
 3           ($300,000)     40.00%      45.00%      50.00%      55.00%
 4         $2,000,000    $900,000    $800,000    $700,000    $600,000
 5         $2,100,000    $960,000    $855,000    $750,000    $645,000
 6         $2,200,000  $1,020,000    $910,000    $800,000    $690,000
 7         $2,300,000  $1,080,000    $965,000    $850,000    $735,000
 8         $2,400,000  $1,140,000  $1,020,000    $900,000    $780,000
 9         $2,500,000  $1,200,000  $1,075,000    $950,000    $825,000
10         $2,600,000  $1,260,000  $1,130,000  $1,000,000    $870,000
11         $2,700,000  $1,320,000  $1,185,000  $1,050,000    $915,000
12         $2,800,000  $1,380,000  $1,240,000  $1,100,000    $960,000
13         $2,900,000  $1,440,000  $1,295,000  $1,150,000  $1,005,000
14         $3,000,000  $1,500,000  $1,350,000  $1,200,000  $1,050,000
15
16
```

Fig. 15-6. Completed Data Table 2 analysis.

ADJUSTING THE DATA TABLE

After modifying assumptions in a data table, you can reperform the analysis by pressing the Table (F8) key.

Once you have created and calculated a data table, 1-2-3 remembers the table range and Input Cell(s) for that data table. So if you want to change some of the assumptions in the data table, you can change the basic "skeleton" and press the F8 (Table) key and 1-2-3 will automatically recalculate.

For example, suppose you want to narrow down the percentage figures in the last example to 48%, 50%, 52%, and 54%. First of all, you need to get back to the Ready mode by Quitting the Data menu. From there, position the cell pointer to each of the existing percentage figures, and type in the new values, as shown in Fig. 15-7. Then, to recalculate the net incomes, simply press the F8 (Table) key, and the entire table will be recalculated with the new values.

In some cases, you may want to make more extensive changes to your data table, such as adding rows and columns or moving things about. 1-2-3 always remembers table ranges and Input Cells once they are created. To change these, you can simply redefine them when 1-2-3 asks for these values in future data table commands. You can also use the Reset option from the /DT menus to make 1-2-3 "forget" previous data table settings.

DATABASE STATISTICS

The database statistical functions perform statistical analyses on data that meet some criterion.

The database statistical commands are similar to the statistics functions in 1-2-3 (@VAR, @STD, @AVG, etc.). However, they include additional capabilities for using database Input and Criterion ranges. The database statistical functions are:

```
B3: (P2) 0.48                                                          READY

              A            B            C           D            E
1   Sales:                            Percent:
2
3            ($300,000)     48.00%      50.00%       52.00%       54.00%
4          $2,000,000    $900,000    $800,000     $700,000     $600,000
5          $2,100,000    $960,000    $855,000     $750,000     $645,000
6          $2,200,000  $1,020,000    $910,000     $800,000     $690,000
7          $2,300,000  $1,080,000    $965,000     $850,000     $735,000
8          $2,400,000  $1,140,000  $1,020,000     $900,000     $780,000
9          $2,500,000  $1,200,000  $1,075,000     $950,000     $825,000
10         $2,600,000  $1,260,000  $1,130,000   $1,000,000     $870,000
11         $2,700,000  $1,320,000  $1,185,000   $1,050,000     $915,000
12         $2,800,000  $1,380,000  $1,240,000   $1,100,000     $960,000
13         $2,900,000  $1,440,000  $1,295,000   $1,150,000   $1,005,000
14         $3,000,000  $1,500,000  $1,350,000   $1,200,000   $1,050,000
15
16
```

Fig. 15-7. Modified Data Table 2.

@ **DAVG(input,offset,criterion)**	Database Average
@ **DCOUNT(input,offset,criterion)**	Database Count of Items
@ **DMAX(input,offset,criterion)**	Highest Number in Database
@ **DMIN(input,offset,criterion)**	Lowest Number in Database
@ **DSTD(input,offset,criterion)**	Database Standard Deviation
@ **DSUM(input,offset,criterion)**	Database Sum
@ **DVAR(input,offset,criterion)**	Database Variance

The Input and Criterion arguments are ranges similar to those used with the /DQ (Data Query) commands. The Offset argument specifies the field on which to perform the calculations. If the offset is zero, 1-2-3 calculates statistics on the first field. If the offset is 1, calculations are performed on the second field, and so forth.

Fig. 15-8. shows a partial list of individuals' ages and their annual incomes (the actual list extends below the bottom of the worksheet window to row 99).

Cells E5 and E6 set up the Criterion range. Cell E5 contains the label 'Age. Cell E6 contains the formula:

A4>39#AND#A4<50

which makes the criteria for performing the statistics all people between the ages of 40 and 49 (inclusive). The resulting statistics show the mean, highest, and lowest incomes for individuals in this age group. The count indicates the number of persons in the group who fit this criterion. The variance and standard deviation (SD) are also calculated. Looking at this same worksheet with the formulas displayed in text format, you see the formulas displayed in Fig. 15-9.

Notice that for each formula, the first argument is always the range A3..B99. This is the Input Range for this database (assuming the rows extend down to 99). The second argument is always 1, which is the offset. That is, the column of interest (income) is one column to the right of the age range. The third argument, E5..E6, represents the Criterion Range, where the formula +A4>39#AND#A4<50 is displayed under the field name Age.

If you changed the criterion formula to:

+A4>29#AND#A4<40

then 1-2-3 would calculate the statistics on incomes in the age range of 30 to 39 (inclusive). Changing the formula into something simple, like +A4>0, would provide statistics for all age ranges (at least, everyone over the age of zero!).

FREQUENCY DISTRIBUTIONS

The /DD (Data Distribution) commands calculate frequency distribution in a database.

Another handy statistic that 1-2-3 provides is a *frequency distribution*, a table that displays how many items in a database fit into various categories. To use this capability, you first need to set up a *bin range*. Fig. 15-10 shows the age and salary data and a bin range. The bin range is in cells D5..D10, and contains the ages 20, 30, 40, 50, 60, and 70. These numbers must have a range of blank cells immediately to the right for the 1-2-3 to fill in, and an extra blank cell at the bottom. The values must be in ascending order.

After providing a bin range, type in the /DD (Data Distribution) command. 1-2-3 will request that you:

Enter Values range:

In this worksheet, the values are in the range A4..A99. Type that in, and 1-2-3 will ask that you:

Enter Bin range:

The bin range in this example extends from cell D5 to D10. Type in D5..D10 and press RETURN. 1-2-3 will fill in the frequency distribution, as in Fig. 15-11 (assuming the data extends down to about row 99).

The frequency distribution shows that nobody in the group is 20 years old or less. Sixteen individuals are in the 21 to 30 age group.

Thirty-eight individuals fall in the 31 to 40 age range, 24 in the 41 to 50 range, 13 in the 51 to 60 age group, and 8 in the 61 to 70 age group. Zero individuals were over 70.

A quick and easy way to fill in the values in a bin range is to use the Data Fill command. Position the cell pointer to the top of the bin range. Type in the /DF (Data Fill) command. 1-2-3 requests:

Enter Fill range:

Type in the range. In the example in Fig. 15-11, D5 to D10. 1-2-3 asks:

Start: 0

put in the lowest value, 20 in the example in Fig. 15-11. 1-2-3 requests:

Step: 1

The step value is 10 in the example, so type in 10 and press RETURN. 1-2-3 then asks:

Stop: 8192

Type in the highest value, 70 in this example. Press RETURN, and 1-2-3 fills the cells in the specified range with the appropriate values. This is also useful for your other applications, such as filling in a range of years (i.e., 1984 to 1994), or for numbering records in a database.

REGRESSION ANALYSIS

Regression analysis lets you analyze the relationship between a dependent variable and up to 16 independent variables.

Regression analysis calculates the relationship between a dependent variable and up to 16 independent variables. You can also create a line graph showing the best-fitting curve of the relationship. In this example, you'll see how well two interest rates (Prime and Triple-A Bonds) predict inflation. Inflation will be the dependent (Y) variable. The Prime and Triple-A rates will be the independent variables (X1 and X2).

The first step is to enter the known data into the worksheet. You can use any portion of the worksheet you like. In Fig. 15-12, the data is entered in the range B3..D10.

Once the data is entered, follow these steps to calculate the regression.

1. Type /DR (Data Regression).

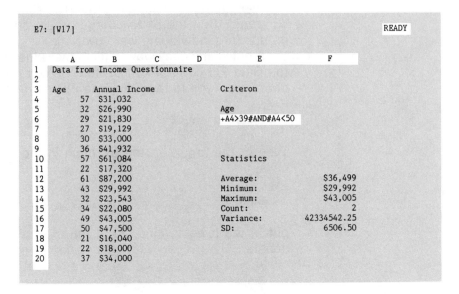

Fig. 15-8. Database analysis with criterion formula exposed.

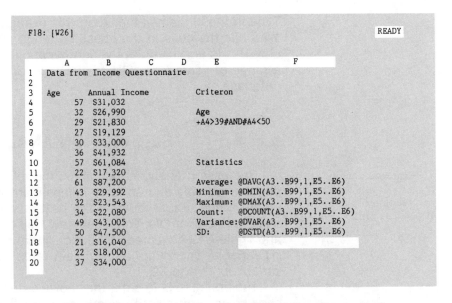

Fig. 15-9. Database analysis with statistical formulas exposed.

2. Select X-Range, and specify the range of the independent
   variable(s) (C3..D10 in this example).

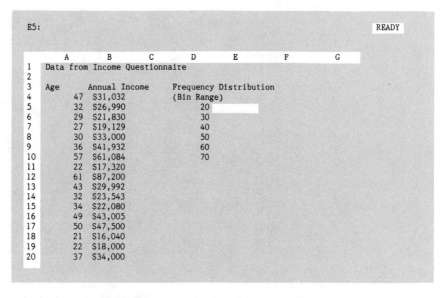

Fig. 15-10. Age and salary data and a bin range.

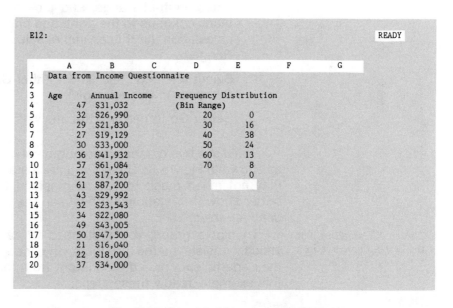

Fig. 15-11. Completed frequency distribution.

3. Select Y-Range, and specify the dependent variable (B3..B10 in this example).

```
A1:                                                                   READY

        A       B       C       D       E       F       G       H
  1                   Prime   Triple-A
  2             Inflation Rate   Bonds
  3              2.30%   6.58%   6.12%           0.131431 -0.11394 0.058513
  4             -3.00%   3.50%   4.55%           0.069910 -0.08471 0.026223
  5             16.20%   1.50%   2.53%           0.029961 -0.04710 0.023883
  6             -0.50%   3.05%   2.90%           0.060921 -0.05399 0.047955
  7              0.70%   4.50%   4.35%           0.089884 -0.08099 0.049921
  8             12.20%  10.80%   8.57%           0.215723 -0.15956 0.097190
  9             13.00%  12.67%  10.05%           0.253075 -0.18711 0.106987
 10              3.90%  11.00%  12.00%           0.219718 -0.22342 0.037324
 11              (Y)    (X1)    (X2)
 12                  Regression Output:
 13            Constant              0.041027
 14            Std Err of Y Est      0.076541
 15            R Squared             0.185496
 16            No. of Observations          8
 17            Degrees of Freedom           5
 18
 19            X Coefficient(s)  1.997439 -1.86184
 20            Std Err of Coef.  2.191800 2.683530
```

Fig. 15-12. Regression analysis.

4. Select Output Range, and pick a cell that has plenty of blank columns to the right, and blank rows beneath, for the calculation. (In this example, select cell B12 as the Output Range.)

5. Select Intercept, and select either Compute or Zero (select Compute in this example).

6. Select Go to perform the analysis.

You'll see lots of labels and numbers appear staring at cell B12, as shown in Fig. 15-12. Unless you are a statistician, these numbers may not mean much to you. A graph of this data, however, will better show the relationship between the dependent and independent variables.

Use an XY graph to plot the best-fitting curve in a regression analysis.

To plot a graph, you first need to calculate the Y-Estimate, which consists of the products, the independent variables, and their coefficients plus the constant from the regression output. In this example, follow these steps:

1. Put the formula:

   +$D$19*C3

   into cell F3. (The X1 coefficient times the first X1 variable).

2. Put the formula:

+ $E$19 * D3

into cell G3 (The X2 coefficient times the first X2 variable).

3. Put the formula:

   + F3 + G3 + $E$13

   into cell H3. This is the sum of columns E and F plus the constant from the regression output.

4. Use /C (Copy) to copy the formulas FROM F3..H3 TO F4..H10. All the calculations will fill in, as in Fig. 15-12.

Now you need to create an XY graph of the new data. Here are the exact steps:

1. Call up the Graph menu (/G).

2. Type T to select the Type option, and XY as the type of graph.

3. Select X, and assign the range H3..H10 as the X-Range.

4. Select A, and assign H3..H10 as the A-Range.

5. Select B, and assign B3..B10 as the B-Range.

6. Select Options Legend and enter:

   Y Estimate

   as the A-Legend. Enter:

   Observed

   as the B-Legend.

7. Select Format, and give the A range both lines and symbols. Give the B range symbols only. Then Quit the Format submenu.

8. Select TF (Titles First) and type in a title such as REGRESSION ANALYSIS. Then Quit the Options submenu.

9. Select V to view the graph. You'll see the graph shown as in Fig. 15-13.

The line in the graph represents the best-fitting curve of the relationship among the variables. The + symbols represent the observed values (actual inflation). As the graph demonstrates, there is a tendency for inflation to increase as the Prime and Bond rates increase.

To try other values, simply plug the new data into the existing raw data (cells B3..B10) as required. Then, select /DRG (Data Range Go) to recalculate the regression analysis, and press the GRAPH key (F10) to observe the effects of the changes on the graph.

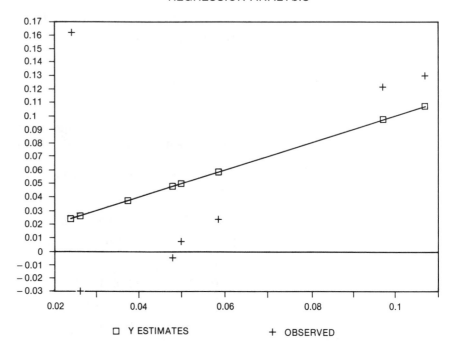

REGRESSION ANALYSIS

□ Y ESTIMATES   + OBSERVED

Fig. 15-13. An XY graph of a regression analysis.

Of course, don't forget to save the worksheet and graph using the usual /FS (File Save) options.

MATRIX INVERSION AND MULTIPLICATION

The /DM (Data Matrix) commands let you invert and multiply matrices.

Some advanced mathematical and statistical calculations require matrix multiplication and inversion. 1-2-3 offers both on ranges up to 90 columns wide, and 90 rows long. In both cases, the ranges must be square (not rectangular).

To invert a matrix, enter the matrix anywhere on the worksheet. Type /DMI (Data Matrix Invert), and highlight the range of values to invert (A1..C3 in Fig. 15-14). Then, when requested, select an output range. A single cell will do, so long as there are enough blank columns to the right, and blank rows beneath, to accommodate the inverted matrix. In Fig. 15-14, cell E1 was used as the Output Range. The inverted matrix appears in the range E1..G3.

To multiply two matrices, type in the two matrices as in the example shown in Fig. 15-15 (First Matrix and Second Matrix). Select /DMM (Data Matrix Multiply). When requested, highlight the first range to multiply (A1..C3 in the example). Press RETURN and

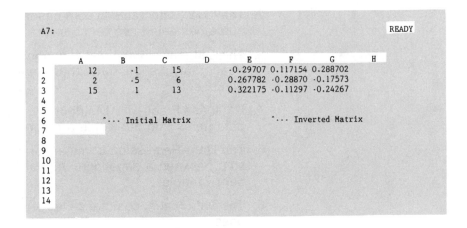

Fig. 15-14. An inverted matrix in E1..G3.

```
A14:                                                              READY

          A        B        C        D        E        F        G        H
 1       12       -1       15
 2        2       -5        6                 <-- First matrix
 3       15        1       13
 4
 5        9        1       19
 6        5        5       -3                 <-- Second matrix
 7       13       -9       -1
 8
 9
10      298     -128      216
11       71      -77       47                 <-- Multiplied matrices
12      309      -97      269
13
14
15
16
```

Fig. 15-15. Multiplied matrices.

enter the second range to multiply (A5..C7 in the example). Press RETURN. Select an Output Range when requested (cell A10 in the example). The multiplied matrix will appear starting at the output range as in the figure.

WHAT HAVE YOU LEARNED?

1. The /DT1 (Data Table 1) commands let you project possible outcomes using a single variable.

2. The /DT2 (Data Table 2) commands let you project possible outcomes using two variables.

3. The Database Statistical functions let you perform statistical analyses on data that match some criteria in a database.

4. Database Frequency Distributions display the frequency of data items that fall within a range of values.

5. The Data Regression commands let you view the relationship between a dependent variable and up to 16 independent variables.

6. The Data Matrix commands let you invert and multiply matrices.

QUIZ

1. To perform a "what-if" analysis with a single variable, you would use:
   a. /DT1 (Data Table 1)
   b. /DT2 (Data Table 2)
   c. /DR (Data Regression)
   d. /DD (Data Distribution)

2. To perform a "what-if" analysis with two variables, you would use:
   a. /DT1 (Data Table 1)
   b. /DT2 (Data Table 2)
   c. /DR (Data Regression)
   d. /DD (Data Distribution)

3. When specifying Input Cells with /DT2 (Data Table 2), Input Cell 1 is for:
   a. Column values
   b. Row values
   c. Range values
   d. The projection formula

4. If you change a few assumptions in a data table, you can quickly recalculate the table using which key?
   a. F6
   b. F8
   c. F10
   d. F12

5. In the database statistical formula @DAVG (A3..B99,1,E5..E6), 1-2-3 will analyze data in which column?
   a. Column A

b. Column B
c. Column C
d. Column D

6. In the database statistical formula @DAVG (A3..B10,1,K5..K6), the Criterion Range is located where?
a. A3..B10
b. A1..A1
c. K5..K6
d. Can't determine from this formula.

7. The /DD (Data Distribution) commands require a Bin Range with which of the following attributes:
a. Values in ascending order
b. Blank cells to the right
c. A blank cell beneath
d. All of the above

8. In a Data Regression, you specify the Y-Range as the:
a. Independent variable
b. Dependent variables
c. Y intercept
d. Correlation Coefficient

9. To plot the best-fitting curve from a regression analysis, you use which type of graph?
a. Line
b. Bar
c. Stacked-Bar
d. XY

10. 1-2-3 can invert a matrix with a maximum of how many columns and rows?
a. 16
b. 32
c. 64
d. 90

MACROS

Chapter 16

MACROS

ABOUT THIS CHAPTER

1-2-3 provides the capability to create macros, collections of keystrokes which can be executed by typing two keys. For example, suppose you have a spreadsheet with five bar graphs. Furthermore, you often try out various "what-if" scenarios with the worksheet, and view the various graphs by typing in the many necessary commands to do so. An alternative to this procedure would be to store all the keystrokes necessary to view all five graphs in a macro. Then, each time you want to view the graphs, you can just press a couple of keys and 1-2-3 will automatically display all five graphs, one at a time, on the screen, and return to the ready mode so you can try out some new assumptions in the worksheet.

MACRO KEYSTROKES

A macro is a collection of keystrokes that can be played back with a couple of keystrokes.

Most commands that you put into a macro appear exactly in the macro as they do typed on the screen. For example, to reformat the worksheet to a global column width of three spaces, you would type in the command /WGC3 (Worksheet Global Column-Width 3), and press the RETURN key. This same series of commands, made into a macro, as in Fig. 16-1 would look like this:

'/WGC3~

The tilde (~) represents the RETURN key in a macro.

The leading apostrophe is a label prefix. All macros must be labels, and therefore the apostrophe is required. The command to set the column widths appears exactly as it would be typed,

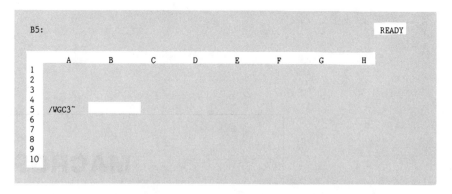

Fig. 16-1. Small macro on the worksheet.

/WGC3. The tilde at the end of the macro is the macro symbol for "Press the RETURN key."

Several keystrokes are represented by symbols in macros. Keystrokes for moving the cell pointer about the worksheet are listed below:

Macro Symbol	Keystroke Meaning
~	Enter, or RETURN, key
{UP}	Up-arrow
{DOWN}	Down-arrow
{LEFT}	Left-arrow
{RIGHT}	Right-arrow
{HOME}	Position cell pointer to home position
{GoTo}	GoTo a cell (F5)
{PgUp}	Page up
{PgDn}	Page down
{Window}	Change window on split screen (F6)
{End}	End key

There are several other macro symbols that provide for other worksheet tasks. These are:

Macro Symbol	Keystroke Meaning
{Del}	Delete Key
{Edit}	Edit key (F2)

{**Abs**}	Absolute Reference key (F4)
{**Table**}	Recalculate a data table (F8)
{**Graph**}	Redisplay a graph
{**Esc**}	Escape key
{**Bs**}	Backspace key
{**Name**}	Display named ranges (F3)
{**Query**}	Perform database query (F7)
{**Calc**}	Recalculate (F9)

In addition, you can use a special symbol to interrupt the execution of a macro, and wait for the user (whomever happens to be sitting at the keyboard while the macro is running) to respond to a prompt. This symbol is the question mark:

| **Macro Symbol** | **Keystroke Meaning** |
| {?} | Pause for input from the user, wait for a press on the RETURN key. |

We'll soon see how this macro symbol can come in handy.

CREATING MACROS

There are three steps to creating and using a macro: (1) Type the macro into an out-of-the-way cell, (2) Name the macro, and (3) Execute the macro. Here is an example using the macro to automatically set all column widths to 3:

1. The series of keystrokes necessary to set the global column width to three spaces is /WGC3 followed by a press on the RETURN key (the ~ macro symbol). In this example, type the macro:

   '/WGC3~

   into cell A5, then press RETURN. Remember to include the apostrophe label prefix as shown.

You can use /RNC (Range Name Create) to assign a name to a macro.

2. Name the macro using the /RNC (Range Name Create) command. Macro names must begin with the backslash character, and have only one letter as their name. In this example, type in /RNC. 1-2-3 will ask that you:

   Enter name:

Type in \M and press RETURN. You can use any other letter of the alphabet for the name, we selected M at random. 1-2-3 next asks:

Enter range: A5..A5

A5 is the macro cell, so just press RETURN.

To invoke a macro, hold down the Alt key and type the letter name of the macro.

3. To invoke the macro, hold down the Alt key (lower left on the keyboard) and press M. All of the keystrokes in the macro are executed, and the worksheet is immediately formatted to column widths of three spaces, as in Fig. 16-2.

Fig. 16-2. Column width globally reduced to three spaces.

This macro is quite simple. Macros can be as large as you like, and can be spread down several rows. For example, here is a long macro to present a graphics slide show:

**'/GNU ~ ~ ~ {RIGHT} ~ ~ ~ {RIGHT}{RIGHT} ~ ~ ~ {RIGHT}{RIGHT}
{RIGHT} ~**

This macro can be made a little more readable by breaking into several separate lines of text, as below:

**'/GNU ~
~ ~ {RIGHT} ~
~ ~ {RIGHT}{RIGHT} ~
~ ~ {RIGHT}{RIGHT}{RIGHT} ~**

When you break up a single macro into several separate lines like this, be sure that you do not leave any blank rows between lines in the macro. You will now have a chance to create a larger macro that covers a few lines.

A GRAPHICS SLIDE SHOW

In this section you'll develop a macro to display a graphics slide show. You'll use the ABCGraph worksheet with three named graphs that have been used in several chapters now. If you have the worksheet available, load it with the usual /FR (File Retrieve) commands. (Don't forget to save the current worksheet first, if one is on your screen.)

The macro will be put in an out-of-the-way cell so it does not appear with the data on the worksheet. Also, a somewhat new technique will be used for naming the macro. Here are the steps:

1. Press GOTO (F5) and enter A21 as the cell to move to. Press RETURN.

2. Type the macro name '\G into cell A21.

3. Place the macro in cells B21..B24 as shown below (the label prefixes will not appear on the screen):

	A	B	C
20			
21	'\G	'/GNU ~	
22		NU{RIGHT} ~	
23		NU{RIGHT}{RIGHT} ~	
24		Q	

4. To name the macro, move the cell pointer to cell A21, type in /RNLR (Range Name Labels Right), and specify A21 as the range label. This command assigns the name \G to the cell immediately to the right (B21).

You can also use /RNLR (Range Name Labels Right) to name macros.

5. For the finishing touch, move the cell pointer to cell A16 and type the instructions:

[Type Alt-G for Graphics Slide Show]

The macro is now complete. To try it out, press the Home key to get back into the data area, then type Alt-G. You should see a graph appear. Press any key to remove the graph, and the next graph will appear. Press any key again to view the third graph, then any key once again to return to the worksheet READY mode. (If the macro doesn't work, check to make sure your ABCGraph worksheet has the three named graphs you developed back in Chapter 10).

The steps that each line in the macro perform are summarized below:

/GNU~   Selects Graph Name Use from the main menu, and the first named graph. The graph is displayed.

NU{RIGHT} ~	Selects Name Use from the Graph menu, and the second named graph (the next named graph to the right).
NU{RIGHT}{RIGHT} ~	Selects Name Use from the Graph menu, and the third named graph, displaying the graph.
Q	Quits the Graph menu.

You can easily extend the macro to present as many named graphs as there are in the worksheet. For example, the line:

NU{RIGHT}{RIGHT}{RIGHT} ~

(or the equivalent NU{RIGHT 3}) will display a fourth graph, and so on. Remember to save the worksheet after creating and testing the macro.

YEAR-TO-DATE ACCUMULATOR

Year-to-date accumulations in electronic worksheets often present a problem. This is because of the *circular reference* issue. A year-to-date accumulation, for example, would have to be the sum of the present year-to-date value (itself), plus the current month-to-date value. Whenever a formula refers to itself, as the year-to-date value does in this example, we say that it performs a circular reference. The problem is that the circular reference grows enormously, because every time a new value is added to the worksheet, all the circular references reaccumulate, even before they should, which usually makes the year-to-date value grow at an inaccurate and rapid rate.

The problem can be solved by making sure that the accumulation procedure only occurs once a month. A macro can take care of this quite well. Observe the worksheet in Fig. 16-3. It presents a simple income statement for a single month. With data filled in, the worksheet might look more like Fig. 16-4.

For the first month, January, the year-to-date values are identical to the month-to-date values. You could just copy them over with the Copy command, but in this example you want to create a macro that can provide a year-to-date update at the end of each month. So, you will use a temporary data file to store the values in the month-to-date column, and then add them to the year-to-date values. For the first month, this must be performed manually. Here are the instructions to do so:

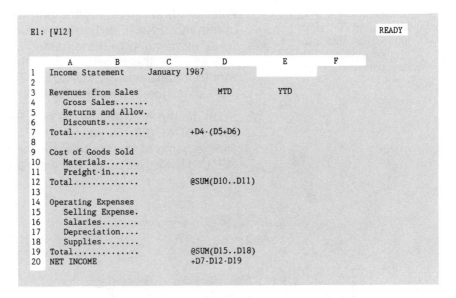

```
E1: [W12]                                                      READY

          A        B         C          D          E         F
 1   Income Statement    January 1987
 2
 3   Revenues from Sales                    MTD        YTD
 4      Gross Sales.......
 5      Returns and Allow.
 6      Discounts........
 7   Total...............            +D4-(D5+D6)
 8
 9   Cost of Goods Sold
10      Materials.......
11      Freight-in......
12   Total.............            @SUM(D10..D11)
13
14   Operating Expenses
15      Selling Expense.
16      Salaries........
17      Depreciation....
18      Supplies........
19   Total.............            @SUM(D15..D18)
20   NET INCOME                    +D7-D12-D19
```

Fig. 16-3. Sample income statement worksheet.

```
E4: (,2) [W12]                                                 READY

          A        B         C          D          E         F
 1   Income Statement    January 1987
 2
 3   Revenues from Sales                    MTD        YTD
 4      Gross Sales.......           $12,000
 5      Returns and Allow.             $500
 6      Discounts........              $750
 7   Total...............           $10,750
 8
 9   Cost of Goods Sold
10      Materials.......            $1,000
11      Freight-in......              $250
12   Total.............             $1,250
13
14   Operating Expenses
15      Selling Expense.            $1,400
16      Salaries........            $2,500
17      Depreciation....              $250
18      Supplies........              $300
19   Total.............             $4,450
20   NET INCOME                     $5,050
```

Fig. 16-4. Income statement with January data.

You can use the /FX (File Xtract) and /FC (File Combine) commands to build macros that accumulate worksheets.

1. After the first month's data is in the worksheet, type in the command /FXV (File Extract Values), and when 1-2-3 asks for a file name, give it the name TEMP (for temporary). 1-2-3 will ask for the range, and in this example it is all the month-to-date values, D4..D20. This will create a small worksheet file called TEMP.WKS.

2. Position the cell pointer to cell E4, and type in the command /FCAE (File Combine Add Entire file). When 1-2-3 asks for the name of the file to combine, type in TEMP and press RETURN. At that point, the worksheet looks like Fig. 16-5.

```
F4:                                                                      READY

           A          B          C          D          E          F
 1  Income Statement        January 1987
 2
 3  Revenues from Sales                        MTD        YTD
 4     Gross Sales.......                    $12,000    $12,000
 5     Returns and Allow.                      $500       $500
 6     Discounts.........                      $750       $750
 7  Total...............                     $10,750    $10,750
 8
 9  Cost of Goods Sold
10     Materials.......                       $1,000     $1,000
11     Freight-in......                         $250       $250
12  Total.............                        $1,250     $1,250
13
14  Operating Expenses
15     Selling Expense.                       $1,400     $1,400
16     Salaries........                       $2,500     $2,500
17     Depreciation....                         $250       $250
18     Supplies.......                          $300       $300
19  Total.............                        $4,450     $4,450
20  NET INCOME                                $5,050     $5,050
```

Fig. 16-5. Income statement after first accumulation.

Once the first month is done, a macro can handle future year-to-date accumulations. The macro can be stored anywhere on the worksheet, and should look like this:

```
{GOTO}D4~
/FXVTEMP~D4..D20~R
{RIGHT}
/FCAETEMP~
```

Once the macro is typed in, use /RNC to give it a name (such as \Y). At the end of each month, typing Alt-Y will automatically update the year-to-date values based upon the current month's data. Let's examine the macro more carefully.

{GOTO}D4~	This step positions the cell pointer to the top of the MTD column.
/FXVTEMP~D4..D20~R	This step selects the File eXtract Values command, names the extraction file TEMP, specifies the range of the month-to-date values (D4..D20), and replaces the existing TEMP file (last month's current values) with the current month's values.
{RIGHT}	This step moves the cell pointer over to the top of the year-to-date column.
/FCAETEMP~	This step selects the File Combine Add Entire file command, and names TEMP as the file to combine. The current month's values will be added to the existing year-to-date values.

In February, you will add some new month-to-date figures. These will not directly affect the present year-to-date values. Fig. 16-6 shows February's income statement prior to performing the accumulation procedure:

F20:   READY

	A B	C	D	E	F
1	Income Statement		February 1987		
2					
3	Revenues from Sales		MTD	YTD	
4	Gross Sales.......		$15,000	$12,000	
5	Returns and Allow.		$700	$500	
6	Discounts........		$650	$750	
7	Total..............		$13,650	$10,750	
8					
9	Cost of Goods Sold				
10	Materials.......		$900	$1,000	
11	Freight-in......		$175	$250	
12	Total.............		$1,075	$1,250	
13					
14	Operating Expenses				
15	Selling Expense.		$1,600	$1,400	
16	Salaries........		$3,000	$2,500	
17	Depreciation....		$230	$250	
18	Supplies........		$400	$300	
19	Total.............		$5,230	$4,450	
20	NET INCOME		$7,345	$5,050	

Fig. 16-6. Income statement with February data.

Now, to accumulate the year-to-date values, just type Alt-Y (the alt key followed by the name of the macro). The macro will send the month-to-date values to the file named TEMP, then add these to the year-to-date column on the worksheet. The result is displayed in Fig. 16-7.

```
F4:                                                              READY

           A        B       C        D         E        F
   1   Income Statement              February 1987
   2
   3   Revenues from Sales                     MTD      YTD
   4      Gross Sales.......              $15,000   $27,000
   5      Returns and Allow.                $700    $1,200
   6      Discounts........                 $650    $1,400
   7   Total...............             $13,650   $24,400
   8
   9   Cost of Goods Sold
  10      Materials.......                 $900    $1,900
  11      Freight-in......                 $175      $425
  12   Total.............              $1,075    $2,325
  13
  14   Operating Expenses
  15      Selling Expense.              $1,600    $3,000
  16      Salaries........              $3,000    $5,500
  17      Depreciation....                $230      $480
  18      Supplies........                $400      $700
  19   Total.............              $5,230    $9,680
  20   NET INCOME                      $7,345   $12,395
```

Fig. 16-7. Income statement after first accumulation.

You must make sure that you only request the updating procedure once a month, or the year-to-date values will increase inappropriately during a single month. For each new month, just type in the current amounts, double check for accuracy, then perform the update using the Alt-Y macro.

BUILDING A MACRO LIBRARY

You can place up to 27 macros in a single worksheet, using the letters A–Z as macro names. Zero (\0) is also a valid macro name, but is a special auto-execute macro, which will be discussed shortly. When developing macro libraries, it's a good idea to use the /RNLR (Range Name Labels Right) options for naming the macros, so you can see the macro names at a glance, and also so that you can name several macros at a time.

For your sample macro library, you will add three macros to the Ten Year Projection worksheet developed back in Chapter 9. If you have that worksheet available, use /FR (File Retrieve) to bring it to the screen.

Macro to Split the Screen

The first macro you will develop will quickly split the screen in two and position the cell pointer for "what-if" analyses. To put the macro in the TenYear worksheet, follow these steps:

1. Move the cell pointer to cell A30, and enter the macro name' \ S into that cell.

2. Enter the macro itself in the range B30..B32 as shown below:

	A	B	C	D
29				
30	\S	{HOME}{GOTO}D1 ~ /WWV{WINDOW}		
31		{GOTO}K5 ~ {WINDOW}		
32		{HOME}{GOTO}B6 ~		

3. You can also type the descriptive label:

Split the screen (Alt-S)

into cell E30.

Let's take a moment to describe each step in the macro:

{HOME}{GOTO}D1 ~ /WWV{WINDOW}

Moves the cursor to the Home position (cell A1) then to cell D1 (using the GoTo key). The macro then uses /WWV (Worksheet Window Vertical) to split the screen vertically. Then the WINDOW key (F6) moves the cell pointer to the right side window.

{GOTO}K5 ~ {WINDOW}

Next, the macro puts the cell pointer in cell K5, which ensures that the right side window will display the last years of the projection. The WINDOW key (F6) then puts the cell pointer back into the left side window.

{HOME}{GOTO}B6~

The last line of the macro readjusts the left side window and moves the cell pointer to cell B6, where the cells used for "what-if" analyses begin.

You will test this macro a little later. First, you will develop a macro to "unsplit" the screen.

Macro to Unsplit the Screen

1. Move the cell pointer to cell A34 and enter the macro name:

   '\U

2. Move the cell pointer to cell B34 and enter the macro:

   {HOME}/WWC

3. Place the descriptive comment:

   Unsplit the screen (Alt-U)

   in cell E34.

This macro homes the cursor then clears the split screen using /WWC (Worksheet Window Clear). You'll get to test the macro in a moment.

Custom Help Screen Macro

The final macro will display some useful instructions for the TenYear worksheet. First, you'll need to create a screen displaying instructions. Fig. 16-8 shows an example. Note that the instructions begin in cell A49. The instructions are just simple labels entered into the worksheet like any other labels. After typing in a help screen as in the figure, type in the macro using the steps below:

1. Move the cell pointer to cell A36 and type in the macro name:

   '\H

2. Type the macro into the range of cells B36..B39 as shown next:

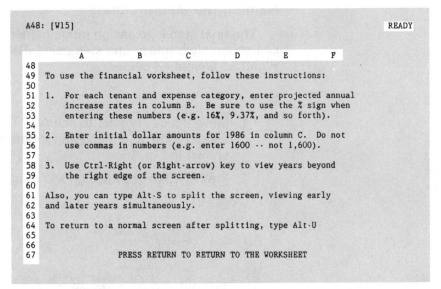

Fig. 16-8. Custom Help screen for the projection worksheet.

	A	B	C
36	\H	{GOTO}A47~	
37		{?}	
38		{HOME}{GOTO}B6~	
39			

3. Enter the descriptive comment:

Help screen (Alt·H)

into cell E36.

This macro displays the "help screen" as follows:

{GOTO}A47~   Moves the cell pointer to cell A47, causing the "help screen" in that portion of the worksheet to appear on the screen.

The {?} symbol pauses a macro until the user presses the RETURN key.

{?}   Pauses the macro until the user presses the RETURN key. (This gives the user as much time as he wishes to view the screen.)

{HOME}{GOTO}B6~   After the user presses return, the HOME key brings the projection data back onto the screen, and the GoTo key positions the cell pointer to cell B6.

Naming the Macro Library

The final step is to assign range names to all three macros. You can accomplish this in one step using /RNLR (Range Names Label Right) as described below:

1. Move the cell pointer to cell A30. Type /RNLR (Range Name Label Right), and highlight (or enter) the range A30..A36, as shown in Fig. 16-9.

2. Press RETURN to assign the range names.

```
Enter label range: A30..A36

           A              B           C         D         E                F
29
30   \S              {HOME}{GOTO}D1~/WWV{WINDOW}      Split the screen (Alt-S)
31                   {GOTO}K5~{WINDOW}
32                   {HOME}{GOTO}B6~
33
34   \U              {HOME}/WWC                       Unsplit the screen (Alt-U
35
36   \H              {GOTO}A47~                       Help screen (Alt-H)
37                   {?}
38                   {HOME}{GOTO}B6~
39
40
```

Fig. 16-9. Macro names highlighted on the worksheet.

The Range Name Labels Right assigns range names in the highlighted range to cells immediately to the right. Therefore, after using /RNLR, cell B30 has the macro name \S, cell B34 has the macro name \U, and cell B36 has the name \H.

To test the macros, move the cursor to the home position (A1). Type Alt-H to test the help screen. (Press RETURN after viewing the help screen to return to the worksheet.) Type Alt-S to split the screen, and Alt-U to unsplit the screen.

Don't forget to use /FS to save the TenYear worksheet after adding the macros.

STOPPING A MACRO

To interrupt a running macro, press the BREAK key, then the Escape key.

To stop a macro prematurely, press the BREAK key (Ctrl-Scroll Lock on most keyboards). Then, press the Escape key to return to the READY mode.

AUTOMATIC MACRO EXECUTION

The macro name \0 (zero) defines a macro that is invoked automatically when a worksheet is retrieved from disk.

If you want a macro to execute automatically as soon as the worksheet is retrieved from disk, just assign the name \0 (zero) to the macro. Use the usual /RNC (Range Name Create) or /RNLR (Range Name Labels Right) to name the macro.

To test the auto-execute macro, save the worksheet with the usual /FS commands, then use /WEY to clear the screen. Then, use /FR (File Retrieve) to retrieve the worksheet. The macro will execute the moment that the worksheet is loaded.

DEBUGGING

Macros do not always perform as you may have expected. 1-2-3 always does exactly as the macro says, which is not always exactly what you meant. When a macro does not perform as expected, you are going to have to change it to get it to work properly. Fixing things that don't work properly in the computer world is called *debugging* (getting the bugs out).

When you create a macro, you should first manually do all the steps that the macro is to perform. Every time you press a key, jot down on a piece of paper the key you just pressed. Then to type in the macro, simply place the same sequence of keystrokes that you wrote on paper into a worksheet cell. The macro *should* perform perfectly, but if it does not, follow these steps:

1. Work through the intended macro procedure manually again. Except this time, follow your own keystroke sequences that you wrote on the paper. At some point, you may notice that you left out a keystroke on the paper.

2. If you had to change the keystrokes you wrote on paper, then you will need to make the same change to the macro. If your handwritten sequence of keystrokes worked fine on the second test, then there is a discrepancy between the actual macro and the sequence you wrote on paper. Study the macro carefully to locate the discrepancy.

3. When you find the discrepancy, position the cell pointer to the cell with the macro in it, and press the F2 (Edit) key. The macro will appear in the control panel, where you can modify it. Press RETURN after making corrections. Try executing the macro again, and repeat these steps until the macro works correctly.

The STEP key (Alt-F2)
helps you to debug
macros.

If that procedure does not help, you can slow down the execution of the macro so that you can watch it happen a step at a time. First, press Alt-F2 to put 1-2-3 into single-step mode. The mode indicator displays the message STEP. Next, type the Alt-(letter) sequence used to execute your macro. 1-2-3 will process one step of the macro, then wait for you to press any key. After you press a key, the next step in the macro is performed, and so on. This allows you to watch each step of the macro in slow motion, and at some point your error should become clear. To exit the single-step mode and resume normal processing, press the Alt-F2 key again.

In general, when you create a large macro, try to make a habit of creating only a small portion of the macro at a time. For a large macro you can enter a small piece of the macro, name it, and execute it. When the little piece works, create another piece by either adding it to the end of the existing macro using the Edit key, or by putting the next step on the line below the existing piece. Create a small macro, test it, correct it, then add a little more, test it, correct it, and so forth. Building your macro in this way allows you to work in small steps which are easy to correct should you make an error.

WHAT HAVE YOU LEARNED?

1. A macro is a collection of keystrokes that can be stored on the worksheet and "played back" at any time by pressing a couple of keys.

2. Special keys on the keyboard are denoted by key names surrounded by curly braces ({ }).

3. The ~ symbolizes the RETURN key on the keyboard.

4. Macros can be separated into several adjacent rows.

5. All macros must be named with a backslash character followed by one of the letters A through Z.

6. You can use /RNC (Range Name Create) or /RNL (Range Name Labels) to name a macro.

7. To execute a macro, hold down the Alt key and type the letter name of the macro.

8. The special macro name \0 (zero) names an *auto-execute macro*.

9. To interrupt a running macro, press the BREAK key.

10. To debug a macro, use the STEP (Alt-F2) key.

QUIZ

1. The macro symbol {?} performs which task?
   a. A press on the RETURN key
   b. Positions the cell pointer to cell A1
   c. A press on the backspace key
   d. Waits for input from the user

2. A macro name must begin with which character?
   a. A slash (/)
   b. A backslash (\)
   c. An @ sign
   d. An ampersand (&)

3. Which commands let you name a macro?
   a. /RNC (Range Name Create)
   b. /WGN (Worksheet Global Name)
   c. /RL (Range Label-Prefix)
   d. /GNC (Graph Name Create)

4. To name several macros at once, you can use which commands?
   a. /RNC (Range Name Create)
   b. /RNL (Range Name Labels)
   c. /WGN (Worksheet Global Name)
   d. /RNR (Range Name Reset)

5. To invoke a macro, you press which key before typing the macro name?
   a. Ctrl
   b. Alt
   c. Home
   d. Escape

6. Which symbol denotes the RETURN key in a macro?
   a. {?}
   b. ^
   c. #
   d. ~

7. Which key interrupts a macro as it is running?
   a. Alt
   b. BREAK
   c. Escape
   d. PrtSc

8. Which name denotes an auto-execute macro?
   a. \A
   b. \F1
   c. \0
   d. \Z

9. To make a macro run a single step at a time, you press which key(s)?
   a. F2
   b. Alt-F2
   c. F3
   d. Alt-F3

10. The macro names for special keys on the keyboard are enclosed by which characters?
   a. [ ]
   b. ( )
   c. { }
   d. "

Chapter 17

CUSTOM MENUS

ABOUT THIS CHAPTER

Besides the basic macro keystrokes, 1-2-3 offers a complete programming language. With the aid of the *macro commands*, you can fully customize 1-2-3 to perform operations that would not otherwise be possible.

The macro commands add a complete programming language to the 1-2-3 worksheet.

Most of the macro commands are for very advanced 1-2-3 users and programmers, and a complete treatment of the topic is beyond the scope of this book. (Indeed, many books have been written about programming 1-2-3.) This chapter covers the most intriguing of the macro commands: those which allow you to replace the usual 1-2-3 menus with custom menus of your own.

A CUSTOM PROJECTION WORKSHEET

You will use the trusty ten-year projection worksheet that was created in Chapter 9 (and modified in Chapter 16) to demonstrate the custom menu capabilities. Use /FR (File Retrieve) to load the worksheet. You'll need to make a few basic changes to the worksheet before you begin add custom menu. (I'll assume you've already added the macros discussed in Chapter 16.)

First, you can use the Alt-M command to bring up the menu, rather than Alt-H for a help screen. So move the cell pointer to cell A20 and change the instructions in that cell to:

[Type Alt-M for menu]

Next, you will add a graph to the menu. Here are the steps to do so:

1. Move the cell pointer to cell C17 (the cash flow for 1986).

2. Type /GA (Graph A) and press End Right to assign C17..M17 as the A-range for the graph. Press RETURN.

3. Select Type and Bar to make a bar graph.

4. Select View to ensure that the graph is there. Press any key after viewing the graph.

If you like, you can add titles and an X-Range to the graph. When you are done designing the graph, select Quit from the Graph menu. Use /FS (File Save) to save the worksheet and new graph. (Use a new file name if you wish to keep the earlier version of the worksheet.)

Next, change the Help screen to reflect the new commands used in the worksheet. Fig. 17-1 shows the modified Help screen, which begins at cell A49.

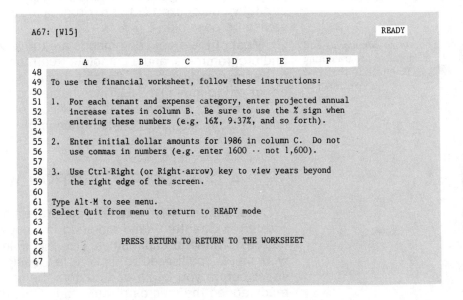

Fig. 17-1. Modified Help screen for the projection worksheet.

You'll be using all new range names in this worksheet, so use /RNR (Range Name Reset) to eliminate the original range names.

So far, you've only made a few changes to the worksheet to prepare it for the new custom menu. Now you can get to the business of creating the menu.

DESIGNING A CUSTOM MENU

In a custom menu, list menu options on the first row, menu item descriptions on the second row, and macro commands, or subroutine calls, on the third row.

Custom menus always consist of menu options with descriptions in the cells immediately beneath. Beneath the descriptions, you place the macro that the menu option performs, or a *subroutine call* to a macro that performs a task. For example, the following menu offers the options Add, Print, and Quit. Beneath each menu option is a brief description of the menu choice. (The description appears on the screen when the menu option is highlighted, just like descriptions appear beneath highlighted menu items on the usual 1-2-3 worksheet.)

Add	**Print**	**Quit**
Add new data	**Print a report**	**Return to READY**
{AddNew}	**/PPG**	**{QUIT}**

The Add menu option calls a subroutine named AddNew. The Print menu option presses the keys /PPG (Print Printer Go). The Quit option issues the macro command QUIT. We'll discuss these in more detail momentarily.

ACTIVATING A MENU

There are two macro commands that activate a menu: {MENU-CALL} and {MENUBRANCH}. {MENUCALL} is used when you want the menu to reappear after the user selects an option. {MENUBRANCH} allows the user to select an option, though does not redisplay the menu. You'll use {MENUCALL} in this example.

Both commands require that you activate a menu that has a range name assigned to it. For example, the command {MENU-CALL Main} activates a menu that starts at a range named Main. Let's create our custom menu for the TenYear worksheet now, using the steps below. First we'll put in the commands to activate the menu:

1. Move the cell pointer to cell A22 and type in the macro name '\M.

2. Move the cell pointer to cell B22: and type in the command {MENUCALL Main}.

3. Put the macro command {BRANCH \M} in cell B23.

4. Put the label 'Main in cell A25.

Next you will put in the menu options Split, Unsplit, Graph, Help, and Worksheet using the steps below:

5. In cell B25 put the menu option 'Split.

6. In cell C25 put the menu option 'Unsplit.

7. In cell D25 put the menu option 'Graph.

8. In cell E25 put the menu option 'Help.

9. In cell F25 put the menu option 'Worksheet.

Next you'll place menu descriptions beneath each menu option. Each description will partially overwrite the previous description, but this won't hurt the custom menu at all. Here are the steps:

10. In cell B26 put the menu description 'Split the Screen.

11. In cell C26 put the menu description 'UnSplit the Screen.

12. In cell D26 put the menu description 'Show graph of cash flows.

13. In cell E26 put the menu description 'Display Help screen.

14. In cell F26 put the menu description 'Return to READY mode.

Next, you'll assign subroutine calls and macro commands to each menu option. Here are the steps:

15. In cell B27 enter the subroutine call '{Split}.

16. In cell C27 enter the subroutine call '{UnSplit}.

17. In cell D27 enter the macro key symbol '{GRAPH}.

18. In cell E27 enter the subroutine call '{Help}.

19. In cell F27 enter the macro command '{QUIT}.

At this point, your menu should look like Fig. 17-2. Notice that the descriptions are run together. (The entire descriptions are there, the narrow column widths prevent you from seeing them).

Next, you need to rename the macros created back in Chapter 16 to their new subroutine names. Here are the steps to do so:

Macro subroutines need not have single-letter names, and can be called from a macro by placing the longer name in curly braces.

20. Replace the label in cell A30 with the new label 'Split.

21. Replace the label in cell A34 with the new label 'UnSplit.

22. Replace the label in cell A36 with the new label 'Help.

Now the macros that we developed in Chapter 16 have *subroutine names* rather than the backslash macro names. Your macros should look like Fig. 17-3.

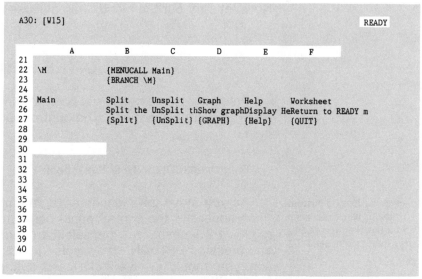

```
A30: [W15]                                                           READY

              A        B        C        D        E        F
21
22   \M               {MENUCALL Main}
23               {BRANCH \M}
24
25   Main             Split    Unsplit  Graph    Help     Worksheet
26               Split the UnSplit thShow graphDisplay HeReturn to READY m
27               {Split}  {UnSplit} {GRAPH}  {Help}   {QUIT}
28
29
30
31
32
33
34
35
36
37
38
39
40
```

Fig. 17-2. Custom menu on the worksheet.

```
A39: [W15]                                                           READY

              A        B        C        D        E        F
21
22   \M               {MENUCALL Main}
23               {BRANCH \M}
24
25   Main             Split    Unsplit  Graph    Help     Worksheet
26               Split the UnSplit thShow graphDisplay HeReturn to READY m
27               {Split}  {UnSplit} {GRAPH}  {Help}   {QUIT}
28
29
30   Split            {HOME}{GOTO}D1~/WWV{WINDOW}  Split the screen (Alt-S)
31               {GOTO}K5~{WINDOW}
32               {HOME}{GOTO}B6~
33
34   UnSplit          {HOME}/WWC                   Unsplit the screen (Alt-U)
35
36   Help             {GOTO}A47~                    Help screen (Alt-H)
37               {?}
38               {HOME}{GOTO}B6~
39
40
```

Fig. 17-3. Menu and macro subroutines on the worksheet.

Next, you need to name the \M macro, the menu, and the subroutines as ranges. To do so, follow these steps:

23. Move the cell pointer to cell A22.

24. Use /RNLR (Range Name Labels Right) to assign labels in the range A22..A36 to cells on the right (highlight the range A22..A36, or type in the coordinates. Press RETURN when done.)

Now, let's try out the menu, then discuss how it works.

USING THE MENU

Press the Home key to get back to the worksheet proper. Type Alt-M to call up the menu. The control panel displays the custom menu:

Split Unsplit Graph Help Worksheet

Select items from a custom menu using the same techniques that you use to select items from the 1-2-3 menus. As you move the highlighter to various options, their descriptions appear in the control panel beneath the menu. As with the regular 1-2-3 menus, you can select an item either by highlighting it and pressing RETURN, or by typing in its first letter. (For this reason, you should always make each option in your custom menu begin with a unique letter.)

When you select Split, the screen splits into two parts. When you select Unsplit, the windows clear. If you select Graph, the graph appears. Press any key to clear the graph. When you select HELP, the help screen appears. Press RETURN to erase the help screen. When you select Worksheet, the menu disappears, and you are back in READY mode. Pressing Alt-M again brings back the menu. Notice that the menu reappears after each menu selection except Worksheet.

When you are done experimenting, use /FS (File Save) to save the worksheet. Now let's discuss how and why all of this works.

HOW THE MENU WORKS

First of all, \M is a macro name. When you type Alt-M, the MENUCALL command displays the menu beginning at the cell named Main (which is the first cell to the right of the label Main). It displays the menu options across that row, and the descriptions beneath when an option is highlighted.

When you select Split, the macro looks for a macro subroutine named Split, then executes that subroutine. Split is subroutine like any other macro, except that it exists as a portion of a larger macro, and can have a full name rather than a backslash name). Whenever a macro sees a name in curly braces (other than a key name like {RIGHT}, it automatically searches for a cell with that name, and attempts to execute the macro. Hence, the command {Split} tells 1-2-3 to find a subroutine named Split and execute it.

After the {Split} subroutine completes its task, the macro resumes processing at the first line beneath the MENUCALL command. In this case, that command is {BRANCH \M}. The BRANCH command passes control to the named cell (\M in this example). Hence, the \M command is issued automatically (just as though you typed it from the keyboard), so the custom menu reappears on the screen.

When you select Unsplit from the menu, the macro looks for the subroutine named Unsplit (because of the {Unsplit command}), and that macro then uses /WWC (Worksheet Window Clear) to clear the window from the screen. Again, control is automatically returned to the BRANCH command which, in turn, redisplays the menu.

When you select Graph from the menu, the macro presses the GRAPH key (F10), which displays the graph. In this case, the macro does not look for a subroutine named GRAPH, because {GRAPH} is the name of a key (just like {RIGHT}{LEFT} and {PGUP}). After displaying the graph and waiting for a keypress, the macro redisplays the menu.

When you select Help, the macro executes the subroutine named Help (because of the {Help} subroutine call) and returns control to the menu when the user is done viewing the Help screen.

The {QUIT} macro command interrupts a macro and returns to the worksheet READY mode.

When you select the Worksheet option, the macro executes the {QUIT} command. {QUIT} is neither the name of a key, nor a subroutine name. It is a macro command like {BRANCH} or {MENU-CALL} that stops the macro and returns you to the READY mode.

AUTOMATING THE MENU

You can make the menu appear automatically by assigning the macro name \0 to cell B22. To keep the original name, \M, and also use the auto-execute name, place the cell pointer on cell B22 and use /RNC (Range Name Create) to name the cell \0 (backslash zero). You won't be able to see the extra name on the worksheet, of course, but it will work. Just save the worksheet with /FS, clear the screen with /WEY, and retrieve it again with /FR. The custom menu appears immediately. After exiting the menu, the Alt-M keys will still bring it back to the screen.

WHERE DO I GO FROM HERE?

As mentioned earlier, it would take at least another entire book to discuss all the macro commands and general programming capabilities that 1-2-3 offers. If you are interested in programming 1-2-3, there are many fine books on the topic. Also, the 1-2-3 Reference Manual discusses the macro commands in detail in the section on Macros.

Try reading the Lotus 1-2-3 Reference Manual again after reading this book. You'll probably find it much easier to understand.

There are plenty of other tricks and techniques besides macros and programming that you can still learn about from the Lotus manuals. If you found those manuals too technical before reading this book, you'll probably find them much easier now that you've had a chance to create and use some sample worksheets.

Perhaps the most important next step, however, is to experiment. Experience is the best teacher, and developing your own custom worksheets, graphs, and databases will probably teach you the most. Use the 1-2-3 Reference manual, the F1 key Help screens, and of course this book to help you find the answers to questions as they arise. With some practical experience and time, you'll find that Lotus 1-2-3 is an extremely powerful, flexible, and even easy to use tool.

WHAT HAVE YOU LEARNED?

1. The 1-2-3 *macro commands* include commands for displaying custom menus.

2. The {MENUCALL} and {MENUBRANCH} commands activate custom menus.

3. A custom menu consists of a range name, a row of menu options, with menu descriptions directly beneath the menu options.

4. Subroutine calls, macro commands, or macro keystrokes associated with each menu item are placed directly beneath the menu descriptions.

5. The {BRANCH} macro command passes control to another portion of a macro, usually specified by a named cell.

6. The {QUIT} macro command terminates a macro.

7. A macro can call a subroutine using the subroutine name in curly braces (e.g. {Help}). The subroutine name is a range name assigned to the first line of the subroutine.

QUIZ

1. Which command displays a menu only once, without the opportunity to redisplay the menu again automatically?
   a. {BRANCH}
   b. {QUIT}
   c. {MENUCALL}
   d. {MENUBRANCH}

2. When developing a custom menu, which portion belongs in the top row?
   a. The menu options
   b. The menu item descriptions
   c. The associated commands
   d. The menu name only

3. When developing a custom menu, which portion belongs in the middle row?
   a. The menu options
   b. The menu item descriptions
   c. The associated commands
   d. The menu name only

4. When developing a custom menu, which portion belongs in the bottom rows?
   a. The menu options
   b. The menu item descriptions
   c. The macro associated with the menu option, or a call to the appropriate macro subroutine
   d. The menu name only

5. When activated, custom menus are displayed where?
   a. On the worksheet
   b. In the same place as the regular 1-2-3 menus
   c. At the bottom of the screen
   d. In the mode indicator

6. In the sample worksheet in this chapter, the {GRAPH} symbol performs what task?
   a. Calls a subroutine named Graph
   b. Presses the GRAPH (F10) key
   c. Calls up the graph menu
   d. Performs a graphics slide show

7. The {BRANCH} command performs which task?
   a. Calls a subroutine named BRANCH
   b. Returns to the READY mode
   c. Passes control to a different place in the macro
   d. Assigns a new name to a range in the macro

8. The macro command {QUIT} performs which task?
   a. Calls a subroutine named Quit
   b. Returns to the READY mode
   c. Passes control to a different place in the macro
   d. Assigns a new name to a range in the macro

1-2-3 INTERNATIONAL CHARACTER SET

INTERNATIONALIZING 1-2-3

You can customize 1-2-3 to use non-USA currency signs, punctuation, date, and time formats using the /WGDOI (Worksheet Global Default Other International) commands. When you select these commands, you are given the options:

Punctuation Currency Date Time Quit

Each is summarized below.

Punctuation

The Punctuation option lets you select punctuation marks for numbers and argument separators in functions. The default 1-2-3 setting is commas for thousands separators, period for decimal places, and commas for argument separators. For example, in /RF,2 (Range Format Comma 2) format, the number 123.45 is displayed as 1,234.56. In an @PMT formula, you'd use the decimal point as usual, leave the comma out of the number, and separate arguments with commas, as in the formula below:

@PMT(1234.56,0.12,48)

The options A through H display the number 1234.56 (using /RF,2) in the formats shown in the left column in Table A-1. The right column shows how you would modify the @PMT formula argument separators for each of the options. Note that option A is the default option. That is, unless you specifically change the numeric punctuation format with /WGDOI, it uses the A option format (American punctuation).

Table A-1. International Numeric Format Operations

Option	Display	Argument Separator	Sample Formula
A	1,234.56	,	@PMT(1234.56,0.12,48)
B	1.234,56	.	@PMT(1234,56.0,12.48)
C	1,234.56	;	@PMT(1234.56;0.12;48)
D	1.234,56	;	@PMT(1234,56;0,12;48)
E	1 234.56	,	@PMT(1234.56,0.12,48)
F	1 234,56	.	@PMT(1234,56.0,12.48)
G	1 234.56	;	@PMT(1234.56;0.12;48)
H	1 234,56	;	@PMT(1234,56;0,12;48)

Currency

The Currency option lets you use currency symbols other than the American $ sign. When you select the /WGDOIC (Worksheet Global Default Other International Currency) commands, the screen asks that you enter a currency sign, as below:

Currency sign: $

You can press backspace then type in any character from the keyboard, or use a *compose key* (Alt-F1) sequence. For example, to use the Yen sign, you would hold down the Alt key and type F1, then type the letters Y = . Compose sequences for foreign currency signs are listed in Table A-2. A complete set of compose sequences appears in Appendix 2 of the 1-2-3 Reference Manual.

Table A-2. Currency Sign Compose Key Sequences

Compose Key Sequence	Currency Sign
ff	Dutch Guilder
C|	Cent sign
L=	British Pound
Y=	Yen sign
PT	Pesetas sign
SO	Section sign
XO	General currency sign

After entering a currency sign and pressing RETURN, the menu displays the options:

Prefix Suffix

Select Prefix to display the currency sign in front of the number, Suffix to display the currency sign after the number.

By using the space bar, you can add spaces in front of, or behind, the currency sign. The currency sign you select will be displayed on numbers formatted with /RFC (Range Format Currency) only.

Date

The Date option lets you define formats for the Long International (Range Format Date 4) and Short International (Range Format Date 5) date formats. These options also affect how data is presented in the @DATEVALUE function. Your options and sample @DATEVALUE formulas are shown in Table A-3. Option A is the default setting.

Table A-3. International Date Format Options

Option	Long International	Short International	Formula
A	12/31/86	12/31	@DATEVALUE('12/31/86')
B	31/12/86	31/12	@DATEVALUE('31/12/86')
C	31.12.86	31.12	@DATEVALUE('31.12.86')
D	86-12-31	12-31	@DATEVALUE('86-12-31')

Time

The Time options let you select formats for date data displayed in the Long International (/RFDT3) and Short International (/RFDT4) formats. The format used to display the time is the same format that you must use in the @TIMEVALUE function. Table A-4 shows the various time options. Option A is the default setting.

Table A-4. International Time Format Options

Option	Long International	Short International	Formula
A	04:27:03	04:27	@TIMEVALUE('04:27:03')
B	04.27.03	04.27	@TIMEVALUE('04.27.03')
C	04,27,03	04,27	@TIMEVALUE('04,27,03')
D	04h27m03s	04h27m	@TIMEVALUE('04h27m03s')

The Quit options from the menus return you to the READY mode.

SAVING INTERNATIONAL SETTINGS

Any changes that you make with the /WGDOI (Worksheet Global Default Other International) settings can be used whenever you run 1-2-3. Enter the commands /WGDU (Worksheet Global Default Update) to do so.

The new settings are stored in a file named 123.CNF (123 configuration). If you've changed the disk in drive A, put the 1-2-3 program disk in drive A before you save the settings. If the 1-2-3 program disk has a write protect tab on it, remove it before saving the new settings.

GLOSSARY

Absolute cell reference A reference to a cell in a formula that does not change when the formula is copied. For example, in the formula @PMT($B$1,$B$2,A5), references to cells B1 and B2 are absolute. The $ (or ABS key) makes references absolute.

ACCESS menu First menu to appear when you enter the command LOTUS at the DOS A> or C> prompt. Provides easy access to 1-2-3, PrintGraph, Translate, and A View of 1-2-3, as well as exit back to DOS.

Anchor cell Cell that remains stationary when highlighting a range of cells. To change the anchor cell, press the period key.

Argument The portion of an @ function that is operated upon. For example, in the formula @SQRT(9), the number 9 is the argument. Arguments are separated by commas in functions with multiple arguments; for example, @PMT(B1,B2,B3).

ASCII code American Standard Code for Information Interchange. A number, from 0 to 254, assigned to a character. Numbers 0 through 32 are nonprinting characters. LICS (Lotus International Character Set) modifies ASCII codes beyond number 127.

Aspect ratio The ratio between the X- and Y-axes on a graph. The standard aspect ratio on 1-2-3 graphs is 1 to 1.38, with the X-axis (bottom) being the larger of the two.

Border The highlighted bar of column letters (A–IV) or row numbers (1–8192) on the screen. Also refers to any column or row that is repeated on multiple pages of a printed worksheet.

CALC indicator When the worksheet is set to manual recalculation using /WGRM (Worksheet Global Recalculation Manual), the CALC indicator appears at the bottom of the screen when the worksheet needs to be recalculated with the CALC key.

Cell A single position on the worksheet that can contain one number, formula, or label. Each cell is referenced by its column letter and row number, from A1 to IV8192.

Cell address A reference to a single cell using its column letter and row number, from A1 to IV8192.

Cell pointer The highlighter on the screen that indicates the current cell in use. The arrow, Home, End, PgUp, and PgDn, and GoTo keys move the cell pointer.

Circular reference   A formula that refers to the cell that it is in (for example, the formula +A2+A1 in cell A1). Usually causes problems because the cell value grows each time the worksheet is recalculated. Causes the CIRC indicator to appear at the bottom of the screen.

Column   A single column on the worksheet, with a letter name from A to IV. Also refers to a single field in a database.

Command   Any option available on the 1-2-3 menus. To select a command, first type / to bring up the main menu. Also refers to macro commands used in advanced macros.

Compose sequence   A series of keystrokes using the Compose (Alt-F1) key which brings special characters to the screen, including foreign currency signs.

Control panel   The lines above the actual worksheet where menus and highlighted cell entries appear.

Criteria   Cell entries used to search (query) a database for particular records. The criteria is placed in the database Criterion Range.

Criterion range   A portion of the worksheet where entries for querying a database are stored. The Criterion Range generally consists of database field names and values to search for. The /DQC (Data Query Criterion Range) commands define the Criterion Range.

Crosshatching   Patterns of angled lines used to identify different ranges of data in 1-2-3 graphs.

Current cell   Cell that currently holds the cell pointer on the screen, and whose name appears in the control panel. When you press the Home key, the cell pointer moves to cell A1. At that point, cell A1 is the current cell.

Cursor   The small underline character that indicates where you are typing in the control panel. Also, the blinking line that appears in the free cell in a highlighted range.

Data   Any item of information placed in a cell on the worksheet.

Data disk   The disk used to store 1-2-3 worksheets and graphs with the /FS (File Save) commands. On a computer with two floppy disk drives, it is usually the disk in drive B.

Data table   A range of cells on the worksheet that is set up in a specific format for using the /DT1 (Data Table 1) and /DT2 (Data Table 2) commands. Allows you to perform "what-if" analyses using a single formula.

Database   A collection of information organized into records (rows) and fields (columns) of information. In 1-2-3, the top row always consists of database field names.

Date format   The manner in which a date is displayed, either DD-MMM-YY, DD-MMM, MMM-YY, MM/DD/YY, or MM/DD. Additional International date formats are available under the /WGDOID (Worksheet Global Default Other International Date) commands.

Debug   To remove the errors from a macro so that it runs correctly. The STEP (Alt-F2) key can help with the debugging process.

Default setting   The setting that 1-2-3 uses automatically if you do not specifically change settings. Examples: Column width of nine spaces, the General numeric format, Left-alignment of labels, and automatic recalculation.

Directory   A subdivision of a disk with its own name and own files. The DOS MD and CD commands create and log onto directories.

Disk   The place where worksheets and graphs that are not currently in use are stored. The currently active worksheet or graph is stored in RAM. To save worksheets to disk, use /FS (File Save). To retrieve worksheets from disk, use /FR (File Retrieve).

Disk drive   The part of the computer that spins the disk, stores information on it, and retrieves information from it. Usually assigned a letter such as A:, B: or C:.

DOS   Disk Operating System. A program that is loaded into the computer automatically when booting up (turning on the computer). Stays in memory and performs basic functions such as transferring information to and from the screen, printer, RAM, and disks.

Edit mode   In edit mode, you can change the contents of a cell using the arrow, Home, End, Ins, and Del keys to position the cursor. To enter EDIT mode, put the cell pointer on the cell that needs correcting then press EDIT (F2). Press RETURN when done editing.

Escape key   The key labeled Esc (or Cancel on some keyboards) which "backs out" of any problem. Anytime you feel lost in 1-2-3, press Escape repeatedly to back out to more familiar territory.

Field   A single column of data in a database. Each field in a database must have a unique name, which appears in the top row of the database.

Field name   The name assigned to a field, which appears in the first row of the database. Each field in the database must contain a unique name.

File   A place on a disk where worksheets, graphs, and databases not currently in use are stored. Each file on a disk (or directory) must have a unique name, eight letters maximum length, with no spaces or punctuation.

File extension   The three letter addition that 1-2-3 adds to a file name, such as .WK1 for worksheets, .PIC for graphs saved for printing, and .PRN for files printed with the /PF (Print File) commands.

File name   A name you assign to a worksheet, graph, or print copy. The file name must be no more than eight characters in length, and may not contain spaces or punctuation. 1-2-3 will add a three letter extension to the file name you assign.

Font   The typeface used in printed graphs.

Formula   A mathematical expression that calculates some result. Formulas can contain operators (such as $+$. $-$, $*$, $/$, and $\wedge$), and @functions such as @IF, @SQRT, and @PMT.

Free cell   The corner of a highlighted range that moves when you press an arrow, PgUp, PgDn, End, or Home key. Pressing the period key moves the position of the free cell.

Function   A built-in formula that performs some task beyond simple addition, subtraction, multiplication, division, or exponentiation. For example, the @PMT function calculates the payment on a loan, given the principal, interest rate, and term.

Global   Any optional setting that affects the entire worksheet. The /WG (Worksheet Global) commands change global settings, which can be overidden in portions of the worksheet with the /R (Range) commands.

Graph file   Any graph saved using the /GS (Graph Save) commands for printing later with the PrintGraph program. Graph files always have the extension .PIC.

Help   The built-in facility that 1-2-3 offers while working online. To bring up Help at anytime, press the F1 key. To return to the worksheet, press Escape.

Highlight   The brighter portion of the screen which indicates the current cell or range in use. Also refers to the bright box on the menu that lets you select menu options.

Insert mode   During editing with the EDIT (F2) key, any new text that you type will be inserted into the existing text if insert mode is on. Pressing the Ins key toggles the Insert mode on and off.

Installation   The process whereby you describe your computer system to 1-2-3 before using the worksheet for the first time. 1-2-3 includes an Installation program which will take you through the process.

Key field   The field used to specify a sort order in a database sort (also called the Sort Key). The /DSP (Data Sort Primary-Key) and /DSS (Data Sort Secondary-Key) let you define key fields.

Label   Any nonnumeric cell entry on the worksheet. If a label begins with a nonalphabetic character (such as the address 123 Apple St.), you must first type in a label prefix such as ', $\wedge$, or ".

Label alignment   Position of a label in a cell, determined by the label prefix, /RL (Range Label), or /WGL (Worksheet Global Label-Prefix) commands. Options are left-aligned ('), centered ($\wedge$), or right-aligned (").

Label prefix   The first character in a cell entry that determines the alignment of the label in its cell. Options are ' (left-aligned), $\wedge$ (centered), and " (right-aligned). Labels that do not begin with a letter A through Z must be preceded by a label prefix.

Legend   The "map" at the bottom of the graph which explains the relationship between crosshatching patterns and data ranges.

LICS   Lotus International Character Set. A special group of characters for using international letters and symbols in a worksheet. Accessible through Compose sequences and the @CHAR function.

Macro   A series of keystrokes stored on the worksheet that can be "played back" at any time with an Alt-key combination. Advanced macros can use macro commands.

Macro commands   Special words used in macros, enclosed in curly braces, that make macros perform more like computer programs.

Menu   A display of optional commands that you can use to manipulate the worksheet. Pressing the / key brings up the 1-2-3 main menu.

Mixed cell reference   A cell reference in a formula that is partially absolute and partially relative. For example, the formula @SUM($B1..$D1) contains two mixed references B1 and D1. Pressing the ABS key twice or more creates mixed cell references.

Mode   The overall state that 1-2-3 is in at any given moment, as indicated in the upper right corner of the screen. In READY mode, data can be entered or edited in a single cell. Pressing / brings up the menu and changes to MENU mode.

Named range   A cell, or group of cells, that has been assigned a name beyond its row and column position. The /RNC (Range Name Create) and /RNL (Range Name Labels) commands assign names to cells and ranges.

Numeric format   The way in which numbers are displayed on the screen, as selected with the /RF (Range Format) or /WGF (Worksheet Global Format) commands. Options include General (1234.56), currency ($1,234.56), Fixed (12345.6000), and others.

Operator   A symbol used to perform arithmetic in a formula such as addition ($+$), subtraction ($-$), multiplication ($*$), and division ($/$). Also, logical operators such as greater than ($>$), less than ($<$), equal ($=$), not equal ($<>$), #AND#, #OR# and #NOT#.

Overwrite mode   During editing with the EDIT (F2) key, any new text that you type will be overwrite the existing text if in Overwrite mode. Pressing the Ins key toggles between the insert and overwrite modes.

Print file   A printed copy of a worksheet stored on disk using the /PF (Print File) commands. Print files are automatically assigned the file extension .PRN.

PrintGraph   A program outside the 1-2-3 worksheet used to print graphs that have previously been saved using the /GS (Graph Save) commands. To run PrintGraph, select PrintGraph from the ACCESS menu, or enter the command PGRAPH at the DOS prompt.

Program disk   The disk which contains a Lotus program such as 1-2-3 or PrintGraph.

Protection A method of preventing unwanted changes to data and formulas on the worksheet. The /RU (Range Unprotect), /RP (Range Protect), and /WGP (Worksheet Global Protection) commands let you protect specific ranges of cells.

RAM Random Access Memory. The portion of the computer that holds the currently active worksheet, graph, or database, and performs all calculations. The /FR (File Retrieve) and /FS (File Save) commands transfer data between RAM and disks.

Range Any group of adjacent cells on the worksheet that form an even rectangular shape. The smallest range is a single cell, the largest range is the entire worksheet. The /R (Range) commands manipulate ranges of cells.

Range address A reference to a group of cells specified by periods. For example, the formula @SUM(M16..Z28) sums all the numbers in the range of cells from M16 to Z28.

Range name A name assigned to a group of cells using the /RNC (Range Name Create) commands. A range name can be up to 15 characters long.

Recalculation The process of calculating all the formulas on the worksheet. Recalculation is automatic unless you specifically change it with the /WGR (Worksheet Global Recalculation) commands.

Record A single row of data in a database.

Relative cell reference A reference to a cell in a formula that changes when the formula is copied. For example, in the formula @PMT($B$1,$B$2,A5), the reference to A5 is relative, and will change as the formula is copied or moved to a new location on the worksheet.

Save To store a copy of a worksheet on disk for future use. Failure to save a worksheet before exiting 1-2-3 permanently erases the worksheet. Use the /FS (File Save) and /FR (File Retrieve) commands to save and retrieve worksheets, graphs, and databases.

Serial Date A date expressed as a number between 1 (for 1/1/1900) and 73050 (12/31/2099). Serial dates can be displayed in more customary formats using the /RFD (Range Format Date) and /RFT (Range Format Time) commands.

Setup string A special code used to set a printer into a special mode such as expanded or compressed print. Setup strings are expressed as numbers preceded by a backslash (e.g. \015) using the /PPOS (Print Printer Other Setup) commands, or preceded by ||\ symbols if embedded in the worksheet.

Sort To rearrange the information in a database into a meaningful order, such as alphabetically by name, or in zip code order for bulk mailing.

Spreadsheet Same as a worksheet.

Submenu A menu that is beneath a higher-level menu. Selecting a menu option often leads to a submenu. Pressing Escape moves backwards from the submenu up to the higher-level menu.

Subroutine   A portion of a larger macro that is called by name. Names are assigned using /RNL (Range Name Labels) or /RNC (Range Name Create). Subroutines are called by enclosing the name in curly braces (e.g. {Split}).

Time format   A way to display time data, such as HH:MM:SS AM/PM, HH:MM AM/PM, HH:MM:SS on a 24-hour clock, and so forth. The /RFDT (Range Format Date Time) commands provide the options. The /WGDOIT (Worksheet Global Default Other International Time) provides other options.

Translate   A program accessible from the ACCESS Menu that translates data to and from version 2.0 of Lotus 1-2-3 and other popular microcomputer software packages.

Value   A number in a cell, or the results of a calculation.

Window   A screen which displays a portion of the overall worksheet. The screen can be divided into two windows using the /WW (Worksheet Window) commands.

Worksheet   The 1-2-3 work area, and what you put into it (synonomous with spreadsheet).

ANSWERS TO QUIZZES

Chapter 1.
1. b
2. c
3. d
4. a
5. d
6. c
7. b
8. d
9. c
10. c

Chapter 2.
1. b
2. c
3. d
4. a
5. c
6. c
7. b
8. b
9. a
10. d

Chapter 3.
1. b
2. c
3. d
4. a
5. d
6. b
7. a
8. b
9. d
10. d

Chapter 4.
1. b
2. d
3. d
4. b
5. c
6. d
7. b
8. c

Chapter 5.
1. c
2. a
3. b
4. d
5. c
6. a

Chapter 6.
1. b
2. d
3. d
4. a
5. c
6. a
7. d
8. b
9. b
10 d

Chapter 7.
1. c
2. a
3. d
4. b
5. b

6. b
7. b
8. c
9. c
10. d

Chapter 8.
1. a
2. d
3. b
4. b
5. a
6. d
7. b
8. d
9. c
10. b

Chapter 9.
(No Quiz)

Chapter 10.
1. c
2. a
3. d
4. b
5. b
6. b
7. a
8. a
9. a
10. d

Chapter 11.
1. b
2. a
3. a

4. b
5. c
6. d
7. d
8. c
9. b
10. b

Chapter 12.
1. c
2. b
3. b
4. a
5. b

Chapter 13.
1. c
2. a
3. c
4. d
5. b
6. b
7. b
8. b

Chapter 14.
1. b
2. d
3. c
4. c
5. a
6. b
7. b
8. c
9. c
10. b

Chapter 15.
1. a
2. b
3. a
4. b
5. b
6. c
7. d
8. a
9. d
10. d

Chapter 16.
1. d
2. b
3. a
4. b
5. b
6. d
7. b
8. c
9. b
10. c

Chapter 17.
1. d
2. a
3. b
4. c
5. b
6. b
7. c
8. b

INDEX

Hard Disk Management Techniques for the IBM®
Joseph-David Carrabis

This is a resource book of in-depth techniques on how to set up and manage a hard disk environment directed to the everyday "power user," not necessarily the DOS expert or programmer.

Each fundamental technique, based on the author's consulting experience with Fortune 500 companies, is emphasized to help the reader become a "power user." This tutorial highlights installation of utilities, hardware, software, and software applications for the experienced business professional working with a hard disk drive.

Topics covered include:

- Introduction to Hard Disks
- Hard Disks and DOS
- Backup and What You Need to Know
- Service and Maintenance
- Setting Up a Hard Disk
- Organizing a Hard Disk
- Hard Disk Managers
- Utilities to Manage Hard Disks, Find Files, UNERASE Files, Recover Damaged Files, Speed Up Disk Access, and Restore and Backup Disks
- Maintenance Utilities
- Security Utilities

472 Pages, 7½ x 9¾, Softbound
ISBN: 0-672-22580-8
No. 22580, $22.95

Lotus® 1-2-3® Financial Models
Tymes, Dowden, and Prael

With this book, Lotus 1-2-3 users will learn to create models for calculating and solving personal and business finance problems using Version 2.0! This book shows how to avoid frustration and delay in setting up individual formulas and allows users to perform any spreadsheet calculation in minutes.

This revision of the popular *1-2-3® from A to Z* includes numerous models or templates for the Lotus user, each preceded by a brief explanation of how the model works and how it can be altered. More advanced business models and an increased emphasis on macros as well as the inclusion of Version 2.0 make this book ideally suited to the business user.

Whether calculating a complex statistical analysis or a home heating analysis, readers can use this book as the one source for the guidance and tools needed to do spreadsheet calculations in the most efficient manner possible.

Topics covered include:

- Personal Models
- Business Models
- Advanced Business Models

Elna Tymes is an experienced computer book author in California with a number of successful books to her credit including *Mastering Appleworks* and *1-2-3 from A to Z*.

300 Pages, 7½ x 9¾, Softbound
ISBN: 0-672-48410-2
No. 48410, $19.95

The Best Book of: Microsoft® Works for the PC
Ruth K. Witkin

This step-by-step guide uses a combination of in-depth explanations and hands-on tutorials to show the business professional or home user how to apply the software to enhance both business and personal productivity.

Clearly written and easy to understand, this book explains how to use such varied applications as the word processor with mail merge, the spreadsheet with charting, the database with reporting, communications, and integration. For each application the author provides a detailed overview of the hows and whys followed by practical examples that guide the reader easily from idea to finished product.

Topics covered include:

- Spreadsheet Essentials
- Exploring the Spreadsheet Menus
- About Formulas and Functions
- Charting Your Spreadsheet
- Exploring the Chart Menus
- Database Essentials
- Filling a Database
- Exploring the Database Menus
- Word Processor Essentials
- Exploring the Word Processor Menus
- Integration Essentials
- Communications Essentials
- Exploring the Communications Menus

350 Pages, 7½ x 9¾, Softbound
ISBN: 0-672-22626-X
No. 22626, $21.95

The Best Book of: WordStar® Features Release 4
Vincent Alfieri

The Best Book of: WordStar includes all of the more than 125 enhancements and revisions found in Release 4.

Readers who want to get the most from WordStar, the most popular word-processing program ever published, are guided step-by-step through a series of real-life problems—from opening a file to sending personalized letters and from simple correspondence to complex tables.

This text shows how to import and export WordStar files to and from 1-2-3 and dBASE III PLUS.

Topics covered include:

- Print Effects and Printing
- Formatting Essentials
- Moving, Copying, and Deleting Blocks
- Finding and Replacing
- Keyboard Macros and Other Shortcuts
- Fun with Multiple Formats
- Editing Features
- Working with DOS and File Management
- Headers, Footers, and Page Numbering
- Controlling the Page
- Boilerplates, Format Files, and Document Assembly
- Math Maneuvers
- A Form Letter Course
- Conditional Merge Printing
- Automated Document Assembly
- Bibliophilic Occupations
- Working with Laser Printers

576 Pages, 7½ x 9¾, Softbound
ISBN: 0-672-48404-8
No. 48404, $19.95

Visit your local book retailer, use the order form provided, or call 800-428-SAMS.

The Best Book of: Microsoft® Works for the PC
Ruth K. Witkin

This step-by-step guide uses a combination of in-depth explanations and hands-on tutorials to show the business professional or home user how to apply the software to enhance both business and personal productivity.

Clearly written and easy to understand, this book explains how to use such varied applications as the word processor with mail merge, the spreadsheet with charting, the database with reporting, communications, and integration. For each application the author provides a detailed overview of the hows and whys followed by practical examples that guide the reader easily from idea to finished product. Quick-reference charts, summaries, and end-of-chapter questions and answers enhance the learning process, and each example is illustrated at important developmental stages.

Topics covered include:

- Spreadsheet Essentials
- Exploring the Spreadsheet Menus
- About Formulas and Functions
- Charting Your Spreadsheet
- Exploring the Chart Menus
- Database Essentials
- Filling a Database
- Exploring the Database Menus
- Word Processor Essentials
- Exploring the Word Processor Menus
- Integration Essentials
- Communications Essentials
- Exploring the Communications Menus

350 Pages, 7½ x 9¾, Softbound
ISBN: 0-672-22626-X
No. 22626, $21.95

The Best Book of: WordPerfect® Version 5.0
Vincent Alfieri

From formatting a simple letter to setting up time-saving macros, this book unravels all of the new features and updates of Version 5.0. With detailed explanations, clear examples, and screen illustrations, it teaches first-time users how to use WordPerfect and helps advanced users learn short-cuts and tips for using it more efficiently.

Covering every new feature and re-examining the old ones, this step-by-step tutorial allows readers to take a self-paced approach to word processing.

Topics covered include:

- Fonts for Special Effects
- Printing and Formatting
- Document and File Management
- Speller and Thesaurus
- Working with Forms
- Headers, Footers, and Page Numbering
- Working with Multiple Text Columns
- Hard Space and Hyphenation
- Footnotes, Endnotes, and Automatic Referencing
- Table, List, and Index Generation
- Merge Features
- For Power Users—Macros, Sorting, Graphics
- The Laser Revolution

700 Pages, 7½ x 9¾, Softbound
ISBN: 0-672-48423-4
No. 48423, $21.95

Macro Programming for 1-2-3®
Daniel N. Shaffer

This book reveals the uses of 1-2-3 Release 2's powerful built-in programming language. With Release 2's expanded macro language, 1-2-3 users can better automate and control routine or tedious worksheet functions, saving time, effort, and keystrokes.

The author shows how to create more accurate, more powerful worksheets that are also easier to use. Concentrating on the practical application of macros, this book gives the reader step-by-step hands-on experience through examples and exercises.

Topics covered include:

- Using Range Names
- Using the Automatic Typing Features of 1-2-3
- Using the Programming Features of 1-2-3
- Easy Data Entry, Results Display, Report Printing, Graphing, Data Storage, and Retrieval
- Making Your Worksheets More Powerful
- Appendices: Summary of Macro Commands, Using the New String Functions, Differences Between Release 1A and 2.0

304 Pages, 7½ x 9¾, Softbound
ISBN: 0-672-46573-6
No. 46573, $19.95

dBASE III PLUS™ Programmer's Library
Joseph-David Carrabis

Written for intermediate to advanced programmers, this book shows how to quickly build a library of dBASE III PLUS code that can be reused many times with only minor modifications. The author reveals universal patterns for editing, adding, deleting, finding, and transferring records in databases, so that dBASE III PLUS tools can be adapted to a variety of applications.

The book has two major parts: The first provides kernels of code that can be used in applications as varied as dental records keeping, fundraising, small business management, and newsletter subscription systems. The second part shows the code necessary to handle such systems, and how kernels and modular programming help you set them up.

Topics covered include:

- What Is a Library?
- The Basic Kernels of Code
- Database Designs
- Advanced Kernels
- Inventory Systems
- Client/Personnel Record Keeping
- Subscription and General Accounting Systems
- Appendices: Clipper Versions of dBASE III Plus Listings, and dBASE III Plus Commands, Functions, and Abbreviations

536 Pages, 7½ x 9¾, Softbound
ISBN: 0-672-22579-4
No. 22579, $21.95

Visit your local book retailer, use the order form provided, or call 800-428-SAMS.